Battle Tactics

of the

German Army

1914-1918

By William Balck

Translated by Harry Bell

Legacy Books Press
Military Classics

Published by Legacy Books Press
RPO Princess, Box 21031
445 Princess Street
Kingston, Ontario, K7L 5P5
Canada

www.legacybookspress.com

The scanning, uploading, and/or distribution of this book via the Internet or any other means without the permission of the publisher is illegal and punishable by law.

This edition first published in 2022 by Legacy Books Press
1

This edition © 2022 Legacy Books Press, all rights reserved.

ISBN: 978-1-927537-69-5

First published in English as *Development of Tactics – World War* in 1922 by The General Service Schools Press, Fort Leavenworth, Kansas.

Printed and bound in the United States of America and Great Britain.

This book is typeset in a Times New Roman 11-point font.

Table of Contents

Foreword... 3

Chapter I – Training in Peace and Reality in War 7

Chapter II – Mobile Warfare......................... 21
    Training and Organization....................... 21
    Tactics of Mobile Warfare....................... 34
    Changes in Organization, Equipment and Armament 42
    Training Regulations for Foot Troops 46

Chapter III – Position Warfare in the West, 1914-1917...... 51
    Origin and Nature of Position Warfare 51
    The Position Battles up to the First Attack on Verdun ... 56
    Lessons of the Battle on the Somme and the Battles in Front of Verdun in the Late Fall of 1916.................. 74
    Utilizing the Experiences Gained.................... 88
    The Battles in 1917 91

Chapter IV – The War in the East and in Italy............ 110
    Russia....................................... 110
    Battles in Northern Italy........................ 119
    Mountain Warfare 124

Chapter V – Technique In War...................... 130

Chapter VI – The Defensive Battle in Position Warfare 151

Chapter VII – German Attacks with Limited Objectives 168

Chapter VIII – Machine Guns........................ 175

Chapter IX – The Infantry Attack in Open Warfare........ 188
    Requirements 188
    Procedure of Attack 191
    Near Reconnaissance 193

Deployment and Development 196
Artillery of the Attack 198
Working Up to the Enemy 200
The Assault 206
Influence of Fog 212
Fighting in Woods 212
Village Fighting 217

Chapter X – Cavalry 221
Cavalry Prior to the World War 221
Views on Cavalry Attacks 223
Employment of Cavalry in War 226
Cavalry Divisions 229
Cyclists 230
French Views Concerning Employment of Cavalry 232

Chapter XI – The Artillery 237
Organization and Combat Principles 237
Co-Operation of Infantry and Artillery 241
Co-Operation Between Artillery and Air Service 245
The Decisive Battle in Position Warfare 246

Chapter XII – The Year 1918 260
Transition from Position to Mobile Warfare 260
Methods of Hostile Defense and German Offensive 262
The Spring Offensive 270
Resuming the Offensive 280
The Last Defensive Battle 286

Conclusion 294

About the Author 296

Foreword

Shortly before the outbreak of the World War, I was engaged in preparing my six-volume "Tactics" (the single volumes of which had already appeared in the 4th Edition), for a new edition. Extensive preparations had been made therefor and valuable material had been assembled, gathered from my essays on Infantry Tactics since 1901 and published in Loebell's Annuals. With the first edition of my "Tactics," I had taken a stand for increased valuation of Tactics and Psychology in troop leading. The World War has confirmed this necessity. My work concerning tactics embraced the viewpoint in tactics of all large military powers prior to the World War, and it is hoped that it will always remain of value in all general questions. The World War brought about enormous changes: It has shown the importance of the penetration, with the million men armies of modern times, as compared to the envelopment. I had very early advocated the unavoidable necessity of the penetration, though I fully knew that, without doubt an enveloping battle, a "Cannae," would be easier, would have greater success, and would probably also be of more decisive effect. 1 well knew; that my opinion and the opinion of military circles differed greatly; I have never denied the advantages of the enveloping battle, but also have always pointed out the necessity of preparing for the penetration. The World War proved that I was right. I attempted from the first days of the war to make myself familiar with all new writings and events in training, and to utilize the lessons shown. If I now attempt to discuss the development of tactics in the World War, I well know the difficulties thereof, because so far little authentic material is available for a basis. Therefore, in the discussion of actual events in the field, from which I was far removed, I have touched upon briefly and have treated principally the events on the Western front from the standpoint of the troop leader. The portrayal of the development has been selected, because it only makes clear, how we arrived at our present day views, which are so very different from those at the opening of the World War.

It is hoped that this work will have its share in emphasizing the experiences of the war that have been purchased with so much blood, and which experiences may easily run the danger of being lost in the dissolution of our old, tried army. May these pages call back to mind what our troops have performed, the equal of which cannot be found in military history, by heavy work against an enemy so superior in numbers and equipped with all possible auxiliary means. But the heroic achievements of our troops were possible only because all members of the army performed untiring and devoted work in time of peace, in the matter of training the men to faithful performance of duty, willingness to assume responsibility and audacity. I have but briefly touched on the end of the army ; my theme ends upon the battlefield ; the awful dissolution process and the failures at home, are beyond the limits of tactics. Therefore, I have purposely avoided touching on the unfortunate struggles in the interior of our country.

This book of mine is not for the purpose of accusing, neither is it for the purpose of excusing errors that have been committed. I have merely touched where it was absolutely necessary. My only endeavor has been to show how our present day tactics had their being and how they, starting from an excellent peace training, adapted themselves to the continually more difficult demands of battle. Though the war could not end with victory on the battlefield, that surely was not the fault of the army, nor of its leaders.

I shall be very thankful for any corrections and additions.

Aurich (East Friesland) the day of the 50th Anniversary of the French Declaration of War in the Year 1870.

Balck,
Lieutenant General, Active Service in the Field,
Commanding the 51st Reserve Division.

Chapter I – Training in Peace and Reality in War

"Our long garrison life has spoiled us, and effeminacy and desire for and love of pleasure, have weakened our military virtues. The entire nation must pass through the School of Misfortune, and we shall either die in the crisis, or a better condition will be created, after we have suffered bitter misery, and after our bones have decayed." Thus wrote the late Field Marshal von Gneisenau under the impressions of the experiences of war in the Year 1806. Only the bloody seriousness of war furnishes a final receipt for long peace labors. If the training of the troops is according to correct principles, so that they can perform anything and everything war demands of them, they will not have to forget on the battlefield anything they have learned in time of peace (I.D.R. 477); also they will not have then to learn anything new. Anyone who possesses actual experience in war may more easily attain such education than another who knows war only from books, or whose remembrances of war have been dimmed during long peace time. The Austrians in 1866 and the British in the Boer War, had materially larger experiences in war than had their opponents, and still neither the one nor the other was inured against disillusions; it may be because they arrived at erroneous decisions based on prior experiences, or it may be because the conception of actual war had been lost by colonial warfare. "*La petite guerre gate le militaire.*"* "The Austrians," wrote Marshal Foch when he was Director of the War Academy — "had so far conducted war without understanding war, the Prussians had studied war and therefore understood it, even without having conducted war."

Just as dangerous as effeminacy is the danger of letting habitual custom gain the preponderance, as is shown by a senseless repetition in training of a well known exercise or a measure that has proven successful in the face of the enemy. The army of 1806 — as von der Goltz calls it "a very industrious, orderly, willing army" — had gone to sleep on the laurels of Frederick the Great. Afraid to break away from the creations of Frederick, we had allowed them to become obsolete by adhering to the strong impetus given by unreliable foreigners, and consequently also adhered to the old time line tactics and the stereotyped formations. The first made the army tactically, the latter operatively clumsy, an enormous disadvantage opposed to the French Army that was not bound down to those tactics. Not in line tactics (for in adopting line tactics the British army was victorious in the Peninsula War over the French column tactics) but in the inaptitude of commanders and troops was to be found the cause of defeat on the battlefield. In the "echelon attack" practiced in time of peace at every opportunity, later commanders perceived the surest guarantee of victory. In Germany we also trained, up to the publication of the Regulations of 1888, by battalion, regiment and brigade. In addition to the free fighting, frequently badly transformed into what we called the "Turkish" method there was a hard and fast formation, which would hardly have been proper in the sixties. The finger marks of this formation was an attack, badly prepared by fire, carried out with insufficient means, and the final result of which was retreat, followed by flight in the face of cavalry and forming squares by battalions. Even the so-called "Schlichting's Seven Wonders" caused fatal, normal formation tactics, until the new regulations swept these misconceptions aside.

---

* "The little war guards the military."

But no matter how advanced these new regulations were, the habitual customary training of earlier times (for instance the preponderous importance of adhering to regular distance) kept up its domination.

Prior to the World War the German army worked faithfully and it was very far from falling into the errors Gneisenau had condemned in 1806. But it was not free from a certain formality, which, as early as 1892 Major von Malachowski pointed out in an efficient study as "Review" tactics. By pointing out the difference between peace engagements and actual engagements in war he showed the "Review" tactics as fatal for the field training of the troops. In the words of Gneisenau "The endeavor to lead the troops well on large parade and muster days is very damaging," and then continuing, "the tactics which expects everything from regulation uniformity, artificially produced on the drill ground, or at the green table, that cannot be used in war is "Review" tactics. In most cases it extends only to a play, or criticism-proof battle exercise. During longer periods of peace it is the most dangerous enemy to field training, by continually attempting to push the field training into the background at all points." And finally he adds warningly "The mask of 'Review' tactics continually changes, the inherent quality of the matter is always the same." Malachowski then turned against endeavors in the army which had for their object to assure a smooth course of exercises. "No normal tactics can replace the military qualities and tactical perception of the leader," he says, "it is absolutely fatal to field training, by continually leading away from the simplicity and the actuality of things." There is but one auxiliary means to meet such abnormal growths, and that is reverting to military historical experiences. The "Review" tactics are satisfied with superficial (exterior) forms, but forgets entirely that war is conducted by men against men and that in war the moral influences are principally of the most decisive importance.

It is very probable that the cavalry especially suffered from "Review" tactics, for it rode charges in autumn maneuvers till shortly prior to the World War. These charges gladdened every military eye, but they could never have been executed in that manner under actual fire. On the other hand, we do not desire to bring forth, as an example to be governed by, the British cavalry in the Boer War, which was nothing but mounted infantry.

Still less did the artillery count in our exercises, unless it laid weight on appearances, as its firing capacities and results could not be portrayed.

Actual experiences in war, which each one can gain only in a limited way, are of inestimable value; but they can produce fruitful effect only if they are thoroughly proven and utilized by the study of military history. And still, how quickly do actual war experiences fade away! We have experienced that fact in our own army. At the opening of the war in 1864 we had lost what had been gained in the Wars of Liberation at so much effort and so much loss of blood. The experiences of Worth and St. Privat should undoubtedly have been sufficient to teach our army what considered new experiences in the Russo-Japan War. In front of Verdun, in 1916, we had for instance, experiences in plenty concerning how horse batteries could follow the infantry across positions — and shortly prior to the Spring offensive in 1918, trials on a large scale were repeated to gain the same old results.

It is not at all difficult to cite a military historical example for every tactical operation. "Especially difficult will be a clear objective judgment, when the question is one of an unfortunate experience in war by our own army. The general adaption of military history to such examples often leads to the most serious errors which, having become accepted rules, spread like an epidemic, which will even take hold of thinking heads, and still will not allow their meaning to be perceived." Thus we can account for the numerous erroneous decisions drawn from events. The Austrians drew from their experiences during the War in Upper Italy in 1859 the necessity of brutal shock tactics; the British, after the Boer War, were not very far from denying the possibility of attack; the desire, to avoid losses, took precedence over the requirement to annihilate the enemy. And finally, the Russians in Eastern Asia had again to gather the same bitter experiences they had gained before at Plevna. Nothing but thorough study of military historical events, omitting the special experiences we obtain ourselves on the respective theaters of war, can prevent commanders from entering a new war with erroneous views of the inherent qualities of present day fire effect gained during long periods of peace. Up to the present day every war has brought surprises, which the troops could master, not through hard and fast rules and formations, but only through the training they underwent in time of peace; and this very fact must be reckoned with in peace time training. Only the inflexible will to be victorious, without regard to sacrifices demanded by battle, will overcome all difficulties. Only thus may we prevent the danger of immediately accepting every new thing happening in a strange theater of war as our guide, and adopting it as a cure-all for success. But, on the other hand, there is a caution, that ought to be considered, contained in the words of the British lieutenant general, Sir Ian Hamilton, based on his impressions of the battles in Eastern Asia:— "What a blessing; the larger and the prouder an army is, the more immobile is it in its firmly-rooted power of sticking to fundamentals so that finally, as a unit, it becomes inapt to absorb the experiences of other armies. Military attaches can discover the most important points for training and employment in a foreign army and urgently recommend their adoption. The majority of their comrades pay just as little attention to them as did Napoleon III pay attention to the reports of Stoffel concerning the Prussian army prior to the Franco-Prussian War." And quite similarly wrote the General of Infantry, von der Goltz, in the second edition of "Rossback and Jena;" — "Even the South-African War has created doubt if we are still on the right road in the execution of our infantry fighting; will our long and dense skirmish lines, with closely following-up supports, carefully nested in the terrain, in the face of rapid fire, not go to pieces, as did in other times, the massed Prussian lines, under the fire of the French skirmishers?" Herewith were pointed out currents of "review" tactics, which threatened to limit the freedom left by training regulations. However, the German infantry could with satisfaction look back on the events of the war in Eastern Asia, for did not the Japanese infantry, trained according to German methods, victoriously fight under very difficult conditions? The Russo-Japanese War had set aside the uncertainty caused by the Boer War in the tactical views, and primarily the doubts concerning the possibility of executing the infantry attack. It made short and thorough work in removing the overestimation of adherence to forms, and of overestimation of the value of the fire power of the defense. However, the superior German leadership in 1870-71 and the passiveness of the Turks in 1877 did not show these two maxims as clearly as was the case in the engagements of the British and Japanese. Thus, these wars did not teach anything else than what could be gleaned from the experiences of the Franco-Prussian and Russo-Turkish,wars, namely: "Conduct of War means attack, attack means carrying forward the fire."

Attack and defense are on the same footing; any one who wants to be victorious and who desires to gain an advantage by physically overcoming the enemy, must attack. But if we desire to resort to the attack, we must train our troops accordingly. The bayonet training — almost preached by Dragomiroff — would have been the very thing in Eastern Asia, if it had been accompanied by thorough training in fire fighting. The form is of importance only, if it materially increases the enemy's losses. The will to be victorious may also offset a discrepancy in numbers; not the stronger, but the one that is more energetic, has the best chances of success. During a long period of peace, which easily causes overestimation of material factors, we cannot too frequently emphasize the fact that the decision to attack is based on the task, not on the relation of strength. This notwithstanding the fact we usually learn the actual strength of the enemy only after a battle, in many cases only after the end of the war, and that all troops are inclined to overestimate the strength of the enemy with whom engaged, and also that intrepid attack weakens the enemy and makes him dependent on our decision. Finally, no one knows if the enemy is actually able to make use of his forces.

These maxims the German army appropriated to its own use. Its location between the two most important military Powers of Europe, in connection with an army which had delayed the opportunity to demand the utmost power of its people in the expectation of a decisive battle, forced the German army leadership to pay special attention to the attack against hostile superiority in numbers. In the absence of experiences in war by ourselves, our army had to draw on the sources of military history for guides in its training, and this was done with success. Military history offers the possibility to properly learn the decisions that were of decisive importance, which, in exercises on the map, or on the drill ground seldom come into account. For conduct of war we have to learn from foreign experiences, our own experiences come too dear and almost always too late. "Military history is no manual containing well-formed theories, is no volume to pass the time in reading, but is a careful teacher, who enables us, if we are attentive, to view things and to conceive their value, as we would never have seen in life. At any moment we may face in the same, or an entirely changed form, questions demanding responsible, decisive and nevertheless immediate action. Of course, military history offers us in outline only the events. But it also offers what the very best theory can never offer, the picture of frictions in war, the picture of the influences of the doubts, of the urgency, of the incalculable chances, of the surprises, of the obstacles; it recounts the road which the commander and practical military knowledge have to take to overcome these difficulties; it prepares the normal counterpoise for the moment of action; it should prepare us also for the unexpected. Military history should take the place of actual experiences in war. Our life is not long enough to gather these experiences up to the moment of action." It does not suffice to merely follow up the regulations laid down; these are only the basis of experiences during a definite, and passed, interval of time, which portray themselves in a far different manner in the brain of the victor than in the conception of the vanquished. Regulations must never descend to the plane of a code laid down for punishments; their details must not be allowed to interfere with freedom of action. Regulations are for the purpose of creating independent thought, but they have to be studied in conjunction with military history, and only what the commander inserts into them in the matter of his personal will and skill, makes them the guide for the conduct of battle. The new arms with which the armies were equipped in the beginning of the sixties, favored, in France, the creation of position tactics, caused von Moltke to consider the combination of the operative offensive with the tactical defensive, while the Austrians, having a one-sided, and in addition an entirely false estimation of the French offensive conduct, in vain endeavored to have victory perch on the Imperial standards by means of brutal shock tactics. Of course, those shock tactics were successful at Custozza over a badly armed and morally inferior army. Tactical theories turn into fatal brain illusions if they influence the commander in his decision beyond the situation.

Mahan, in his "Influence of Naval Power on History," writes as follows: "We will make the observation that changes in tactics will occur not after the introduction of new arms as is necessary, but also that the period of time between the two changes is relatively very long; this, undoubtedly, is caused by the fact that the improvement of arms has its origin in the skill of one or two individuals, while for the change in tactics the inclination to stick to customs on the part of an entire class has to be overcome, which class endeavors to adhere to what exists now. This is a grave misfortune. It can be overcome only by acknowledging each change willingly and voluntarily." The history of tactics in the 19th Century shows this "inclination to stick to established customs," from the disputes between field and review tactics, and we could cite more than one case thereof.

The reason that, no matter how farseeing any regulations are constructed in their inception, they become obsolete after a time, may be found in the very spirit of the training regulations. Emperor Napoleon measured that time to be ten years. In any case, frequent changes are a mistake, if we do not want to interfere with the tranquility of tactical development and if we want to avoid friction in the composition of our mobile army consisting of the regular levies, reservists and landwehr. On the other hand, regulations must follow suit, if the conditions on which they are based have changed. In his military phantasies, the Prince de Linge wrote in 1783:— "A paragraph that ought to be incorporated in all regulations, and that we omit, I do not know for what reason, is that we should occasionally act contrary to regulations. We must teach action contrary to regulations just as well as we must teach disorder among troops, for it will happen in battle."

To be out of touch with present day requirements is always dangerous. Troops will have to pay later on with streams of blood for knowledge gained under the fire of the enemy. Of what use was it to the Austrians in 1866 that they charged in utter disregard of death, imbued by the firm will to be victorious, but did so in tactical formations which were then obsolete and in the face of the

Training in Peace and Reality in War   15

newest improved arms? The willingness to sacrifice themselves on the part of the troops and strictest discipline, encountered an impassable obstacle in the rapid fire of an unshaken infantry. The experiences in war on the part of our regiments show that bullets quickly write a new tactics, that bullets make short work of obsolete formations and create new ones. But at what cost! In the Franco-Prussian War superior leadership and a better artillery permitted us to pay the price.

At the outbreak of war the usual custom is to prepare troops, that have been trained under obsolete regulations, for fighting on a strange theater of war by certain "Field Service Regulations." After the battle of Montebello in 1859 Napoleon III made his troops quickly acquainted with the peculiarity of the terrain and the method of fighting on the part of his opponents, and the Austrians neglected to do this. In 1866 Benedek was forced to change the tactics that he had recommended in his field service regulations, before his excellent views could be of any general benefit to the army. The tactical instructions of Kuropatkin were without any effect whatever in the Russo-Japanese War and individual experiences were disregarded. It is very desirable that the first experiences in battle become the general property of all concerned as rapidly as possible.

In 1870 we did not do this, and all units had to gather their own experiences. As late as August 18, 1870, the 85th Fusilier Battalion advanced in columns toward the center, though the campaign in Bohemia had shown that that formation was completely obsolete. In the World War, the experiences gained at some one point were printed and thus quickly became the general property of all. The impulse to gain and spread experiences worked especially well on tranquil fronts. Extraordinarily much was accomplished by establishing schools in order to make officers of all ranks, under officers of the special arms, familiar with the latest experiences. But this method sufficed only when the troops, by the method of their training in peace, had gained the necessary ability to adapt themselves thereto. Training regulations should not emphasize the matter of formation, they should induce every one to practical co-operation.

Troops that are thus trained and trained theoretically, and who are not afraid of losses, will soon evolve new tactics. What a difference there was between the method of attack of the Guard at St. Privat and at Le Bourget, and the charge of the Royal Grenadiers on Chateau Geisberg and of the Baden Body Grenadiers on the railroad embankment at Nuits! The Russian experiences at Plevna were similar to ours in August, 1870, except that with the Russians the fear of losses gained the upper hand; they considered the fire effect of the Turks as a certain unchangeable factor, declined the freedom of operations, and sought only means to lessen their losses. In no instance must the troops at the first sudden impression of the hostile fire effect accept that fire effect as a stated factor and passively submit to it with the thought that it cannot be helped, and that the main consideration is to lessen the losses. In that case we forget that the impressions are the same with the enemy. The effect of these impressions is naturally larger if we have, before the war, underestimated our opponent. The Russians sought to draw lessons for mechanical conduct in battle, as they also did subsequently in Eastern Asia; but entirely different factors co-operated decisively. The application of the best lessons as to utilization of our own fire power, as to formations and conduct against the influence of moral factors, is impossible. We must never lay down the law, or accept as a maxim for our action, that procedure which proved itself in war, or in battles, as immediately the best, or which brought about the victory. Conditions, under which that procedure was correct, play too large a role, and among these numerous and different conditions the moral status of the troops and of the commander play the leading role. What one may permit himself to do and what, because he permits himself to do it, leads to success, is for another who adopts it, the very cause of defeat. Studying wars and battles does not furnish recipes for victory. It increases the knowledge of the commander of troops only when it causes him to perceive the connection between cause and effect. It is not difficult to perceive the effect, that lies open to the view, but to correctly cull the causes, requires not only a clear view and study, but thought and knowledge of the characteristics of war. It is important also to know that chance plays a great role in all military actions, and that chance favors permanently him only, who deserves it. It is therefore wrong to condemn any action because without "luck" success could not have been possible. Such an event teaches merely that we must have the mental conception that luck easily passes one by, and that we must have manhood enough to grasp it in passing.

Superior in rifles and guns, trained in fighting the mountain inhabitants of the Indian frontier, and in defense against numerous swarms of the false Mahdi, the British entered the campaign against the Boers with full confidence. No one doubted a glorious victory; but, in the dark December days of 1899 ill-success succeeded ill-success, not only in the matter of defeated attacks, but — what the heart of a soldier had to feel most poignantly — even capitulations in the open field. Up to then it had been unheard of in British military history, that in the first six months 182 officers and 4984 men capitulated, while only 168 officers and 2124 men were killed or wounded. It is said that the tactics pursued by the British had their origin on German ground. But, German troops defeated, with German tactics, in South-Africa, an enemy equally as good as the Boers; our troops there in any case understood how to quickly adapt themselves to new conditions. Colonial wars and inapt training in the home country had led the education of British commanders into wrong channels. Absence of the firm will to insert even the very last man for victory, dearth of willingness to assume responsibility on the part of the higher commanders, absence of independence on the part of the subordinate commanders and the inability to execute attacks by combined units supported by artillery, are the real causes of the British disasters. As the British had, at the start, underestimated the Boers, the weight of the impressions gained was the heavier. Underestimation is followed as a matter of course by overestimation. In England, they went even so far as to question the possibility of any attack, and only gradually the spirits rose again. We must bear witness to the fact that the British in the World War attacked especially well. Through the misconception of inherent things in the Boer War, we attempted in Germany to follow the forms of the Boer attacks for a time (as a matter of fact, the Boers never attacked), until we again thought of our own experiences and employed only the most valuable of the experiences gained in the South African War.

A similar thing happened in the Russo-Japanese War. The tactical causes of defeat were the same as in the Boer War, and thereto were added faults to be found in the character of the Russian peoples. Bitterly did they pay for their underestimation of the enemy. And this very fault is hard to avoid, as leaders and troops take their own achievements as a model. Only sharp criticism of our own action can save us from underestimating the enemy.

On the Japanese side also, the first successes had been bought with relatively small losses and just as in the FrancoPrussian War, a change of the procedure of attack took place, as we can see from following up the battles of the First Army. As with us in the year 1870 the endeavor was to arrange a looser formation. "But the course of war, without definite rules, caused all tactical formations prescribed by regulations to be forgotten. As was the case with the Germans in 1870, the Japanese battle action gradually lost its uniform character and adapted itself again and again to the changing situation. In larger as well as in smaller units, down to the battle unit, the same applied. Thus, the Japanese tactics became more and more clearly acting according to circumstances, without regulation formations, and without official basis, all depending on the peculiarity of the leaders."

Knowledge of the inherent peculiarities of a people, of their military establishment and tactical views is therefore absolutely required of every leader. Thus, the tactics of the French 1st Corps at Worth ought not to have contained anything surprising to us, as those tactics had been minutely discussed in German military literature prior to the war, and the fire effect of the chassepot rifle, which we belittled (probably for reasons of training), ought not to have been unknown to the troops. The annihilating effect of hostile arms must not be allowed to offer something new to our troops. Proper target practice must make known the effect of arms to the troops and get them accustomed to have the artillery and other arms fire over their heads. As far as possible, the primary battle impressions must not be foreign to the troops. Dragomiroff's method of training, to strengthen the will and the heart, was correct, though it had been completely misunderstood in Russia.

The leader must be able to see his troops bleeding, but he must also know how to save them from unexpected high losses. The more individual the training has been in time of peace, the more the will to gain victory has been fostered, the more the readiness to assume responsibility has been developed, the better will the troops behave under the first impressions in battle. The individual will perform more, the more he is trained in the use of his arm, and the more he is imbued with the feeling that he is superior to the enemy in its use. In prior wars the British, the French, and the Russian boasted of their superiority to all other armies, in the use of the bayonet. This conviction in a way hurt them, as it merely fostered the desire to seek the decision in hand to hand fighting. Similarly, in the World War the conviction of the superiority of the German infantry in close range fighting which was proven in the very first battles, and thereafter spread throughout the army, played a great role in the stubbornness of defense and in the relentless attack. Under the surprising impression of the effect of hostile fire we quickly discount the effect of our own fire, when it becomes the "safety valve of our own nervousness," as when the skirmisher fires only to deaden his hearing, or to be doing something. Here the influence of the subordinate commanders and of quieter and better educated men must make itself felt, to attain a slow, well-aimed fire. The moral value of the individual is the decisive factor.

We must not forget the importance of drill. It may be possible that other peoples do not feel its beneficial influence. But we require drill by all means. We should never forget that it was nothing but the drill which helped the Guard at St. Privat gain the victory with the employment of obsolete formations and in spite of enormous losses. When imminent danger of death overpoweringly awakens the striving for salvation, when the frightful impressions of the battle cloud the clear understanding, then the often-heard word of command must electrify the soldier and make him capable to perform his duty. Therefore we cannot go too far in demanding the utmost endeavors in time of peace; but not in the forms of a senseless marching around the parade or drill ground, but in the forms used in battle. We foster the drill, not for inspections, but for war.

However, the army has no community life for itself alone.

Prior to the World War, the army was the school through which a very material portion of the people went. Army and people are, and must be, one. Education of the entire people for efficiency in war and willingness to sacrifice is a political and national necessity, and at the same time the main basis for the successful training of an army equal to all conditions.

We were not saved from surprises in the World War, as will be shown later on. But we did not treat them merely passively, we became master of them and utilized them. That was possible only through the manner of our peace training, through rapid dissemination of all experiences, and through never slacking up in our work during the rest pauses between the battles. "It has always been moral factors which have decided a war, even before it began, and it will always be moral factors that will do so. In comparison with them everything else, organization, numbers, armament, and even leadership, are but secondary considerations. And that is even true of leadership, as has just been said, because in an army in which every individual is trained to perform his highest duty, the leadership cannot be bad. And even if leadership sometimes commits an error, which is but human, what are those errors as compared with the efficiency that overtops everything, and the moral strength?

"But let us not believe that at any time any technical inventions, even if they are ever so enormous, will be able to change even the very least bit of the nature of war. It is true that they may change the forms, but they will never touch war's inner core. The capability to be victorious is not naturally inherent to any people. It cannot be borrowed from nature for eternity. No, the capability for victory must be educated into the people and into the army and must be maintained by strict performance of duty. Maintenance is frequently more difficult than acquisition. Two races, two nations, may be physically equal and have the same intelligence, but if in case of one of them the capability of greater sacrifices by the individual, and thus by the entire people, is less than is the case with the other, it is as certain as the sun rises in the morning and sets at night, that war will pass its hard judgment on the lesser sacrifice."

Chapter II – Mobile Warfare

Training and Organization

The German leadership sought the annihilating battle as quickly as possible; and in order to be able to conduct it at the decisive point, satisfied itself with defensive procedure on minor fronts, or with giving ground, prior to the decisive battle. The training of the infantry in time of peace was in full conformity with those intentions. Training in peace was based on the excellent drill regulations of May 5, 1906, which of course had their origin in 1888, but which had been revised several times. Special preference to training in mobile warfare sought to foster the spirit of attack on the part of the infantry in every possible manner. The leaders saw the basis of all military success in independence, properly checked by tactical training and education, in increased firing ability and marching capacities, as well as in drill intelligently carried out. We cannot blame the troops for their inclination to a so-called "attack-agitation" in carrying out the attack. This however prevented the co-operation between infantry and artillery which would have produced the fullest effect. Insufficient time was given to battle reconnaissance, to the establishment of means of communication, and it cannot be denied that there was a great preference for dense skirmish lines. But this peace training had such a permanent effect that the regular soldier and the reservist could not be distinguished in their capabilities within a few days. The officers of the furlough class were prominent by their knowledge and faithfulness to duty. The effect of the training course, held before the war on the drill grounds, could be plainly felt. Only the aims should have been set higher. It must be attributed to the youth and incomplete training of many officers who had been promoted on the battlefield, that they not always found the proper "tone" in their relation with the older soldiers whom they had been with but shortly before in ranks, and to whom they were now superiors. The difficulty in preserving the status as superiors, placed the new officers in a difficult position often erroneously considered as supercilious; it probably might have been better to transfer these officers, on commission, to other units. It was far from those officers to be cold to their subordinates, though they were blamed for that. Many of the newly appointed officers failed. Instead of setting an example to their men, they thought more of their ease and pleasure, which could be procured behind the front by any one with sufficient means. The subordinate had sharper eyes than the superior. The danger to consider single instances as the general rule, lay near. It cannot be denied that in selecting the provisional applicants for commissions we did not always exercise sufficient care, and on the other hand, we were frequently too slow in promoting acting officers. How frequently, however, have we seen that in battle the men preferred to follow the youngest lieutenant than the older well-tried noncommissioned officer.

The necessity to carefully husband our material for commissioned officers which compelled us to cut out a "leader reserve" before battle, encountered small comprehension; the great loss in officers show that very plainly.

In the course of the World War the conditions of replenishment became worse. Younger levies at home had grown up uninfluenced by the older men in the field. The irresponsibility of youth in Germany increased and the short time for training at home by officers that were not of the best grade offered no counterweight.

To this were added difficulties in the matter of subsistence. Increases in wages made the relations more acute between employers and employees and between superiors and subordinates. Through this new levy, and through the influence of men of the field army, home on furlough, mistrust was sowed between the recruits and the officers, which was not fully perceived in the first two years of the war. It was strange, but in the officers, people saw only "Prolongers of the War," who were believed to expect higher rank from the longer duration of the war, while as a matter of fact, a major general, for instance, remained a full year longer in that grade than he would have in time of peace, before being promoted to lieutenant general. The talk that officers procured at the cost of the men, advantages which were denied the men, was easily believed. We do not want to deny, by any means, that irregularities happened, that through the method of appointing officers much was made easier for them. But in general the officers can be proud of the fact that they took good care of their men. Mistrust existed, factory workers believed that preference in the matter of granting furloughs was given to agricultural workers, while the latter objected to the numerous claims of well paid factory workers for exemption from service. All this ill feeling was increased by the advanced cost of all necessities at home; and many men returned to the field army disgusted with conditions at home.

As was the case during the Franco-Prussian War, the losses in officers were extremely high in the first battles, so that young officers quickly became company and even battalion commanders. It was soon perceived, that it would have been wise to train every officer in time of peace for the duties of the next higher grade. Intense desire to attack on the part of the troops and bravery of the officers, never fearing bodily harm, helped the troops to overcome many difficult situations. "All hail to that army where untimely bravery is frequently shown; it may be a rank growth, but it is a sure indication of fruitful ground."

The German defense held to a single line, fortified in depth as much as possible — and generally strongly occupied — sought the decision by the attack of its main reserve. Advanced positions, which had been occupied under the experiences of the fortress warfare (Regulations for fortress warfare, August 13, 1910, p. 123) assumed a doubtful importance and the question arose, due to increasing development of aerial reconnaissance, of advanced positions being replaced by false works. Under the conviction that infantry that can attack well, can also defend itself well, we had not paid as much attention to the technique of the defensive battle as should have been done. Leaders and troops paid little attention to the defense. The soldier does not love the spade. Troops that had participated in fortress maneuvers however were better trained for the close range battle in the use of hand grenades and minenwerfers.*

The infantry was armed with the rifle model '98 (magazine under the barrel and pointed bullet). The complement of machine guns was not sufficient. There were only 6 guns to the regiment. The fire effect was excellent, but the sled mount was too heavy; protective shields intended to offer protection to the men in the fire fight and during fire pauses, betrayed their location by their size.

The intrenching equipment had been augmented shortly before the war by the addition of an intrenching tool wagon for each regiment (field train) containing 230 long handled spades. With the small intrenching equipment, suitable only for digging trenches of little depth, 1 company could construct a trench of 150 meters. The supply of wire cutters and wood working tools was inadequate.

Hand grenades, introduced by the Russian infantry, were used only by pioneers.

The "protective coloring" of the field equipment was not correctly done. The various arms betrayed themselves by different colored insignia. Officers fell because of their equipment, order clasps, belts, sashes, and especially the officers' long side-arms.

To each infantry regiment were attached 6 telephone squads with 18 kilometers of light wire (not field wire as in case of telephone battalions), and there were an additional 12 kilometers of light wire on the infantry ammunition wagon. Of special importance for mobile warfare was the equipment of mobile field kitchens. The Russians had these rolling kitchens but not the

---

* A type of short range mortar that launched mine shells, a high explosive ordinance often used to clear obstacles.

French nor British.

The Jäger battalions, composed of picked men, and intended for the support of the army cavalry, had been reinforced by 1 cyclist and 1 machine gun company each. They performed excellent services due to their increased fire, their training and the excellent material of which they were composed.

The German cavalry had excellent well trained animals, though a little sensitive against extremes of temperature. The troopers, trained by 3 years' service, were armed with the carbine and tubular steel lance as principal weapons; the "thrusting" saber, fastened to the saddle was little suited to the German cavalry for their "strike and cutting method." Our cavalry could meet the French and British cavalry with full confidence. France believed that the German cavalry had a great love for fighting dismounted. The regulations of March 4, 1909, rightly warned against fighting on foot in only a half-hearted manner. These drill regulations also mentioned the possibility of carrying on attacks on a larger scale dismounted (C.D.R. 456) but laid particular emphasis on the general rule, that the cavalry fight should in general be mounted (C.D.R. 389); also that cavalry must always try to solve its task mounted. "Only where the lance is out of place, the cavalry resorts to the carbine. ..... In an engagement of all arms, small cavalry units may achieve local success by vigorous action at the right moment. Decisive participation in the course of a battle, either in the beating off of a hostile attack or in the support of our attack, is possible only by insertion of large masses of cavalry. The enemy is very vulnerable to a cavalry attack on his flank or rear. Merely threatening an attack in such a direction has a serious effect on the hostile troops. But the cavalry must not be satisfied with mere threatening. Operations against the lines of communications of the enemy to the rear can have valuable results; but these operations should never divert the cavalry from its battle task. If a battle ensues, then the watchword for each large and small cavalry unit must be "participation in the victory." (C.D.R. 393-395.) Success against unshaken infantry is considered possible "if the cavalry has come up close and can attack by surprise" (C.D.R. 441). An attack against shaken infantry will always be successful. Attack direction and attack formation are of less importance in this case. (C.D.R.

443.) Where possible, charges against infantry from several sides may be executed with depth formation, in which the leading waves are deployed. In attacks against artillery the advice was given to attack the flanks rather than the rear. Artillery under cover can be charged in front also, under certain conditions, without material loss (C.D.R. 444), and heavy artillery was pointed out as an especially vulnerable target (C.D.R. 448). In the service of reconnaissance the attack was especially emphasized, the impression created on an enemy by the offensive action of patrols and reconnoitering detachments was valued especially high. It was believed that no valuable information could be gained by making detours. The enemy undoubtedly would endeavor to hide important measures from our view, which could only be overcome by force of arms. To foster the offensive spirit, stress was laid on the fact that our mounted messengers could find their way back only after the hostile reconnoitering detachments had been driven from the field.

The composition of the larger units (army cavalry) was consistent with the demands of reconnaissance and battle; higher cavalry commanders were instructed to cause the consolidation of several cavalry divisions on the battlefield into 1 cavalry corps (C.D.R. 523), in so far as this had not been done during the course of the operations (C.D.R. 229). The cavalry division consisted of 3 cavalry brigades, each of 2 regiments, 1 machine gun battalion, 1 pioneer detachment, and 1 information detachment. Some cyclist troops and a Jäger battalion were attached.

During the year prior to the war, the German artillery had been increased so that each infantry division had the disposition of 2 regiments, of 6 batteries and 2 light ammunition columns each; 1 battalion thereof being equipped with light field howitzers. Corps had the disposition of a heavy howitzer battalion of 4 batteries. We could count on the attachment of mortars (21-cm.) and heavy guns in battle. At the beginning of the World War the field batteries had 6 guns and caissons; horse batteries, 4 guns and caissons, heavy field howitzer batteries, 4 howitzers with 8 caissons, and mortar batteries, 4 mortars and caissons. During the course of the war all field batteries were limited to 4 guns, without any disadvantages accruing thereby, as far as military literature shows. In the 6-gun battery there were 136 rounds per piece available, in the French 4-gun battery 312 rounds for each piece. The field gun, model '96, with its very effective shrapnel, was considered the main fighting weapon, and less importance was attached to the shell, as shown by the supply thereof carried by the battery. The light field howitzer with high explosive shell was to be employed principally against artillery targets behind cover, villages, and troops in dense forests. "It is able to pierce most of the cover found in the field, and to fire on captive balloons and airplanes at high altitude." (F.A.D.R., 356.) The heavy field howitzers, drawn by heavy draft horses, broken to fire, was considered an especially effective gun to fire on artillery under cover and on strongly fortified positions. Only when the crisis of battle demanded it were the heavy field howitzers advanced at the trot. The principal projectile was the percussion shell (instantaneous and delayed fuse). The employment of the mortar battery was made more difficult by the parts of the gun being carried separately on the march — barrel, cradle and trail. It required about five minutes to assemble the piece. Equipped with a mobile and efficient heavy artillery the German Army was presumed to have a material superiority over its opponents. It could, "delay by its long range pieces the advance of the enemy; could force him to make detours; could block or keep open defiles." "It also can take up the battle against heavy hostile artillery and thereby facilitate going into position of light batteries at effective range." (F.A.D.R. 388.) As the battery that is in the open can be rapidly destroyed, the development of the telephone and the indirect laying method, caused the field artillery to generally be found firing from covered positions. Causing the officers of the furlough class to attend courses of instruction in field artillery schools of fire, had disseminated knowledge of indirect laying and the new firing procedure to a very great extent. Regulations demanded that the field artillery should at times disregard the advantages of covered positions, and should fire from the open to bring about the decision in the infantry battle. (F.A.D.R., 367.) In such emergency even the hottest infantry fire was not to be feared. Emphasis was laid on the fact that the battle activity of infantry and artillery must be of the closest and that the main task of the latter is to support the infantry (I.D.R. 44, 446,

F.A.D.R. 366). Co-operation of these two arms was demanded, but it was left to the training in peace time to find the suitable means therefor. (I.D.R. 447, F.A.D.R. 368.) That requirement left much to be desired. We intended to force the defender to leave his position and show his troops by having our infantry advance and attack (F.A.D.R. 494, H.A.D.R. 454). Then the task was left to the artillery to annihilate the enemy with its sheaf of projectiles. Contrary to this method, the French Regulations contemplated but a portion of the artillery firing on the attacking infantry, while the mass of the guns were to engage the hostile artillery. Conduct of the artillery battle was left to the commander of the artillery. Employment by regiment and by battalion was the rule, without however prohibiting the employment of single batteries and platoons. It was recommended that instead of dispersion, employment by groups be resorted to, for the better utilization of the terrain for facilitating fire control (F.A.D.R. 366). Hostile artillery was to be engaged by field fire and heavy artillery combined, though we did not deceive ourselves in thinking that locating batteries under cover would be easy. If we did not succeed in locating the hostile batteries, firing on observation posts that were visible might promise success. (F.A.D.R. 438.) In any case the infantry had to become used to the belief that the attack must be made even when the artillery did not succeed in gaining fire superiority.

The infantry division formed the battle unit; 2 to 6 infantry divisions were formed into an army corps or group, which could be reinforced in artillery according to the situation. All fighting arms were combined in the infantry division, while corps headquarters reserved to itself the disposition of the heavy artillery, information detachments, columns and trains. Dividing the infantry division into 2 infantry brigades of 2 regiments and 1 artillery brigade, also of 2 regiments (a corresponding number of infantry and artillery regiments) undoubtedly assisted in the proper co-ordination of these arms. This co-ordination was interfered with by the assignment of a light field howitzer battalion. The organization of the infantry into 2 brigades was disadvantageous in so far as the brigade unit became disrupted in deploying for battle from the march column. One brigade commander became superfluous. A better solution, and one corresponding to the battle object, was attained by decreasing the units into 3 infantry regiments and 3 artillery battalions (1 of the latter a light field howitzer battalion). Experience soon showed this organization corresponded best with the demands of battle, even if the overhead, in comparison with numbers of troops, became larger. Many instances happened where field guns and light field howitzers were found in the same battalions.

It was a grave error to send the 22d and 27th Reserve Corps in October, 1914, to Flanders and Poland, after a short period of training, without attaching strong artillery to them. Only a few commanders, with war experience, could be assigned to them by transfer, at the last hour and the number of seasoned soldiers in those corps was very small. Intense enthusiasm could not offset training and equipment. These corps went to pieces in Flanders under heavy losses. This was the more serious, as in these corps the men were from the well educated classes and we lost considerable material that could have been used later on for commissioned officers. We thus gained the same experiences as we did in the Wars of Liberation, in forming volunteer corps. Events of war proved that new organizations of young troops, Landwehr and Landstrum, require a more liberal supply of artillery, to give them the same fighting power, as active and reserve organizations. No one can foretell in arranging war organizations when units will be compelled to fight at a decisive point.

The divisional cavalry originally organized into 3 squadrons, still possessed a certain fighting strength. This strength proved itself unnecessary the more the cavalry confined itself to message service and near reconnaissance.

In the matter of technical troops, only 1 pioneer company with division bridge train was attached; this sufficed for mobile warfare, but was not sufficient as the change was made into position warfare. There were no division information detachments, and only 1 sanitary company.

Ersatz units, at mobilization received an insufficient instructor personnel. When the loss in officers became so great these units very soon lost their active officers by transfer. This loss was very bad for the training of the Ersatz troops. The retired officers detailed as instructors, did not comprehend the requirements of modern war. This increased the difficulties in training at home, so that units in the field were satisfied to have only primary drill and training take place at home, while the actual training for work in the field was undertaken by divisions independently, in field recruit depots gradually established. In any case these replacements could be furnished quicker from division depots than to be brought from home. For this the army authorities should have made arrangements in time of peace. All experiences gained in war proved that field recruit depots were necessary in the theater of war. The training in the field recruit depots was enhanced by the military atmosphere; by the immediate use of campaign experiences and lessons; and by life within the midst of hostile peoples. According to the progress of their training the men were formed into companies. Strict orders had to be issued that the men subsequently were sent to join their former organizations or in case or recruits, to whose home district they belonged. This was especially important in consideration of furthering esprit de corps. In the battles on the Hochberg near Rheims in 1917 one battalion of my division was almost annihilated. Within three days it had been filled up again from our field recruit depot, and by transfer of officers, and was again ready for employment. We generally allowed eight weeks for training in the Ersatz battalion, four of which was for company training. In that short a time nothing thorough could, of course, be accomplished. The greatest difficulties encountered were to make good the losses in officers. The Ersatz battalions commenced very early to train younger acting officers and officer aspirants. As compared with the old noncommissioned officers, who in most cases were far more advanced in years, they lacked experience in military service and in the field. It might probably have been better to promote efficient first sergeants and sergeants major to commissioned rank, as rapid promotion of young men causes bad blood very quickly. In the field mental education alone is without value. If the young officers were assigned to a unit of well trained troops, their value in the field grew gradually. It was no illusion whatever that such a short time of training could not suffice to create a unit of war-trained troops. A superficial training, deceiving the layman, can be

Mobile Warfare 31

attained, but we can never create the cohesion and the morale, which assures the primary battle value of troops. Campaigns clearly showed the importance of a well trained peace army. Even the training of Kitchener's armies does not justify a militia system. Training was had under the pressure of military events. There was a nucleus of units that had been trained in peace, furthered by the sporting sense of the entire nation. The primary training was not for the difficult mobile war, but for mere position warfare, in which the troops were supported by superior artillery. The war situation permitted the high command to designate the time for recruits to be sent to the front according to the status of their training. Complaints that the army, with its young officers, was not able to cope with the difficult situations, were frequently heard. Sporting rifle clubs and military training in the schools and colleges of the nation are absolutely necessary for an army that has but short period of service in peace time. Athletic and similar training are not only for bodily training, they are, for the mind also, of great value. They not only further the will power but demand within a stated time the greatest exertion of all mental and physical powers. Thus they directly increase the value of our youth for service in the field.

Labor Battalions modeled after those of Japan, were organized by us early in the war. These units relieved the fighting troops from detaching large numbers of men and preserved their fighting strength. The Russians learned this lesson to their sorrow through the difficulties they encountered in bringing up recruits in Eastern Asia. Men, who were unsuited for active service in the field under arms, were enrolled in the labor battalions, and under efficient officers, performed excellent services.

The infantry, as a matter of course, had to bear the heaviest burden. In active officers of infantry, the 7th Army Corps lost 70%, 60% of officers of the furlough class, and 40% of the men. The corresponding numbers in field artillery were 45%, 35% and 7%.

The tactical views of the Austrian Infantry, after they had been purged of false ideas of the lessons of the Boer War, were in general in accordance with the tactical views of the German leadership. The Austrians did not fully understand the method of German training, in which prime importance was laid on good training in firing and marching. However a portion of the Austrian Infantry was well trained for mountain warfare. In time of peace each regiment had 2, in war 3 machine guns with tripod and collapsible shields carried on pack animals. It was believed machine guns could replace artillery at short range and their employment in defense as a fire reserve in widely separated positions was recommended. Regulations of 1911 laid emphasis on the value of training in close formation in order to increase discipline. This however without limiting the front to be covered in the various exercises. The Regulations designated "the inflexible will" as the power that would mainly decide the battle:— "In case the attacker does not succeed in gaining fire superiority, even after inserting all his rifles, the commander must always remember that even in apparently hopeless situations success will come to the side which is the more stubborn. Tenaciously persisting is far better, and causes less losses, than retreat. ..... When during a costly, stubborn infantry engagement the enervating influences of the battlefield have caused the utmost exhaustion on both sides, that side will gain the victory whose iron discipline and stronger will power enables him to better withstand that exhaustion, and who continues the fight with unshakeable persistence, until he has forced the enemy to desist. ..... Upon the sure, firm will of the commander reflects all actions of the troops. If he vacillates in his decision, his uncertainty is transmitted to his subordinates. He must let his will permeate to his subordinates, and must always take care that his will turns into action." The importance of independence was especially emphasized. In the excellent words of our field regulations, par. 38, "Inactivity is criminal." It was pointed out that the decision being made and knowing its objective, the energetic execution of the decision makes high demands on character. That often after success these demands must be increased. "After every battle the vital point is for the commander, and for the troops as well, to force themselves to overcome the mental, physical and moral tension, which, after fatigue and danger, may easily lead to being satisfied with a half-success. Only a forceful, inflexible will can overcome this weakness. In most cases the commander must demand, after the success, a further extreme effort by all forces to complete the victory and annihilate the enemy. Only thus can he avoid renewed heavy sacrifices in subsequent battles."

The regulations of 1903, written under the fresh impressions of the Boer War, placed too high a value on fire effect, and credited fire as the only decisive element. The regulations of 1911 took into account the fact that the opponent would display tenacity and persistence, which all leaders demand. "Infantry, imbued with the will to attack, physically and morally well trained and well led, can fight successfully under the most difficult conditions. The infantry batters down the enemy with its fire, then with the bayonet breaks down his last resistance." Good infantry must always look to the bayonet fight as the last resort, it is frequently indispensable to gain the decision. The final appeal to the bayonet, omitted in prior regulations, is found again in the new regulations. In its preparation for war the army suffered much from the small appropriations. A portion of the infantry (Landwehr) consisted mainly only of skeleton organizations so that the excellent plans for training of the drill regulations were of little use, the more so as the replenishment of officers had not been sufficiently prepared. The number of guns and machine guns of units did not correspond to the requirements of modern times. Still less than in Germany was the population, fit to carry arms, made available for service in the army.

The Austrian Cavalry was excellently trained as such. Its regulations corresponded to those of the German cavalry. The artillery had been for years the elite arm. Theoretically well trained, it suffered from having a small number of guns. In an army corps there were only 8 gun batteries, 2 light and 2 heavy field howitzer batteries, a total of 84 guns against 160 in the German army. Austria's artillery had not been sufficiently trained for the tasks of fire control in large scale battles.

At the opening of the war the Imperial Austrian army was not a valuable instrument for war. The value of the army was decreased by the composition of the States from which men, with different racial qualities, and different political aims were drawn. German and Hungarian troops were decidedly superior to Slavic troops. High losses in the first battles, for the replenishment of which little preparations had been made, the absence of an old, well-tried corps of noncommissioned officers, the mixture of non-

German with German troops, with no common language, the unreliability of the Slavic troops, an indisputable effeminacy on the part of the officers, decreased the value of the army still further. "In the instruction of officers training in will power was neglected, knowledge and education were rated higher. More dutiful subordinates, than independent, forceful superiors were trained; we systematically accustomed the officer to be dependent and to await leadership. In the general staff, knowledge was the prime requisite; the general staff dominated the forms of troop leading and the issue of orders, but was insufficiently acquainted with the instrument with whose help it intended to utilize its knowledge." In 1916 an exchange was tried with German officers; it was hoped to give the Austrian army a greater degree of power of resistance through the increased influence of German officers in its training, and through the insertion of German troop units into the Imperial Austrian units of the army. But it was too late for that. The army lacked strict discipline, lacked the enormous driving power, and lacked the sense of duty, of the German troop units which never failed in the first four years.

Tactics of Mobile Warfare

The rapid advance of the German Armies in the West made a material change in the method of fighting impossible; the troops attacked as they had been taught in peace; after the first experiences the skirmish lines were kept thinner. Troop leadership sought to give plenty of time for the absolutely necessary battle reconnaissance, and for a better co-operation with the artillery. Proper utilization of the terrain progressed under the stimulus of the hostile fire. On the eastern front the training of the German infantry was so superior to its opponent that here also a change in the method of fighting was not considered necessary. It must be said that the Russians had many excellent qualities. Its infantry especially showed the benefit of the experiences gained in the Russo-Japanese War in its use of the hand grenade and field fortifications. While demanding the strictest discipline, our regulations had educated the troops in initiative and the will to attack. It had given them the means to adapt themselves to the changing forms of battle. Where high losses occurred, the reason could invariably be traced to non-observance of the maxims laid down in regulations.

A material difference in the conception of the infantry attack in Germany and in France existed prior to the World War in the value laid on utilizing infantry fire. Regulations for the training of the French infantry published immediately prior to the World War did not mention the necessity of gaining the infantry fire superiority, the artillery rather was to hold down the hostile guns, and then to facilitate the advance of the infantry by heavy fire on the defender's infantry. "Infantry is the main arm; it fights through fire and on the move. Only the forward movement, leading to hand-to-hand fighting, is decisively irresistible, and usually an effective and strong fire has to open the road to pierce the enemy..... Artillery fire, which has only a very slight effect on an enemy under cover, can never by itself drive the defender out of his position. The advance of the infantry must compel the opponent to show himself and to offer targets. The artillery supports the advance of the infantry, by annihilating everything that might hold up that advance." Infantry must resort to its protecting arm if the hostile fire prevents a continuation of the forward movement, which, as soon as possible, should be resumed.

Our German regulations considered "the most excellent means for working up, (prerequisite to going forward) to be gaining fire superiority" (170), "which will be perceived by the decreasing hostile fire, or by the enemy firing too high" (336). In this, errors were possible, as fire pauses, ordered by hostile commanders, due to firing with incorrect sight elevations, might only too easily be mistaken as due to the results of our fire. The demands of the Infantry Drill Regulations (374), to not make the execution of the infantry attack mainly dependent on first gaining artillery fire superiority, seldom furnished a basis in field exercises to execute an attack with our own infantry weapons. We waited until our attacking artillery had gained fire superiority. During the Russo-Japanese War it was reported of Japanese attacks that they had been executed without the Japanese artillery having gained fire superiority. Reports from the Balkan war made us study the statements according to which Bulgarian and Serbian infantry had worked their way up to within 200 to 300 meters of the enemy without firing a shot. By deploying into small detachments and under efficient support by the attacking artillery, a well trained unit might get close to the enemy and take up the fire fight only at close range. This was successfully achieved by the 43d Infantry Brigade (General v. Hülsen) on September 9, 1914, at Gerdauen.

French reports available at this time praise the rapid advance of our infantry and their excellent utilization of the terrain, without waiting for the artillery preparation. They state that the fire effect of the infantry was annihilating and that the machine guns were used effectively at every opportunity and with surprising skill. The effects of the field artillery were considered less favorable. The reports further say that the superiority of the German tactics was especially noticeable in the open terrain during the battle of Saarburg. The hostile divisions were annihilated in a frightful frontal attack, though the French infantry utilized the terrain most excellently and could barely be distinguished. The Alpine Chasseurs and the colonial troops fought very well. The skill of the French in defending a village was especially noticeable, while at the start the fire of the French infantry and machine guns did not come up to our expectations. That may have been because we valued the artillery effect too highly and believed that it could overcome every halt that was forced on us. Though the fire was good by itself, the French sought every opportunity to attempt a flanking movement, and was seen to be especially adept in finding good firing positions, unperceived by the enemy, in houses, barns, sheds, etc.

The French positions also had a great depth, the leading line consisting of single rifle trenches, connected by false works, and the foreground excellently arranged. Farming implements that had been left in the fields, scarecrows, and trees were utilized to designate the range.

In the British Infantry were found many excellent marksmen, who acted independently. Much attention was given to flanking fire; loopholes and embrasures in the trenches, arranged so as to allow firing obliquely to the line of retreat had the preference; trenches were generally well hidden, were constructed in sawtooth shape or wave-like, so that the attacker could be taken under oblique fire, while the enemy's fire, straight from the front against the loopholes had no effect. The trenches usually lay 300 to 500 meters below the crest or behind hedges. The troops made much use of night firing.

Subsequent to the first battles much was heard in Germany of the insidious conduct of the French and Belgians; it was said that each soldier (?) had a suit of civilian clothing in his knapsack, to evade difficult situations or to carry on the war as a bushwhacker. Long range ricochets caused the suspicion that inhabitants had fired from houses, and it was also assumed that the entire population took part in the information service. Cases of that kind certainly did happen, but should not be taken as the general rule. There is no doubt that the Germans were much inferior to their opponents in the employment of permitted and forbidden war ruses and tricks, and our men did not consider it fair that the enemy should resort to placing sharpshooters in trees, and neither did they consider the conduct of the British sharpshooters posted in cabbage fields as permissible. At the start our men were not suspicious enough and they trusted the inhabitants too much. Subsequently they saw in each inhabitant a traitor.

The German rifle fire had an enormous effect, probably being the result of carefully firing each round in the manner taught in peace in connection with the training in the continuous rifle fire, increasing and decreasing according to the situation. The main fire fight was carried on at about 800 meters range, then the lines advanced in long, broad rushes, to close with the enemy quickly without awaiting for our artillery to gain fire superiority in each instance.

Under the impression created by this advance, hostile fire effect soon diminished, and in most cases the French did not await the contact but retreated when the attacker came to within 500 meters, thus offering excellent targets to the artillery. Our troops felt superior to the enemy in short range fighting. The example set by the officers and by a few courageous men, who in time of peace had not been numbered amongst the best subordinates, was of decisive influence. In battle everyone went straight ahead and everyone fired straight to the front. In the very first battles the importance of independence could be seen.

Fire control, developed in peace time to perfection with its precise words of command, was practiced only in the most favorable instances at the opening of fire. The noise of battle is generally such that we cannot hear our own commands. Targets — almost exclusively a strip of the terrain from where the noise of firing seems to come — and elevation, will be designated by the platoon commander as long as practicable, but very soon the fire control will slip out of his hands, and his place is taken by the squad leader and finally by the individual skirmisher. This is of no very great importance, provided the individual correctly observes the effect, husbands his ammunition, increases the fire rapidity when the target becomes more favorable, and decreases it when the target fades, and ceases fire at once when the target disappears. The command "fire slower, fire quicker" merely indicates inattention or insufficient training.

In carrying the fire forward to the enemy, in gaining the fire superiority by infantry, supported by the fire of the artillery, the Infantry Drill Regulations saw the surest means of success, and demanded that infantry open fire only at mid range even in a terrain devoid of cover. In battle the conviction gained ground more and more, that to bring the defender into a condition where he could be charged, was the principal task of the artillery and that, considering that the infantry could rapidly entrench, fire preparation by infantry was a minor matter. Besides the terrain, the possibility of our own and of the enemy's fire effect controlled the manner in which infantry worked itself up to charging distance. But even under the most favorable conditions artillery will not be able to open a road for the infantry to victory, even if reliable connection is maintained during the entire attack between the two arms.

Insufficient support of artillery forced the infantry to resort to the spade to hold the ground it had gained. The infantry soon perceived that incautious conduct on the part of the staffs and troops soon drew the hostile artillery fire, and that fire was then directed also on points where in the opinion of the enemy commanders, German troops were moving and where they might be halting. The fire was then in the shape of a sweeping fire up to the longest ranges. This occasionally caused material losses to an incautious unit, but a cautious unit could avoid it, as the method of fire was distinguished by regular uniformity. The French artillery designated buildings, woods, and rows of trees as "artillery traps." Frequently the fire commenced with a well prepared fire-surprise and the effect then might be very great. The artillery took pleasure — being covered in front against the German artillery — in firing into neighboring sectors.

Reconnaissance and scouting that attracted no attention was now of importance, in order to cross the long and mid-ranges by smaller units with irregularly formed skirmish lines, to gain a firing position at about 400 to 500 paces from the enemy. The skirmish lines were made denser by supports rushing forward from cover to cover. It was also found to be well to bring the reserves up in skirmish waves. Massing the reserves at points that could be seen from afar, proved to be an error. The success of the attack was based on the efficiency of the lowest commanders; battalion and regimental commanders had their hands full in inserting the troops and keeping up connection with the artillery, as well as with efficiently bringing up the reserves, and could not therefore supervise all the minor details of troop leading.

Night engagements very soon assumed increased importance; their success frequently became questionable by reason of insufficient preparation and by the fact that no attention was being paid to the lessons of war that had been compiled during peace. Dense skirmish lines, with scouts far to the front, were found to be of advantage, or any formation in close order with narrow front extension. It was found best to execute the advance with pieces unloaded. All distances were shortened. The decision was sought in the charge with cold steel and without shouting. If the enemy was encountered, an immediate charge was always of advantage. As the enemy undoubtedly was prepared to fire, it was well to draw his fire by false movements and to conduct the charge in another direction, but in any case to clear the roads. Charges that were to pierce deep into the enemy, required formation in depth. Conduct in case of artificial illumination (agreed-on signals or signs for our own illumination or our own information) and co-operation with searchlights (light signals, flank protection) required special training. In the defense, fire must be opened only if the enemy is recognized beyond doubt. The practice, recommended by Regulations, of laying guns and rifles during daylight for firing at night, was hardly ever resorted to; night fire was as a rule executed by machine guns, not by riflemen. Frequently it was found better not to occupy the skirmish trenches, because the defender, standing lower was of a disadvantage against the attacker standing higher; it was found to be best during the night to have the unoccupied trenches as an obstacle in front of the line.

The newly organized reserve corps employed in Flanders in October, 1914, did of course utilize the experiences of the Western front, but suffered from the difficulties inherent to all new organizations, when they have been insufficiently trained and incompletely equipped. The first battles caused heavy losses among the young, inexperienced troops, but by early summer of 1915 they had been trained in the following attack method. Approach to within about 800 meters of the enemy with patrols, which reconnoiter and find out everything necessary for the battle activity. Advance by the company on a narrow front in skirmish waves, companies 200 meters in rear of each other. Intrenching in the first firing position, reinforcing with machine guns, and men making the firing line denser to an interval of two paces between skirmishers. Working forward by squads up to the next firing position, which again will be entrenched. From the firing position close to the enemy the charge starts under all available fire protection, the captured position being immediately arranged for defense against a counterattack that is sure to come.

The French First Army (Dubail, November 27, 1914) demanded that troops, as the result of the first lessons gained in the war, abandon, the march column 10 to 12 kilometers from the enemy and continue the further advance deployed; that the infantry, in open terrain, should not show any unit in close order at 10 kilometers range from the hostile infantry, but work up to 500 meters in the smallest units and these intrench when they could no longer advance. In covered, close terrain and in hazy weather, each battalion in the first line was to send ahead 1 company, followed by 2 companies echeloned to the flanks, and followed in turn in their center by the reserve company. For fighting in woods it was laid down that the companies in the second line should at once turn against the enemy. It was recommended that in night fighting an advance be made by half platoons in column of fours.

A German report concerning the French method of attack supplements these Regulations. "Frequently individuals rushed forward, assembling again in squads at the nearest cover. Stretches of open terrain were crossed in this manner in very thin lines, echeloned, and offering a very poor target. The supports and even the reserves following the skirmishers separated into small groups, never more than a platoon, with large intervals. The endeavor seemed to be to reach the mid ranges without material losses and there to form skirmish lines that could take up the battle in force. The fire of these skirmish lines usually was very strong, but was of little effect as soon as it met our infantry fire."

The French infantry was excellently supported by its artillery, which utilized its long range guns to the utmost. Its skill was very great in finding and taking up covered positions, in frequently changing positions and in observation. Batteries, platoons and single guns took position with very irregular, different intervals and in echelon. It appears that the French entirely abandoned the normal position with regular intervals. Detaching of platoons or pieces for the direct support of the infantry or for the purpose of flanking the leading lines was frequently observed. The French laid the greatest value on flanking fire. The endeavor was very plain on the part of the French artillery, to cover itself frontally against German artillery firing straight to the front by this method of taking position, either using the terrain (ridges, villages, buildings) or by the use of masks (strips of wood, rows of trees, hedges). Each French gun carried a saw in its limber, by the use of which it procured for itself a line of sight through these masks and, covered frontally, fired obliquely, and mostly into the firing sector of its neighbor, and thus effectively flanked the neighbor's attack target. Therefore the French batteries were hard to locate by the German batteries, and could but seldom be perceived by our infantry in the front line, causing it frequently to assume that it was being fired on by its own artillery.

Mobile Warfare

Changes in Organization, Equipment and Armament

Based on the experiences of the war, changes in organization and armament had been made in the summer of 1916, which were to make their influence felt on the method of fighting. The divisions were organized into 3 regiments of infantry, 1 regiment of artillery of 9 batteries (3 of them light field howitzers) and 2 pioneer companies; the strength of the divisional cavalry had been reduced to 1 squadron, but the information troops had been permanently increased. Heavy artillery was assigned to the division from time to time according to need, so that in tranquil position warfare each division generally had 3 heavy field howitzer batteries, 1 mortar battery and 2 heavy gun batteries. The number of machine guns had been materially increased, each battalion receiving 1 machine gun company of 6 guns. By changing the construction of the gun carriage (wagon) the guns per company could subsequently be doubled. The introduction of automatic rifles whose importance the German infantry had found during the fighting on the Somme, took place in the Summer of 1917; the introduction of "firing cups" for throwing grenades from the rifle, took place in the Spring of 1918, after specially constructed grenades had proved to be too heavy for mobile warfare.

Each man was protected by a steel helmet, in addition received a gas mask and in many cases a long-handled spade, which was valued also as a means of hand-to-hand fighting. Every man was equipped with hand-grenades; the originally adopted ball or disc grenades were not good, and they were replaced by grenades more easily handled, and the lighter egg grenades, which were carried in the attack in sandbags slung across the shoulder. There is no doubt that both sides overestimated the effect of the hand grenade and attached more value to it than to the rifle. An automatic pistol — "long pistol" — (16 per company) was supplied for trench warfare. For connection with the artillery colored light rockets served, and for connection with airplanes colored lights and large cloths (panels) were used. Shocktroops, minenwerfers and flame throwers taken from the position war, could also be employed in the mobile war. The artillery had made great progress in flash and sound ranging methods. Much more use was made of the shell, than had

Mobile Warfare 43

been expected before the war. In gas shells artillery possessed a fighting means, independent of the direction of the wind, to neutralize hostile batteries and to gas stretches of the terrain. Airplanes increased in importance through armament, equipment with cameras and wireless apparatus. The means of communication were materially improved. In addition to the telephone there came into use intermittent lights, ground and wireless telegraph, light and sound signals, information projectiles, carrier dogs and pigeons. In February, 1918, the divisions received wireless battalions (also for ground telegraphy), and the personnel with the troops was organized into troop message detachments as follows: each infantry regiment, had 1 regimental information platoon, consisting of 1 officer, and 13 men; each infantry battalion had 1 battalion information platoon, consisting of 1 officer and 21 men; each independent battalion (cavalry rifle regiment) 1 battalion information platoon of 1 officer and 30 men. Employment, traffic and co-operation was in charge of the information officer under the direction of the regimental (battalion) commander.

As early as 1915 the French commenced to organize their battalions into 3 infantry and 1 machine gun company of 8 guns, and to attach automatic rifles — up to 16 — to the companies. By the law of September 27, 1916, the company organization was fixed. Each company, not counting officers, had a subsistence strength of 194, the fighting company proper having a strength of 168 men. This number did not include 4 older noncommissioned officers and 22 men, used for runners, signal men and infantry pioneers. The men throwing hand and rifle grenades were designated "grenadiers," the gunners of the automatic machine guns were designated "fusiliers," and the rest as "voltigeurs."

The fighting company was divided into 4 platoons of 2 half-platoons (sections) each. Of the half-platoons, the first always contained rifle grenadiers, hand grenade throwers and fusiliers, the second contained the voltigeurs, 4 rifle grenadiers and 2 cartridge carriers (*pourvoyers*). All men were trained as hand grenade throwers. The fighting company numbered 32 hand grenade throwers, 16 rifle grenadiers and 8 (12-16) gunners for automatic machine guns.

The rifle grenade (*Vivien Bessieres*) fired from a firing cup, was very effective. With 16 rifles arranged with the appliance a barrage could be thrown with 150 rounds per minute at from 80 to 150 meters. In village fighting they replaced absent artillery, cut off the retreat of the enemy, prevented supports coming up, and defeated counter-attacks. Fire unity was sought. The possibility of fire by the automatic rifle on the move forced the enemy under cover in the final phases of the charge. Of course, the machine gun could not be entirely replaced, but the automatic rifle was especially useful in accompanying the infantry, to secure terrain that had been taken, to stop counter-shocks, and enable the bringing up of machine guns without undue haste.

The 37-mm. gun attached to the battalion was so mobile that it could follow the infantry in all battle situations; its fire was exact, easy to regulate, had a range up to 1500 meters, and could be fired from a covered position. The projectile had the effect of a shell, as solid shot pierced three sandbags, or steel plates. It was especially suited for annihilating invisible machine guns. In the attack waves the gun was not to be used, as there it would be easily seen and destroyed.

In order to gain the highest efficiency of the company after its first organization, all war implements must act in co-operation, the supply of ammunition must be assured and the complement well trained. In the training the machine guns and the 37-cm. gun directed their fire on targets above ground, the hand and rifle grenades against skirmishers or targets under cover.

In the deployed line the interval between files was 4 to 5 paces. The platoon had an extension of 60 to 75 meters. In depth it was formed in two waves following each other at 10 to 15 meters distance, the grenadiers and fusiliers in the first wave, the grenade carriers and voltigeurs in the second. They were followed by the *nettoyeurs* (trench moppers-up) at 10 to 20 meters distance, and the latter, at a distance of 40 to 50 meters, by the company reserves. The fighting front of one company was 300 meters.

By the law of September 10, 1917, the peculiar organization of the platoon was even extended to the half-platoon "as after the filling up of the first line the battle is conducted by half-platoons; therefore these should not only in case of need, but at the very start, combine all infantry auxiliary and fighting means and have

Mobile Warfare

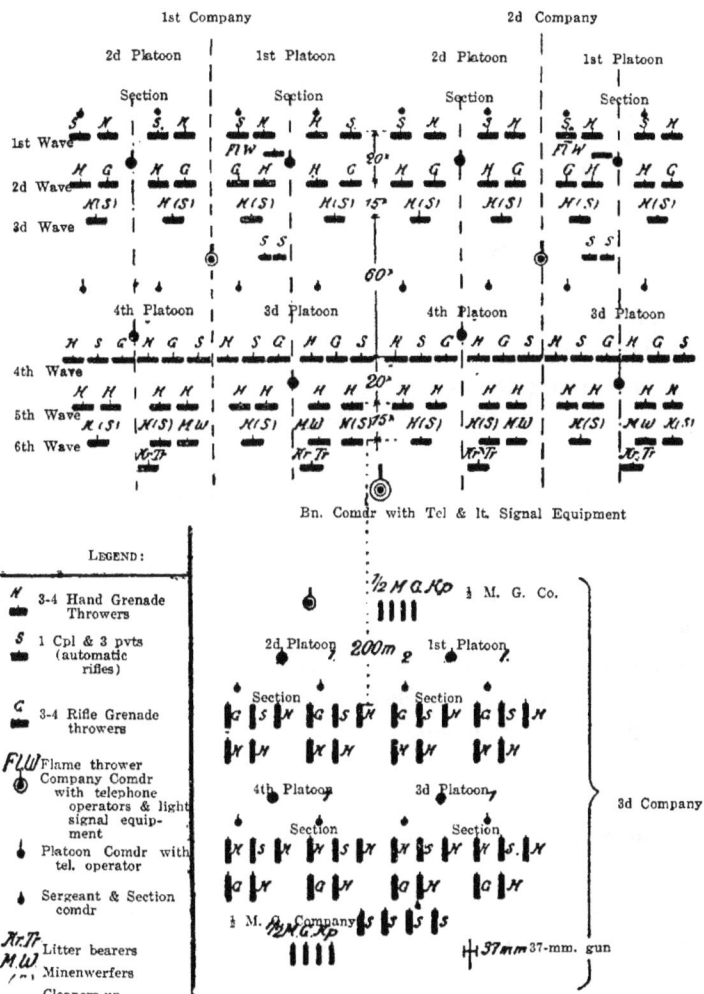

French Battalion in Attack Formation
Extension—400 to 500 meters

the auxiliary weapons within themselves be able to take formation in depth." Each half-platoon had 1 sergeant and 14 to 18 men, with one automatic rifle attached. After the automatic rifles had been distributed to the half-platoons, the 8 guns remaining comprised the materiel reserve — 4 to the company, 4 at the disposition of the division. There was no difference made in half-platoons between grenadier (hand grenade throwers) and voltigeurs. The half-platoon consisted of a complement (1 corporal, 3 men, fusiliers), of automatic rifles, of grenadiers V. B. (grenade gun) with 2 to 3 firing cups divided between the two squads. It was directed that an elite company be formed in each regiment. In the attack the half-platoon was formed into 2 waves with 10 to 15 meters distance, in the first wave the riflemen and the automatic machine gun squad, in the second wave the rifle grenade throwers and skirmishers. In the attack the platoon inserted its half-platoon either alongside or behind each other; in the latter case the first half-platoon was the *vague d'assault* (attacking wave), the second the *vague de renfort* (support), distance 60 to 100 meters, extension (half-platoons in rear of each other) 40 to 45 meters. The *nettoyeurs* (trench moppers-up) were furnished by other than the attacking unit, which after the completion of their task formed the security detachment of the trenches.

In England the same mixing of men took place. Each tactically independent platoon (28 to 44 men) consisted of 4 squads; riflemen, hand grenade throwers, light machine gun (Lewis gun) and rifle grenade throwers. Half of the men, were trained in the use of the machine gun, the other half in the use of the rifle grenade.

Training Regulations for Foot Troops

At the close of the battles of the Somme in the Autumn of 1916 the lessons of the mobile and position warfare that had been gathered were thoroughly examined. These were published to the troops in January, 1917, in the shape of an outline of "Training Regulations for Troops in the Field." The mobile war has proven the correctness of the general rules of our previous training and field exercises, and thus it was only a question of minor changes of our

Mobile Warfare

Field Service Regulations. The few directions however contained in our F.S.R. concerning position warfare, required material revision and extension. The importance of drill, as means to an end, to teach the individual the absolute necessity of the strictest obedience to his superior, had come to the front everywhere, especially in difficult battle situations. Troops, trained and educated in a strict school, fought well. This fact had to be adhered to in the new Regulations, but on the other hand, the fact was not to be lost sight of that thoughtless drill, carried to excess on the drill ground, had a damaging effect. The increase in auxiliary arms and the necessity of making the "shock-troop procedure" the very life of the troops, led to the publication of a second outline edition in January, 1918.

The Regulations treated of training, not leadership. Rigid adherence was held to careful, strict individual training as a basis for the schooling of the unit, and all was left out which was not absolutely required in war. The training of the individual was to be furthered at every opportunity, either while at rest, or in the trenches. Special attention was paid to rigidity, exactness and order, in all close order drill. Double time in cadence, present arms, the manual of arms for the charge, and the use of signal flags was omitted.

In extended order the formation in platoon columns was omitted, the line was the principal formation for the company. Drill ground formations were no more to be expected of the company, than skirmish fire in close order. Volley fire and the charge, gaining direction on guides sent to the front, the transition from line into column of squads while on the move, as well as different kinds of deployment for firing were done away with. A new designation was given to the single column (column of files) and also column of twos, as column and double column.

The most important formation in close order was the company column, in which the platoons are in column of squads, in double column, or single file with 1½ pace interval, which can be increased according to need (see plate).

The company must be able to take up, in addition to the regulation formations, a formation adapted to the terrain and the available space. The formation of the platoons need not be the

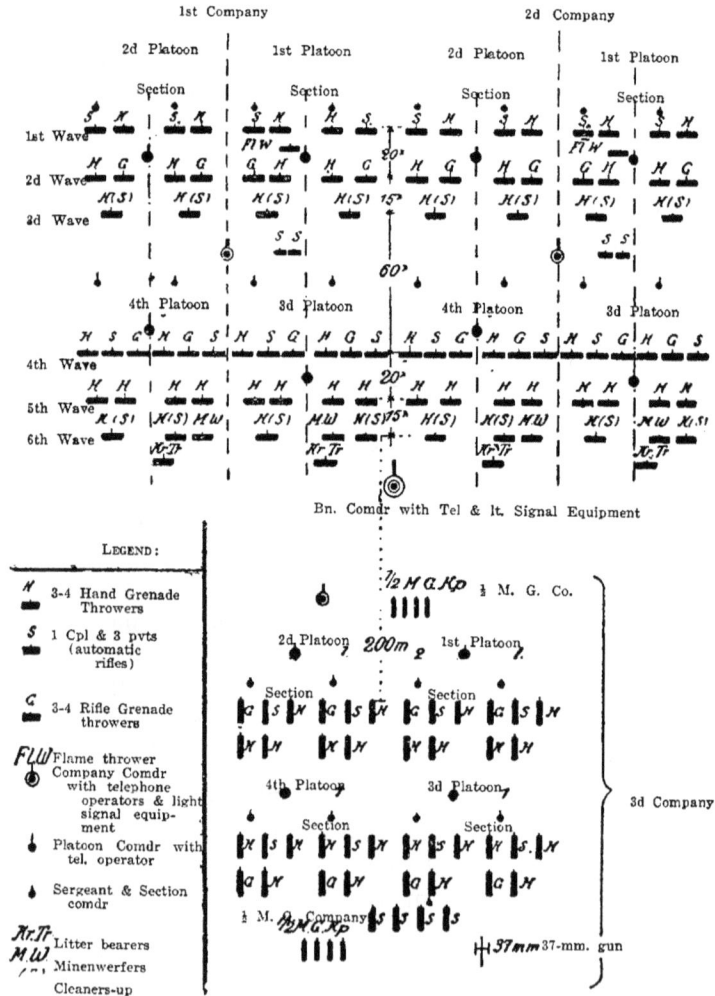

Mobile Warfare 49

same in that case. The main point is that the company must be ready for employment in any direction according to existing conditions. By attaching the automatic rifles, the company received a materially changed appearance. Training Regulations (first edition) provided for the formation of a 4th platoon, in which the charging troops, the hand grenade throwers, the sharpshooters, and the automatic riflemen were consolidated, "so that the fighting power of the company would be kept at the highest degree." This plan permitted at the opening of decisive battle, selected leaders and men to be a special platoon at the disposition of the company commander. But more correctly. Training Regulation Number 2 objected to composing the platoons of rifle carriers and specialists as in England and France. Every man was trained in the use of hand grenades and rifle; the squad was trained for skirmish fighting as well as for shock-troop fighting. The automatic rifles were inserted on the right wing or at the head of the platoons and half-platoons.

The machine gun complement had to be selected on the basis of the reliability and independence of the individuals. For each machine gun at least 1 complement and 2 ersatz complements should be trained. The men were armed with pistols, the ersatz men with rifle or carbine. The complement (Numbers 1 to 4) and the best ersatz complement formed a machine gun squad under a machine gun squad commander. On the march the machine guns were loaded on the machine gun wagon of the company. All officers and noncommissioned officers of each company were trained in the service of machine guns. Special importance was laid on timely opening of fire, so the machine guns were inserted on the right wing or at the head of their platoons or half-platoons.

The battalion consisted of four companies, one automatic rifle platoon, one information platoon, and machine gun company. The battalion assembled in companies alongside or in rear of each other, the companies in march column, in line or in company column. The machine gun company consisted of three platoons of two half-platoons each, the two guns of the half-platoon carried on one gun wagon. The following formations were designated for the machine gun company: the line, single file, and march column. Drill was never to be in the line formation. It was proper to have the platoons march in line in rear of each other or in single file column abreast of each other. When the guns were taken off the wagon in each instance it was ordered whether the gunners were to carry the protective shields, the water, or cartridge chests. To decrease the weight of the heavy machine guns, the sled was replaced by an auxiliary mount or even by a sandbag. Loading and unloading at night with gas-mask was practiced. Movements of heavy machine guns, after having been unloaded from their wagons, was generally executed with the gun assembled, but in all cases without cartridges in chambers differing from the automatic rifle, in which movements with loaded guns was permissible.

All movements were at the walk. Trotting was confined to exceptional cases. By order of the company commander, when the battle situation demanded haste in entering the action, portions of the complement rode on the machine gun wagons (for instance noncommissioned officers and gunners Nos. 1 to 3 of one platoon distributed on the 6 wagons). Employment of machine guns in battle, will be discussed later on.

Chapter III – Position Warfare in the West, 1914-1917

Origin and Nature of Position Warfare

The prime importance of the initial success upon the entire course of a campaign, as illustrated by the wars of the 19th Century, which generally ran a rapid course, led Germany to rapidly assume positions in readiness at the outbreak of war and to simultaneously insert all available forces. Strategic reserves were discarded. They consisted of troops (new organizations) condemned to a slow mobilization, or of allies who entered the war later on. If neither of the opponents has sufficient forces to break the other's resistance, position warfare results. It lies in the very nature of the offensive war that, after relentlessly gathering the fruits of the initial success, the heavy expenditure of strength forces the victor to a halt, also, in order to protect what he has gained.

Such a culmination of victory is shown in the World War by the first battle on the Marne with the resulting retreat and defense, which was fought against a strong superiority of the Entente. In the subsequent course of the World War, which developed for the Central Powers into the most magnificent operation of all times on interior lines, the situation forced them upon the defensive on one front in order to beat the enemy by an offensive on another. The length of the lines was so extensive that the disadvantages of a central location were of no importance. A favorable railroad net made it possible to shift the forces from one to the other theater of war. Thus position warfare had its origin in the East and in the West.

Military history shows that only by inserting fresh forces, or by voluntarily abandoning a large part of the position followed by an offensive against the pursuing enemy, is the inertia of position warfare overcome and mobile warfare resumed. The effect on the morale of the enemy and our own troops and the difficulties of overcoming rapidly constructed field fortifications, requires serious consideration prior to voluntarily abandoning a portion of our position and starting a counter-attack against the enemy who may have taken our position.

The extension of battle fronts of today seldom permits any envelopment, and leads naturally to a penetration of the position, the execution of which makes great demands upon leadership and troops. The commander requires strong forces to gather the fruits of a penetration after the first battle success.

No commander will voluntarily choose position warfare, and will hardly consider blocking off in time of peace a certain portion of the terrain after the method of the Roman Lines or by means of a Chinese Wall. The decision lies in the attack. The fortified lines of the 18th Century did not meet expectations. They held confined extraordinarily large numbers of troops and these never did make a good stand. Today aerial reconnaissance can furnish the basis for the attack of fortifications. Another point must not be left out of consideration and that is that the sphere of action of the enemy into the home terrain by means of airships and long range guns has increased immeasurably, whereas in the 18th Century the effective range of hostile guns reached only some few hundred meters within our position. By such procedure (choosing position warfare) we abandon every possible war objective, delay the decision into the distant future and increase the economic pressure on our own people. Sufficient protection of valuable economic terrain can be secured only by carrying the war in the enemy's country.

Position Warfare in the West, 1914-1917

Brief examination of the military events in the past forty years may cause us to assume that position warfare became the rule; mobile warfare, the exception. But we must in each case carefully ascertain whether the position warfare was selected on account of inferiority of numbers, in order to delay defeat until other States could participate (expected British participation in the Russo-Turkish War, 1877-78), or until the arrival of reinforcements (Russo-Japanese War, 1904-05), or whether the position warfare was forced by special conditions. Position warfare lengthens the war and thereby increases the suffering and, in spite of the smaller losses in separate engagements, the aggregate losses total far more than results from a battle in the open. Only overestimation of our auxiliary means and underestimation of the moral influences, could lead to the conclusion that in the future position warfare will be the rule. Only an attack (not considering the influences of an economic war) is able to break the will of the enemy. For any commander seeking a decision, position warfare is but an auxiliary means used to let the enemy wear himself out and to gain time. The earlier the attack is undertaken and the greater the forces employed, the less time will the defender gain. Most time will be gained by the defender if the attack is made with insufficient means (Plevna, 1877). The commander must be thoroughly prepared for position warfare but must strive with all means at his command for mobile war and carry that through.

Field Marshal von Moltke, as is known, had advised as early as 1865 a strategic offensive in connection with a tactical defensive, and in 1874 had again insisted on that procedure; but in war, not counting the battles on the Loire (Coulmieres, Beaune la Rolande, Loigny) the Field Marshal had been unable to transmute his ideas and recommendations into action, under the pressure of events. But Moltke surely had in mind a procedure that was to be voluntarily adopted, even before the climax of the victory was attained. After the September battles on the Marne in 1914, and in the summer of 1918 we were forced (in France) to choose the defensive after a successful offensive. We by no means appreciated the advantages of that situation. In 1914 the frontal attacks of the enemy were defeated on the Aisne, and then commenced a race "to the sea" each opponent with the intention of gaining the flank of the other. The Entente had gained freedom of action by stopping our forward movement, and they were able to recuperate from the heavy fighting of the Summer of 1914. In England an army had been created from nothing and their divisions at the front had been equipped with heavy guns and modern battle means.

In position warfare attacker and defender are opposed to each other at close range and both of them are forced to the same construction of positions. While the attacker has to take the terrain as he finds it, the defender seeks to increase his fighting strength by choice of a favorable terrain, fortified by artificial means and he certainly will not give up that position without good reasons. Therefore possession of the terrain gains increased importance in position warfare. As the attacker desires to avoid the frontal attack, he seeks to lead the attack against a flank or, as was the case in the 18th Century with smaller armies, to maneuver the enemy out of his position and to attack him in the open. The defender is thus offered the opportunity of counter-attacking with strong forces, holding the position with weak forces merely as a shield. However, the importance of possession of the terrain held good only as long as the defensive means of the defense proved themselves superior. All battles show that the attacker is successful, and even with far less losses, in gaining the first penetration. The defender has to decide whether to hold to the terrain under great loss or to avoid a decision, abandoning his labors and the terrain — but which have forced the enemy to time-consuming expenditure of material and personnel — and to resume the battle at some other place.

It cannot be stated whether modern weapons favor the attacker or the defender, but the attacker has the advantage of being able to choose the place and time for the attack and to bring the assaulting troops into the effective fire zone of the defender only a short time before the hour of the assault. On the other hand the defender must keep his troops in readiness at all times awaiting the attack. For that reason, surprise on a large or small scale increases in importance. Attack preparations that have not been observed avoid counter-measures. A surprise in the commencement of the assault delays the hostile barrage fire and prevents timely occupation of the hostile fire trenches. But we cannot reckon on surprise as a certainty. It is difficult to hide from aerial observation the placing in readiness of personnel and materiel employed in an attack, on a large scale, even if we can succeed with our surprise at other points. The statements of a single deserter may easily nullify all preparations. Thus we cannot plan an attack on surprise alone. Surprise is merely a material auxiliary means for success. In attacks on a very large scale the statements of a deserter immediately prior to the attack still may have no materially bad consequences. Transmission of messages requires much time, as well as the transition from decision to execution. Our military channels seldom have anything important to report. Even "reliable reports," meaning such as confirm a pre-arrived at opinion, cause little attention to be paid to other reports that are not in conformity therewith.

A certain monotony is combined with position warfare, which can easily lead to indifference and apathy and finally to acceptance of a "Peace within the precincts of a castle" or "leave me alone and I surely will do nothing to you" policy. Such a conception which is as far as heaven is from the earth from the conception of actual war, must be combated with all possible means. The most extensive damage must be done to the enemy. In the foreground, up to the hostile obstacle, no patrols must be permitted. Fortification labor in the open and movements in the open by detachments or vehicles must be made impossible by fire. If that is not done we will finally see an agreement between the pickets and thus "trench friendships" will be created which in all cases are of the gravest danger to loyal troops. In the French divisions the maxim was generally adhered to that troops, once relieved, should never again be placed in the line at the same point, thereby increasing the difficulties of fraternizing. Monotony will be prevented by firing as a general rule on all visible targets, laying a sweeping fire by day and night upon the hostile rear areas and frequently executing operations of some kind. In position warfare, as we have learned, discipline, capacity for marching and desire for operations suffer under the hard work of throwing up fortifications and officers of all and every grade have to do their very best to prevent a "tiredness for war." The value of cover is easily overestimated. As numerous complete reports indicate the troops accustomed to the cover of a position system in many instances can no longer accommodate themselves to the uncertain conditions of mobile warfare.

The Position Battles up to the First Attack on Verdun

When, after the battle of the Marne in the Autumn of 1914, the German troops resorted to the spade, they had sufficient high-trajectory artillery. It therefore was sufficient, as the enemy lacked minenwerfers, to arrange for protection in the trenches against small arms and shrapnel fire. The importance of aerial reconnaissance was insufficiently appreciated at that time.

The first positions in which infantry and artillery worked in many cases without proper connection, showed, with a long range field of fire, a line according to the profile of the reinforced rifle trench, constructed in most cases by far separated groups. Differing from the French and the Russians, we rejected any formation in depth. The center of gravity lay in the most advanced trenches, beyond which a few shallow trenches for sentries were located. The demand, to defend only one line, was based on the proposed conduct of the defense which anticipated that the attacker would be held up by the fire fight of the defender, and the decision sought by the counter-attack by the reserves. There was no time for false works. There were but very few routes of approach and covered trenches. Shelters were to provide security at the most against straight hits of field artillery, otherwise only against shrapnel fire. The importance of flanking from open trenches was not generally appreciated. Fortification by squads or groups led to the reestablishment of the supporting points (which had been omitted in the "Field Pioneer Service Regulations for all Arms") which, constructed in the shape of "kraals," allowed deployment of the firing line up to 400 meters, but resulted in violating of the general rule of the line being defended only by weak forces. Obstacles were to be placed so far from the trenches, that they could just be watched from the latter (about 50 meters). "If they are located close to a position, they will be within the effective zone of dispersion of the hostile artillery fire laid on the position; and in addition they will not provide sufficient cover for the garrison against hostile hand grenades" (Field Pioneer Regulations, 348).

The applied forms of fortification were in absolute consonance with the Regulations of the Field Pioneer Service, in the preparation of which we might have reckoned with the possibility that the enemy would quickly bring to the front heavy batteries employing high-angle fire, and that we would also have to encounter heavy guns of large caliber using flat-trajectory fire. In any case the 15-cm. calibers were soon outclassed by heavier ones. Also new weapons, hand grenades in the hands of the infantry, minenwerfers, gas shells and gas projectors, made their importance felt which caused a complete change in the forms of the fortifications.

It was very soon seen that the attacking artillery, if in sufficient strength and liberally supplied with ammunition, would be capable with increased volume of fire (drum fire) to annihilate any position that it could observe; that thereby narrow, deep skirmish trenches would be transformed into flat depressions in which the artificial works disappeared beyond recognition, and that shelters and covered trenches with insufficiently strong roofs were in danger of being filled up. A remedy therefor was had by increasing the strength of cover first, then by constructing more covered and connecting trenches, whereby it became possible to construct numerous shelters, distributed in breadth and depth, so that in the rear of the front trenches several lines were created, to which the garrison that was being heavily fired on could go for shelter. Where the ground was firm, very narrow and deep trenches were preferred. Such were not fit for defense at all points without additional preparation. They required special arrangements for firing and for drainage; could not be used indefinitely without proper wall supports; and finally, the rescue of the men who had been covered up by trenches caving in, was made more difficult. We rightly asked ourselves if the extensive labor connected with the construction of such trenches was justified by the protection which they could offer the garrison after a continued "drum" fire. If we assume that any position within reach of the hostile artillery can be annihilated by the enemy, then second and third positions, against which the hostile artillery would have to deploy again, gained special importance; thus we discarded the view: "as a general rule only one defensive position will be selected and fortified with all available means." (Pioneer Regulations, 216.)

Very properly all regulations pointed out the necessity of making the parapet as low as was possible from the nature of the terrain, the character of growth covering the ground, and condition of the ground. But following the directions of regulations alone did not suffice as soon as hostile artillery could observe the trenches, which could not be hidden from aerial observation, and which betrayed themselves by the obstacles. False works offered only a minor remedy. Thus in the first months of 1915 we took a step farther and abandoned the long range field of fire by drawing back the firing line from the forward slope of the plateau, in many cases even to the rear edge of the plateau, and merely observing the forward slope of the plateau by sentries, who frequently were posted in false positions. The advantage of being able to defend positions having a good field of fire with only a small number of skirmishers became of small consideration as a powerful hostile artillery would prevent skirmishers from using their rifles. It is certain, however, we mainly secured protection against hostile artillery fire by this method, but as a matter of fact, we limited the co-operation of our own artillery and gave the enemy increased facilities for finding the range. In a short time the hostile artillery could bring its observers to the abandoned, or only weakly held heights; and then, from a covered position and unhindered, could without difficulty smash our infantry by its fire.

It is true that the observation stations of our artillery could be placed for temporary purposes beyond our own position, but for the decisive battle they had to be located within the position. On account of the immense dust and smoke clouds caused by the drum fire, observation from flank positions and from positions in rear gained in importance. It became more and more evident that the location of the observation was of the utmost importance in the selection of the fighting line.

The non-successful battles of the Entente — in Flanders and in the Champagne starting with the 16th of February, 1915 — differed from the prior attacks only by the stronger artillery preparation that had been increased to "drum" fire. This preparation was to enable the attacking infantry, advancing in dense skirmish lines and followed at 100 meters distance by companies and battalions in columns, to take possession of the battered position without fighting. It is said that in the Champagne 18 to 20 rounds were thrown on each lineal meter of positions, but the success did not accord with the expenditure of ammunition because, according to the views of the leaders, the assaulting mass was not broad and deep enough and there were no reserves.

"Experiences in war concerning field fortifications" demanded that a portion of the infantry should be trained in throwing and manufacturing suitable hand grenades. The ball (time-fuse) hand grenade, the disk (percussion-fuse) and the steel handled grenades (time and percussion fuses) were all employed. Only the steel handled grenades (time-fuse) were found to be serviceable and also a lighter egg-shaped hand grenade with throwing ranges of 30 and 40 meters. It was recommended that in stubborn defense, at least two positions, one in rear of the other, be taken up, each consisting of several lines (50 to 100 meters distance), with organization in depth to prevent a rolling up after the enemy had broken in. Not much emphasis was laid on the value of a large field of fire, but it was recommended that machine guns and light field pieces be placed in the forward trenches and thoroughly covered at the most important points; that the trenches be arranged for defense toward the rear as well as toward the front ("closed rifle trench," separating the two trenches by 50 meters); and that they be surrounded by obstacles. Construction of loopholes was left to the discretion of the defender. Smaller shelters were provided in the front trench; larger ones holding as much as one platoon in the rear trench. Head-cover was not required in rifle trenches, except in observation stations, because it interfered with the use of the rifle and bayonet. If, in exceptional cases, head-cover was desired, one with a continuous horizontal loophole was considered best. Closed works were of no use; straight lines rather were preferred, as it was not possible to depend on securing flank fire. When the flanks of a position have to be drawn back, it should be done by echeloning the rifle trenches. Machine guns had better be posted on the flanks and, if possible, under cover. They should not expose themselves prematurely in order to avoid early destruction by artillery fire. In many cases the front trench was designated the fighting trench, the

FORTIFICATIONS PRIOR TO THE AUTUMN------------

Dugouts (fox-holes, for about 4 men sitting)

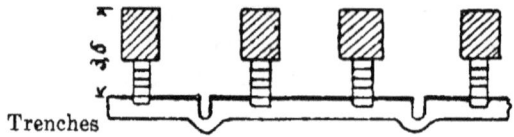

Trenches

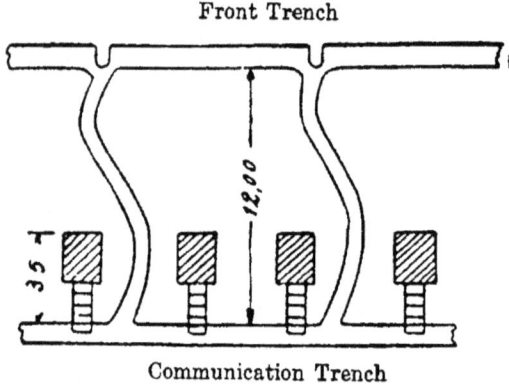

Front Trench

Communication Trench

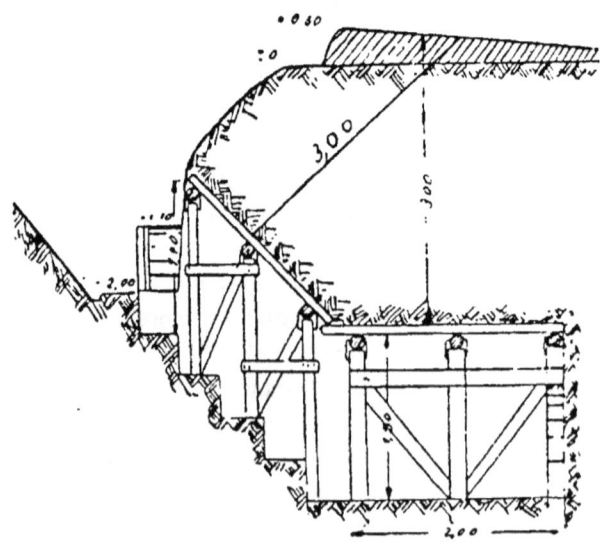

BATTLE IN THE CHAMPAGNE

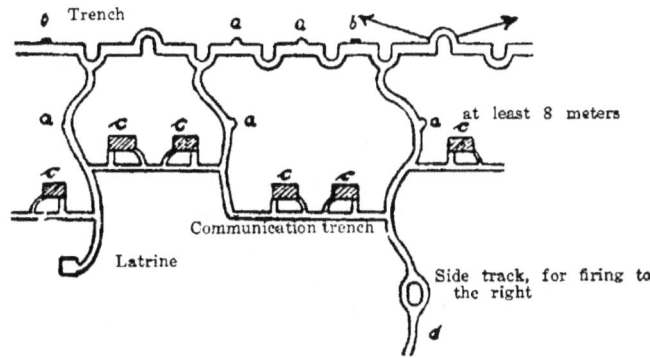

a Riflemen's niches
b Splinter-proof shelters
c Shelters on larger scale (warming places, Command stations, rest stations, dressing stations)
d Route of approach

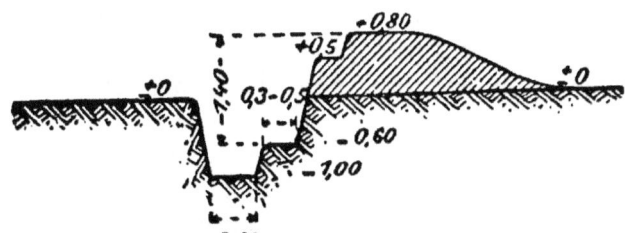

Reinforced trench as infantry position. To be constructed in one night in favorable ground

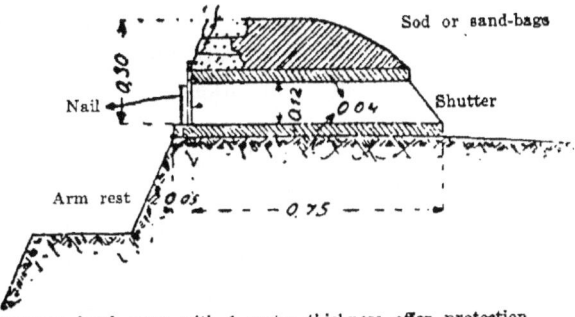

1 Concrete head cover with 1 meter thickness offer protection against shells fired from mortars
2 Trenches in the shape of reinforced trenches. Approach trenches 2½ meters from floor to ceiling

rear trench (12 meters distance), the communication trench. The strength of cover against light field howitzer projectiles was given as 2 meters (using alternate layers of stones, logs, etc., of 1.5 meter). Using concrete the cover was 0.5 to 1 meter thick. The necessity of having two exits from shelters was not sufficiently emphasized. Obstacles were to be constructed not farther than from 20 to 30 meters in front of the trenches, and to be in 2 to 3 bands, each 6 to 10 meters wide. They were to protect against sudden attack and to force the attacker into the spaces swept by our fire. Several bands of obstacles proved themselves just as good as obstacles placed in depth. High obstacles betrayed themselves clearly on aerial photos. Close co-operation between infantry and artillery was absolutely necessary.

Posting the artillery at a designated time and place was absolutely required for attack as well as for defense. Today infantry cannot fight unless the artillery has fully prepared the way. But the artillery effort is in vain, if it is not utilized by the infantry at the correct time. The effect of the artillery fire supplements that of the infantry and vice versa, and both must work in close conjunction.

The French positions, exclusive of those in unimportant sectors, as a general rule consisted of three lines of which the first line — strongly constructed but weakly held, — was designed for security. The second line, 150 to 200 meters distant, was the main line of resistance, in rear of which were located a series of supporting points prepared for all around defense. 400 to 500 meters in rear of the line of main resistance, the reserves were held in secure shelters for use in the counter-attack. Special consideration was given to carefully planned flanking works for all lines. Sector reserves, labor and park battalions, were employed in constructing a second position.

French generals ascribed the cause of the success of the German attacks to the fact that the front lines of the positions were always too strongly occupied, though Joffre as early as January 5, 1915, had cautioned (to reduce the loss) against crowding defenders into the front line. The men in the front line were merely to report the assault and delay it; the decision was to be sought in the counter-attack by the reserves. This created the need of a

Position Warfare in the West, 1914-1917

position system, with carefully planned formation in depth in which strong obstacles and a powerful flank defense played an especial role. The difficulty in gathering together the widely distributed garrison of the front line for attack purposes, led to the construction of covered assembly places. Numerous captured documents show that the French were slow to accept the very correct views of Joffre. Similar views, as we will show later, encountered stubborn resistance in the German Army.

The British, not caring much for a long range field of fire, tried to hide the fortifications from the view of the enemy. In many instances they were constructed on reverse slopes and in the cover of hedges. Their position consisted of three lines, connected by approach trenches. The front rifle trench was as narrow as possible (45-cm.) and 90-cm. (or more) deep, with shelters and breastworks. 15 yards in rear was the communicating trench, 45 to 60 meters long and 1.8 to 2.1 meters deep. 25 yards in rear of the communicating trench was the cover trench with a breadth of 60 cm. and with a depth as great as practicable, under special conditions, 4.8 meters. The earth dug out was scattered and smoothed off or used for the construction of false works. For protection against explosive shells, a parados was required. Simple arrangements were provided for fixing the rifles with proper sight elevations, for use in night attacks.

The experiences gathered and lessons gained by the Allies in the Winter engagements were arranged and compiled by General Joffre into the Regulations of April 16, 1915, entitled: "Aims and Prerequisites of the General Offensive," which shortly after publication fell into German hands. The procedure established therein was that the troops, after a concentrated heavy artillery fire of all calibers ("drum fire") lasting for from four to five hours and concentrated on a very limited space with great rapidity of fire were to be brought up under cover to assault distance (150 to 200 meters from the enemy) and placed in readiness under cover and in the assembly trenches. During the night preceding the attack a line of departure for the attack was to be constructed. If the fire preparation proved insufficient to annihilate the materiel and moral resistance of the defender, then the fire was to be extended to several days. The attack was to commence with the assault.

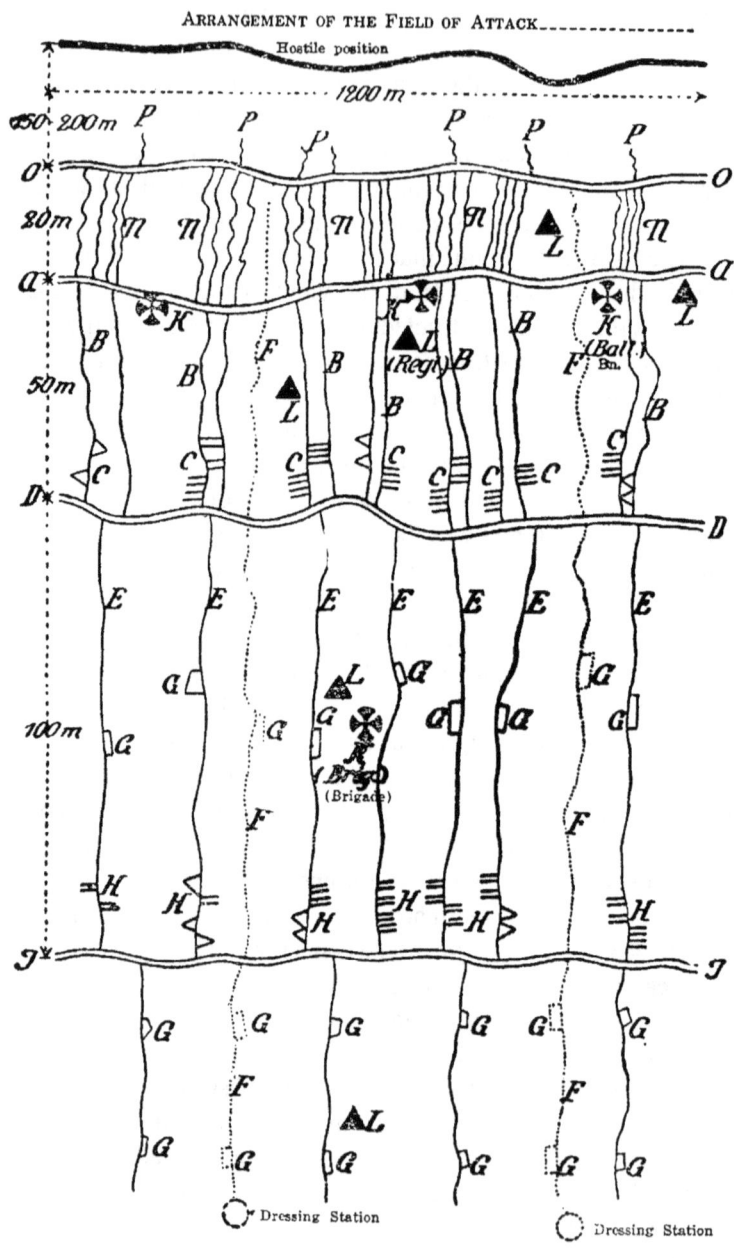

Position Warfare in the West, 1914-1917

---------------------ACCORDING TO JOFFRE'S PLAN

LEGEND:

P = Advanced trenches

O = Exit trench (Paralle de Depart) 1 meter broad

N = Approaching trench

A = Trench of the 1st Line, 1 meter broad

B = Approach trenches, 1 meter broad
two for each company

C = Assembly stations of the 1st Line
two each for one platoon

D = Communicating trench, 2 meters broad

E = Approach trench, 2 meters broad, one for each company

F = Evacuation trench

G = Side tracks

H = Assembly stations of the 2d Line

J = Connecting trenches, 2 meters broad

✠ **K** = Headquarters location (Bn, regt, Brig., Div.)

▲ **L** = Observation Stations of Artillery

POSITION IN READINESS TO ATTACK
German Front (about 600 rifles)

1200 m

150 m
200 m
*6 companies of each of the 1st regiments in a single dense skirmish line—2400 rifles

300 m
**6 companies of the 2d regiments in same formation as those of the 1st regiments—1200 rifles

Distance variable, at head of field of attack.   6th Co., 2d Regiment

Second Brigade at rest, but in readiness

The attack is made in the start by the 1st Brigade only with 18 companies, i.e., with 3600 rifles, placed in readiness on a stretch of ground 122 m. broad and 150 m. deep.

It was intended to overrun the hostile line on a broad front (1200 to 1500 meters for each division) and in strong formation in depth, column of brigades and regiments. By continuous advance of successive echelons the movement was to be kept up to a designated attack objective deep in the hostile position. The attacking waves followed each other with little distance and consisted of entire companies deployed with intervals of only half a pace between skirmishers, so that 3600 men were together on a space of 1200 meters extent and 170 meters deep. The attack was initiated only by the 1st Brigade, while the 2d Brigade remained on the alert in its quarters. Placing the regiments in column led to a complete mixing of units and prevented the exercise of command. Penetrating a position is impossible by successive waves, as the ones following in rear cannot find any room to pass through the halting masses of the leading lines. It is evident that there is danger that the supports will be hung up in the first line on account of the small intervals. Joffre's procedure changed the division into a single unwieldy phalanx which, once started moving could only advance straight ahead or turn back in complete disorder. In this illogical scheme no opportunity for leadership or exercise of initiative was allowed. A minor portion of the artillery was to hold down the hostile artillery, one-third of the field artillery being assigned to destroy the obstacles and two-thirds to prepare the hostile trenches for the assault. In this, to each 200 meters two 75-cm. batteries were assigned with 80 to 100 rounds per piece. Of the heavy calibers 40 to 50 rounds for each 220-mm., 50 to 60 for each 150-mm., and 60 to 80 for each 120-mm. piece were allotted. This plan of attack precluded all surprise, though as late as March 1st the army had seen in surprise the "indispensable factor of success." The plan of attack was based on the effect of superior expenditure of ammunition and the weight of the assault by superior infantry that had been saved therefor. It demanded the time-consuming removal of enormous quantities of earth and forced the command to attack only where the two opponents were at assault distance. To defeat such an attack the German measures were: Great distance between the rear lines protected by obstacles and supplied with numerous shelters which had to be occupied simultaneously with the front line; full utilization of the flanking effect of machine guns and single field pieces; the enemy's penetration to be answered by an immediate counterattack; hostile batteries that could be seen, to be engaged prior to the attack; demolition of the hostile assault works by heavy guns of high angle fire and minenwerfers for the purpose of delaying the attack; during the attack the heavy artillery to keep up its fire on the hostile front trenches to cut off the hostile supports.

Joffre's army orders of September 14, 1915, designated "the present moment as especially favorable for the offensive." Found by the Germans, these orders pointed out the danger, while at the same time the results of the German ground and aerial reconnaissances as well as the statement of prisoners and deserters furnished valuable information of attack preparations against the line Auberive — Ville sur Tourbe, that was then held by only four divisions (33 kilometers) . General von Castelnau led the attack. On September 27, at 7:00 A.M., reinforced artillery fire opened which the defender sought to reduce by regular firing on the hostile batteries. Gas was liberally used by the attacker. French airplanes ascertained the effect of the fire, and sought to interrupt traffic in the hostile rear by dropping bombs. The French attack divisions had been in the front line a short time to get familiar with the terrain and the position, and had then been taken back to the vicinity of Chalons for rest. Thus it was that as early as September 22d we knew 18 of the 30 hostile attack divisions. Completely fresh troops, that had the advantage of the superiority in numbers and materiel were to make the attack against the weak German first line divisions which for the most part had been in the trenches for several months. The preparations for the attack were completed by the 22d. Thorough preparation to the minutest detail was absolutely essential for success. Improvement of the approach and assembly trenches was demanded. Even preparations for concealed assembly places for and provision for advancing the cavalry divisions in columns of twos, had been made. The morning of the 24th the drum fire was suspended for a short time, so that reconnoitering detachments could ascertain its effect. The grouping of the French, different from Joffre's attack method was the same along the entire front. In each front line division 3 regiments were placed abreast with the 4th in reserve. In the regiments the battalions were in column, each in dense skirmish lines at 50 meters distance. The first wave was preceded by hand grenade squads and followed by detachments to clear the trenches (*nettoyeurs*) and detachments to salvage captured material, to break any surviving resistance and to bring back the prisoners.

Some battalions were accompanied by 65-mm. mountain guns to fire on machine guns. In order to have the artillery distinguish their own troops the men wore white cloths sewed on their backs.

Along the 33-kilometer battle front the French had deployed 1285 light and 650 heavy guns, or 40 light and 20 heavy guns per kilometer. Prior to the attack the 50th Infantry Division (German) had only 12 gun batteries, one Russian 15-cm. gun battery, and 2 heavy field howitzer batteries; the 15th Reserve Division (German) had only 6 gun batteries, one 10-cm. gun battery, 4 heavy field howitzer batteries and 4 mortar batteries. Thus the French superiority in artillery was ten to one.

During the night of the 24-25th, trench work on a large scale took place to provide assault positions. Routes of approach permitted reserves to be brought up under cover to within 4 to 5 kilometers. In order to have the entire day for development of the success, and after a drum fire that had lasted 72 hours, at 9:15 A.M. the attack started with 22 divisions in the first line and eight divisions in the second, along the front Massiges — Auberive (33 kilometers) against the position held by four German divisions after the artillery fire about 7:00 A.M. had again been increased to maximum volume.

The French assault positions were about 80 to 400 meters from the foremost German trenches. Generally the distance was about 200 meters, which was still more decreased by the leading French waves which in order to avoid the defensive barrage, had, shortly before the attack, taken position lying down in the open ground in front of their trenches. Considering this short distance, the defender could not man the fire positions at all points at the proper time; but the resistance was not broken thereby. Each squad, each individual kept on fighting. The 53d Infantry Regiment (50th Infantry Division) which had furnished 4 companies for the corps reserve, held a sector of 2250 meters front with only 3 companies in front, 3 companies in rear and 2 companies in second line. The

Position Warfare in the West, 1914-1917

attack of 4 French regiments with 8 battalions was directed at that point, these battalions close alongside each other. The front lines were overrun by the attacker, it is true; but the stubborn resistance of the 53d Regiment was broken by envelopment and attack in the rear. All honor to this brave regiment, which here succumbed to superiority in numbers, but the remains of which, reinforced by a few reserves held their place until the evening of October 1st. From September 22d to October 10th the regiment lost 56 officers and 2583 men. In consequence of the superiority in men and materiel and of the stubborn resistance of the front line, heavy losses in prisoners could not be avoided. The French army communique of the evening of the 26th, reports for the entire front 16,000 unwounded prisoners, 200 of whom were officers and 24 guns captured. The evening of the 29th they reported 23,000 prisoners and 121 guns captured.

The excellent conduct of that regiment stands by no means alone. I shall cite only the stubborn resistance of the 2d Battalion, 65th Infantry, under an efficient cavalry captain on Hill 196 at Le Mesnil, in a reverse slope position which could not be reached by the flat-trajectory guns. The troops, though attacked in flank and rear, held their position; gained time by counter-attacks; and by the evening of the first day of the battle had captured 300 prisoners and 2 machine guns from the enemy, they themselves losing 8 officers and 180 men (only 60 killed) and 5 prisoners.

We cannot emphasize too much in peace training that threatening and envelopment of the flanks are of themselves no justification for withdrawing; that a well constructed trench system can be held even under very unfavorable conditions, while retreat across an open terrain will almost always lead to annihilation. On the French side the main cause for the failure of the attack was attributed to the efficient employment of the German machine guns.

It appears that the main plan was to break through along the four main roads leading northward. The objective of the attack was to be the Vouzieres — Rethel road, about 24 kilometers distant. We will not go into details here. However, a deep penetration succeeded only on both sides of the Souain — Somme road for a width of 17 kilometers and a depth of 3.5 kilometers. At another point the French had penetrated only to a depth of 1500 to 2000 meters. The German defense was by means of barrage fire. Though this fire did not break up the first waves, it still had the effect of delaying the succeeding waves; and in many cases stopped them. Where the penetration had been successful, advancing reserves strove to gain the fruits of that success, regardless of the losses they suffered.

This resulted in the mixing of units and in confusion which was increased by the French fire and the stubborn defense of the intermediate ground by the German troops held in readiness. In the evening the battle came to a halt in front of the second position, which had been located, after the experiences of the Winter battles, on the rear slope of the hill. Attempts by the cavalry to exploit the success met with a bloody defeat. The attack preparations had been thoroughly planned up to the penetration and regulated to the minutest details; and from there on the command left everything to the initiative of the subordinates, who failed.

The next few days passed in minor actions with no results. The artillery required till October 4, 1915, to deploy in new positions. The attack, resumed then, gained no success, as by that time sufficient German reserves had arrived. The battle died out by the end of the month.

Prior to the attack it had been presumed that the German resistance would be completely broken by the artillery fire. This presumption did not materialize. The artillery support, in connection with support of airplanes, had been excellent; the "drum fire" had annihilated all works that could be seen; but after the penetration, connection with the artillery was entirely lost. The skill of the individual French infantryman in clinging to the ground and in rapidly and skillfully strengthening the terrain, showed up advantageously; but less successful was the leadership from the company commanders up, for the leaders did not understand how to keep their men in hand. The effect of the artillery fire was disappointing, for in spite of the enormous expenditure of ammunition, it did not have the power of annihilating a very numerically inferior opponent.

It was deduced from the Autumn battle, as far as position warfare is concerned, that each defensive system must consist of at least two positions, which should be so far separated that the enemy cannot overcome by his artillery fire the second from the first; and that the main purpose of the second position is to prevent the attacker moving by the flank after penetrating the first position in order to extend his success. Each position should consist of two lines, separated by a distance of 50 to 100 meters and connected by numerous trenches capable of being defended. The most advanced line, in which the larger portion of the machine guns should be, should form the main battle line. It was found that flanking fire along the front of the line was especially important. Obstacles should be placed in several rows rather than in a single row. Although it is desirable to assume formation in depth to decrease the losses, this should not lead to splitting up commands. A trench garrison, attacked from all sides, must hold out at all costs in the expectation of relief by a counter-attack that is certain to come. Narrow, deep rifle trenches, if well revetted, endured on quiet fronts. Deep and broad trenches lasted better under artillery fire. Loopholes were also used. Dugouts had to be proof against the continual high-angle fire of the 15-cm. pieces. The entire garrison of the first and second line had to be given protection against artillery fire. Machine guns should be placed in casemate-like shelters and sited for flanking fire. The advantages of taking position on the rear slope, just behind the crest of a hill, had been clearly shown. The decisive factor in the selection of the position continued to be primarily the location of the artillery observation stations, from which it should be possible to observe to a considerable depth the terrain over which the enemy would advance, and secondarily the possibility of organizing our own artillery positions in sufficient depth. Part of the artillery was assigned for the general defense and part for closed defense against the assaulting troops. The latter, distributed by platoons or pieces, was to be kept hidden from hostile observation up to the time of the assault; but in most instances it betrayed itself by the size of its cover; and being placed in the front line, it was always sacrificed during the preparatory drum fire. The generally weak artillery of the defense did not justify such a detachment on a part of the artillery.

The first German attempt to break the position warfare was the attack on Verdun, which had originally been planned for February 12, 1916; but was postponed to the 21st on account of bad weather; and executed after a drum fire lasting for 24 hours on the bank of the Meuse. Whether this attempt should not have been made earlier and in an effectual manner, we shall not discuss here. Of course surprise had not been fully safeguarded. Nevertheless, the enemy lacked time to prepare counter measures. The advance commenced (according to French reports by the 3d, 18th and 7th Army Corps) on the 22d on the 12-kilometer front, Consenvoye — Azannes. The French positions were overrun on a 10-kilometer front for a depth of 3 kilometers. Then a second advance started from the direction of Etain. On the 25th Fort Douaumont and the village of Vaux were taken. From the middle of March, the attack was also conducted on the west bank of the Meuse. Unfortunately army headquarters had neglected to place reserves at the disposal of the attack. Toward the end of March the front of attack had been decreased, by pushing in the arc, from 72 to 55 kilometers. The advance on that front was carried to a depth of 8 kilometers. Early in April, on the east bank of the Meuse, 6 German corps and on the west bank, 9 German corps carried on the offensive while the French gradually placed in the line more than 30 corps. The French command attempted in vain to throw back the Germans. In the shifting of the location of the attack lay the possibility of surprise for either opponent. By the middle of July, the battles came to a standstill on the recommendation of the Crown Prince, on account of the enormous expenditure of forces. The French command had conducted the battle as offensively as possible; but the employment of artillery and the power of the German infantry proved superior to the French defense in a battle terrain that had been prepared in time of peace and during 18 months of war and was densely covered with woods in many places. The forces available were insufficient to carry on the defensive battle on the Somme and at the same time force a decision on the Meuse. The lessons learned by all arms were of special importance in subsequent attacks. They pointed out before all else the necessity of the closest cooperation with the artillery, pioneers, and aerial forces. Minenwerfers proved themselves to be an auxiliary means especially well suited for the attack. As large a number of men as possible should be trained in the employment of machine guns and hand grenades. Everywhere it was learned that best method of advance of the infantry in assault was on a broad front and in waves following closely the preparation by the artillery and minenwerfers, and accompanied by machine guns, pioneer detachments, and artillery. Intervals between skirmishers should be about 3 meters; distance between waves, about 30 to 50 meters in order to pass through the barrage fire. Every advantage that offers itself, such as gaps in obstacles and favorably situated shell-holes, must be utilized in the attack. The stubborn French defense from pill-boxes and dugouts located in woods and the failure of the attack under the fire positions arranged for close defense but unknown to and unobserved by the attackers, compelled the employment of *"assault groups"* of a strength of 1 to 3 infantry squads in conjunction with a pioneer squad, machine guns, minenwerfers and flame throwers. The "assault groups" were specially trained; and in the attack remained in rear of the front line at the disposal of the company commanders. In place of the rigid skirmish line which was too easily stopped by organized resistance, the employment of series of small assault detachments was considered, in which the personality of the leader, on which everything depended, was brought into greater use. Adopting this method, on July 7, 1915, the Bavarian Ersatz Division captured a position of 1800 meters front to the 4th line within twenty-five minutes after an artillery preparation of only seventy-five minutes, the same procedure having had satisfactory results on May 5th and 14th. The one rule governing the attack is rapid advance, utilization of the smallest success, and advance as far as the effect of our own artillery, the broken morale and the losses of the enemy will permit. Artificial construction of an attack forces us, in attacks with a limited objective, not to cross the established line. From an artillery viewpoint, the defense was organized on barrage fire lasting initially three or four minutes and then decreasing and counter-offensive preparation in which stretches of hostile trenches are fired upon and which secures relief for our heavily pressed infantry. The realization of the necessity for offensive employment of the artillery, even in defense, had not yet become general. In the attack, the hostile artillery was to be held down effectively, while the infantry was to work its way up close to the place where our artillery projectiles fell. "Our infantry must absolutely rid itself of all nervousness when our own artillery fire strikes close to them. Co-operation between heavy and field artillery should be improved. Our artillery fire should be supplemented by minenwerfer fire." The superiority of the enemy in the matter of heavy flat- trajectory guns was sorely felt by us. Aside from consideration of the kind of gun and organization of mixed artillery groups proved uniformly advantageous in the solution of tasks and facilitated cooperation with the infantry. For support of the infantry only the common tasks, frontal and flanking effect combined, as well as conditions for observation and communication, but not the location of the batteries, are decisive. With this understanding the issuance of clear orders and satisfactory liaison are gained, and personnel (observers, artillery liaison officers, telephone operators) and implements are husbanded. To facilitate co-operation with the infantry it became necessary to locate the command posts of artillery group and infantry regimental commanders as close together as possible. These requirements in the defense led to a well advanced long-range artillery group taking the hostile artillery as its principal target and a close range group, kept farther in rear, to fire on the hostile infantry. All artillery groups were under the orders of the artillery commander. Whether that artillery commander should be under the orders of the division or corps commander was a matter of discussion for a long time. Finally, differing from the French policy which placed the main portion of the artillery under orders of the corps commander, our entire artillery, except the heaviest artillery, was placed under the orders of the division commander.

Lessons of the Battle on the Somme and the Battles in Front of Verdun in the Late Fall of 1916

After the Autumn battle the Allies, while still employed in defense against the German attacks on Verdun, started preparations for a new battle on both banks of the Somme, which was to be a joint operation by British and French; but considerations in the matter of training the British troops compelled the attack to be postponed to the end of June. The Russian attack in Volhynia occurred in the meantime.

It may have been thought that the cause of the failure in the Autumn battle was insufficient ammunition supply, but now, in addition to a pronounced superiorly in the air which made its importance felt in the observation of fire and in the participation by airplanes in the ground battle, such an amount of ammunition was to be supplied that according to all human calculations the resistance of the defender should be completely broken. Thus was created the "Battle of Materiel" which could be fought to a finish only by timely and maximum exertion of all munition industries. Delays at home reacted bitterly on the troops that had to face that storm. The ammunition brought from home in the first weeks was hardly sufficient for the barrage fire and for the absolutely essential support of the infantry. There was no ammunition for counter-battery work. In addition the attention of the supreme command was fixed completely on the battles around Verdun when the first signs of another serious battle on the Somme became noticeable. Thus the German defense was from the very beginning under very unfavorable conditions; but what did it not achieve in spite of these!

According to French reports the leading German position consisted of 3 main lines of a total depth of 500 tc 1000 meters, between which there were underground shelters and machine gun nests. A second position, consisting of 1 or 2 main lines and protected by excellent obstacles, was 2 to 4 kilometers distant from the first, so that the artillery of the attack would be forced to change position. Between the two positions preparation had been made for conduct of the battle by "lock" trenches.

In April, a systematic artillery fire took place on the British wing; the road net was extended; positions reinforced; mine warfare started; and plenty of ammunition and subsistence stored. By the end of April the German command no longer doubted that an attack was to be expected here. On June 22, 1916, the artillery preparation began. During the concentration of the hostile artillery, however, the German artillery had been able to cause heavy losses. The number of allied guns was materially larger than in the

Autumn battle in the Champagne; the method of the bombardment differed by the fire being more concentrated against single stretches of trenches; and strong gas bombardment was interspersed "from June 24, 1916, to July 1, 1916, on a front of 25 kilometers in forty different places." (Haig.) Our drum fire, fire against the Somme bridges and gassing the ground in rear, occurred from June 25 to June 30. Hostile reconnaissance operations, started in the last week prior to the attack, proved excellent. They furnished important information concerning the effect of the fire on trenches and batteries. On June 25th battle airplanes made an attack against German captive balloons, destroying 9 of them. The attack, which was to start on June 30th according to the statement of a deserter, started at 7:30 A.M., July 1st south of the Somme, and two hours later, north of the river. It was apparent that thereby the attention of the German reserves was to be distracted; but that two hours' space of time served only to preclude surprise on that part of the battlefield.

Joffre's systematic conduct of attack, reckoning only on mechanical means and merely frontal pressure by masses, declining the use of cover offered by the terrain and favoring the mixing of all units, was changed in this Somme battle. Front line units stood alongside each other with great formation in depth. Thus in each regiment 6 companies no longer were formed abreast in a dense skirmish line; but only 8 half-platoons from 4 companies were formed abreast in light skirmish lines, with intervals from 4 to 5 paces. The regular construction of trench system had been abandoned. More attention had been paid to surprise. Stress was laid on the necessity of the artillery accompanying the infantry by fire in such manner that the fire would be lifted to positions in rear only immediately preceding the penetration. Airplanes were employed as "infantry observation planes" to locate the positions of the infantry in the terrain. Joffre's demand of a penetration deep into the enemy's lines, to connect the operative penetration with the tactical penetration, could not be carried out in the Autumn battle and the French attacks came to a stand-still in front of our weakly held second positions. In the Battle of the Somme this procedure was followed as a fixed rule. The enemy contented himself with attacks against a fixed objective, renewing the same procedure after renewed artillery preparation. This "eating through" the entire position system was characteristic of the Somme battle. The French attack carried the first position, but then encountered serious resistance. The British attack, preceded by explosion of mines and accompanied by smoke clouds, did not initially have the same success, though its objectives were only 6 kilometers distant. The successes of the center and the right of the attack were exploited by the employment of reserves, so that finally the left also made progress. According to Marshal Haig's report a night attack on a large scale took place on July 14th. After a march covering 1200 meters a position was taken, at a distance of 250 to 400 meters from the enemy, under cover of security detachments on a front of 6 kilometers and the attack started at 3:25 A.M. against the Trones woods, Longueval and Bazentin le Petit. After the artillery preparation that had started on July 11th, the attack resulted in the capture of the Trones woods. It is stated that cavalry performed excellent service in this attack. On July 1st the defense had, north of the Somme, five German divisions on a 36-kilometer front; and south of the river, four divisions on a 33-kilometer front. From July 19th on, the defensive front was formed into 2 armies in place of 2 army corps as previously, separated by the Somme. On the average, 1 German division held 7 to 8 kilometers, against which the enemy brought 3 to 4 divisions. Placing fresh troops into line and thereby changing the sector limits did not prove advantageous to the battle command.

On September 15th tanks were used for the first time. In the beginning they gained success by surprise, which however did not last long. Far more annoying was the firing on the trenches by low flying battle airplanes equipped with machine guns. The fear of being seen by the airplanes and then annihilated by the hostile artillery fire started by the information given by the airplanes, prevented the infantry for some time from taking countermeasures until they became convinced that this fear was groundless. Automatic rifles of the allies played a very important and effective role during the attack. Locally they proved of great value in the defense, wherever buildings with cellars were available for defense. Thanks to its "catacombs" Combles was held from September 15th to 26th, when it was voluntarily evacuated by the

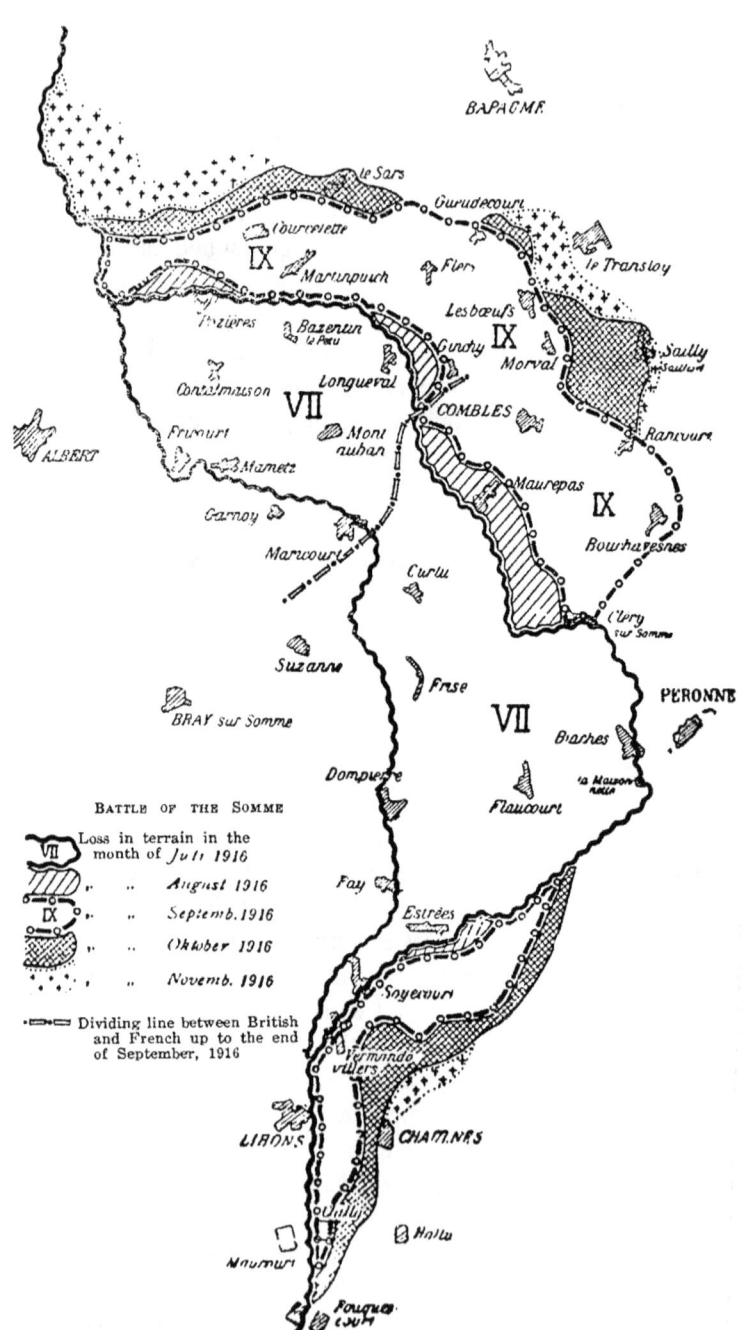

few German defenders. An opportunity offered during the evening to the cavalry held in readiness in an advance by way of Sailly eastward, was not noticed by the British.

The Somme battles concluded with a heavy attack on November 11th. The penetration had not been accomplished; but the object of the British command in the attack, of holding the German forces had been accomplished.

For their success, the Allies had to thank the enormous expenditure of ammunition and their superiority in the air, which could only be offset gradually. A numerically inferior artillery can in the end hold down a superior artillery if it has superior aerial observation facilities. But an artillery superiority should make itself doubly felt if the enemy, as was the case on the Somme, is superior both in number of guns and aerial forces. But in spite thereof the Allies had not been able to destroy the weak German artillery, but only lessened its effectiveness. In place of the destruction of the hostile materiel, the attack demanded annihilation of men or even only the reduction of their power of resistance for the decisive moment of the assault. This led to gassing shelters of the defense. The German infantry, though inferior in numbers, understood how to evade the hostile fire by moving forward or sideways; and was not shaken to the extent the enemy had expected. It is true that the trenches were in a very short time changed into a field of shell-holes; but the deep shelters with overhead cover six meters thick, held out and were found useful as long as the entrances were kept open. The artillery defense consisted mainly in firing a barrage which however was ineffective when the signals from the front line were not observed or when the larger portion of the guns had been destroyed by the hostile artillery preparation. This caused ceaseless complaints concerning the lateness of the barrage or its lack of density. The infantry, trusting entirely too much to the barrage, easily failed to defend itself independently. Orders from higher headquarters at this time compelled the artillery defense to be conducted offensively before the attack proper started. The exhausted German divisions needed relief. Though the quickly exhausted infantry could be withdrawn the relief of the weak artillery could not be accomplished. Thus units were disrupted. As a result the commanders of the infantry and the artillery were not personally known to each other any longer. Fresh divisions arriving after the loss of the first position found very bad and weak fortifications, which contained nothing necessary for a successful defense. Labor within the zone of the hostile fire was impossible. Still those troops held out bravely, cheered by the example of their officers. It is no wonder that the infantry during these heavy battles in which it had to suffer patiently under the heaviest kind of fire, deteriorated in battle efficiency. Only timely relief, thorough training during the rest periods and offensive conduct of the defense could return to the German infantry its former superiority over the enemy. The hostile airplanes found special difficulties in locating for their artillery the German lines in that shell-torn ground, so that the latter had to be content with merely sweeping certain portions of the terrain. Losses for the defense were thereby decreased. Positions, that could be definitely determined by the airplanes, were destroyed and obliterated in a very short time. This explains why our men were much opposed to converting shell-holes into trenches. At any rate, the losses increased as soon as the trenches appeared on the photos taken by the airplanes. Trenches thus rapidly constructed could of course, not offer the same protection as would trenches on which weeks of labor had been expended. The troops soon adopted the expedient of digging trenches in rear of the shell-holes that were to be defended. This diverted the fire from the occupied shell-holes; and during lulls in the battle and at night, offered protection against weather. It was a question whether on the whole it would not be better to abandon the time-consuming construction of trenches and confine ourselves to the mere construction of obstacles and shelters. Though this might have been justified in case of the first construction of works in rear, it was on the other hand, extremely dangerous to abandon trench construction completely. Command, subsistence of the men, care of the wounded, issuance of orders, and the service of information would have been made more difficult. In addition, there was the rapid consumption of man power in the damp Autumn weather. In the shell-holes the men were in no way protected against the weather and often stood in water up to their waists. As obstacles were lacking in the shell-torn terrain the dispersed troops were open to attack by any hostile patrol and it would have been difficult to organize a counter-attack. The difficulty of giving our artillery the exact location of our men, decreased the possibility of laying the barrage exactly in front of our line. In addition in a position in the shell torn terrain there was continuous movement caused by relief and by the inclination of the men to evade striking projectiles. This caused loss of contact and co-operation with adjacent troops. As we have learned, contact by eye alone with the neighboring units does not suffice in general. The commanders must consult and agree on combined action. Troops holding their place stubbornly in a frontal attack pay no attention to the flanks, if they know supporting troops are there. If an adjacent unit gives way and the attacker follows him up and turns toward the flanks, the troops holding their ground will find themselves in a precarious situation, which they can overcome only by withdrawing (defense of Combles) or by a counter-attack. The points of contact of two units become weak points, against which the enemy preferably directs his attack and which the defense meets by placing in readiness a special connecting detachment. The necessity of reducing the effect of the hostile artillery led to a distribution of all works in depth. It was found best to post the machine guns, withdrawn from air observation, between the first and second positions, especially when it was possible by constructing obstacles, to guide the attack into definite directions. In the intermediate terrain nothing was shown which would draw the artillery fire; and on the other hand, false works may have a good effect in diverting the hostile fire. The artillery also had to form its observation stations and battery positions in depth with numerous alternative positions, so that the hostile infantry could not reduce them in one effort. In this disposition, of course, we had to reckon on the loss of the foremost batteries.

There is no hard and fast rule governing the strength with which a position should be occupied. At Gommécourt the defender believed he would be able to get along in trenches without shelters employing 1 rifle to every 3 meters, whereas prior to the attack of July 1, 1916, in the well constructed sector of Fricourt, there were 800 rifles and 8 machine guns for each 1000 meters and this was believed insufficient. The more the offensive defense is prepared in advance, and the more the hostile fire strikes only the leading trenches, the smaller the garrison of the leading trenches may be. In the 12th Infantry Division (German) it was found sufficient to have on a front of 6 kilometers, 1 battalion per 500 meters. 2 companies of each battalion were in the front trenches, each company having 1 platoon in the front line, 1½ platoons in the second line, and ½ platoon in the third line. 1 company of each battalion was in battalion and 1 in regimental reserve.

On the German side, it had been sufficiently perceived that a serious attack, involving a penetration, could be stopped only by a position of great depth, so that it was immaterial to absolutely hold the first trenches requiring dense skirmish lines and resulting in increased losses. It was seen that it would be far more advantageous to conduct the defense offensively by giving way under the hostile fire, and then seeking a decision by an independently organized counter-attack by the troops in readiness and by the position reserves, so that at the end of the battle the trenches would be again in the hands of the defender. At the Somme there was an absence of reserves at many points, but wherever a counter-attack struck the enemy immediately after his entry into the position, success was complete and nullified the entire artillery preparation of the attack (Fricourt, July 1, 1916). If the counter-attacks executed by the troops in readiness immediately behind the position within about 400 meters, are not successful, then commanders of all rank must immediately do everything they can to prevent the extension of the penetration. Extension in depth must be prevented by using the lines in rear, extension toward the flanks by the use of approach trenches; and around the enemy's nest we must immediately create a certain "locking" position, the most threatened comers requiring special reinforcement. The commander must be at once notified of the creation of such a nest. Frequently, because of human reasons the extension of the penetration is reported as a minor one, and that fact leads to arranging a counter-attack with insufficient forces. And just those very "French nests" that had been created by penetration facilitated the subsequent hostile attack very materially, because they were made points of departure of new operations.

Position Warfare in the West, 1914-1917

It was found urgently necessary by army headquarters to have fresh divisional and army artillery in readiness for insertion. Only thus was it possible to withdraw the infantry and artillery simultaneously from the fighting line and to give them some rest for recuperation, for replacement of men and for training prior to putting them in line along a quieter front. During the Somme battle this was impossible and had its effect on the morale.

The Battle of the Somme led to a complete change of views concerning the conduct of the defense. The passive endurance of the hostile fire ceased. A fresh, offensive spirit was incorporated in the conduct of the defense. On August 29, 1916, Field Marshal von Hindenburg, who had been promoted from Colonel-General was assigned to the supreme command and General von Ludendorff was appointed First Quartermaster General. At once, in a new regulation "the Defensive Battle," the new method of fighting was presented: "The object of battle defense consists in letting the attacker wear himself out, bleeding himself white, but saving our own forces. The defense will be conducted not by putting in line large numbers of men, but mainly by inserting machines (artillery, minenwerfers, machine guns, etc.) . At the same time, in addition to the question of numbers, organization, employment and co-ordination, all bear an influence. In the distribution of forces, the fundamental consideration is saving of personnel." The troops only reluctantly accepted the general rule of weakly holding the front line because it was feared that that line could be retaken only with difficulty. But with the very short assault distance over which the attacker passed, it happened only too frequently that the strong garrisons could not leave their shelters in time and were captured. In addition to the thin occupation of the front line, narrow sectors (250 meters for a company of 150 men, on quiet fronts 500 meters) and great depth formation were ordered to facilitate a stubborn resistance.

The Autumn Battles Around Verdun became of special importance. The enormous German attack in February was followed by French counter-attacks, which made great progress only when General Nivelle, a colonel, commanding an artillery regiment at the outbreak of war, was assigned to the command of the army group at Verdun. The battles of October 24 and

December 15, 1916, showed a very peculiar method of attack, by thoroughly discarding the Joffre method based on a systematic procedure, declining the use of the cover of the terrain and by assigning deeper objectives to the attacks then had been the case in the battle of the Somme. The first attack-shock was to end at least in the hostile artillery position. Difficult points of attack were to be covered sparingly by infantry but thoroughly covered by artillery. Weak points, especially in defiles and depressions were to be penetrated by strong forces which, paying no attention to what happened on the right or left, took possession of important sections of the terrain. Everything that still held on the flank of or in rear of these shock columns which had pushed far ahead, had to fall by flank and rear attacks. "If we have once opened a door in a wall that has to be crossed, then nobody would possibly think of climbing over the wall." From this resulted quite naturally the organization of the units into assault units and reserves, corresponding to the points to be attacked. The front of the assault columns was dependent on the battle task; the deeper the troops were to penetrate into the hostile battle position, the narrower the front and the greater the depth. The zone of attack of a *"division de breche"* of 9 battalions was to be 2000 to 2400 meters wide, according to Joffre's views only 1200 to 1500 meters in case of 12 battalions. The division might be formed either in column of regiments or with regiments abreast, the latter in column of battalions separated by a distance of 500 meters. The attack proceeded automatically so that the leading battalion halted on reaching its objective, the succeeding battalion passed through to a more distant objective. The reserve divisions followed at distance of only 2000 meters. In the uninterrupted advance by the troops lay the best help for adjacent troops, should the latter not advance rapidly enough or be held up. As the initial penetration was almost always easy, the determining factor lay with the reserves. It was their duty to conduct the subsequent attack. They must follow up as rapidly as possible and deepen the penetration. Nivelle counted on the fact that second positions are not completely occupied, and that in all cases gaps would be found through which detachments under skilled leaders could work. As the attack was made on a broad front, an abundance of artillery was necessary. On the one hand, artillery protection for the infantry was attained by a rolling barrage, automatically advancing 100 meters every four minutes, and on the other hand, by forming a mobile artillery reserve, which was taken from divisions not designated for the attack. Success of the attack rested primarily on surprise, and then on artillery effect. Surprise required that we abandon all thoughts of time-consuming earthworks, such as routes of approach, bomb-proof battery emplacements and reserve trenches, and especially the position from which the attack is to depart be not advanced. It is better to make the attack across an extended open stretch under protection of the artillery, than to lose the advantage of surprise. For that reason the air forces should not be increased prematurely on the attacking front. A planned attack against the hostile captive balloons should not be started earlier than one day prior to the artillery preparation. Counter-battery work is of particular importance. The hostile artillery must be neutralized before the artillery preparation proper begins; then the hostile artillery must still be kept under fire. Nivelle planned an artillery preparation, dependent on battle conditions, of 6 days. An increase in the volume of fire prior to the attack was not to take place. Special emphasis was laid on the necessity of using fresh troops in the attack, which had been trained in the rest area behind the front. Weak points are encountered in every position. If the attack finds them, a penetration of the position system is possible in case the position lacks sufficient depth. This shows the necessity of special protection for the artillery of the defense. The batteries should at least have some machine gun protection in order to give the artillery an opportunity to participate in the fighting for the intervening terrain (with positions for observation close to the batteries) . Thus too, is evident the necessity of previously prepared plans for strong and timely counter-attacks, which, however, can be effective only if arrangements for prompt transmission of information have been perfected.

Prior to the December attack the 4 French Divisions (37th, 38th, 126th, 133d) had been trained from 5 to 6 weeks, commencing with the school of the soldier and ending with division maneuvers, in a terrain similar to that over which the attack was to be made. The attack was to be made from the east bank of the Meuse to the village of Vaux in a northerly direction towards Louvemont, Hill 378 and Bezonvaux on a front of 9 kilometers. On December 11, 1916, the assault divisions were brought up by auto trucks. The artillery preparation began at the same time. On the night of December 13-14th the divisions took their places in the line; and early on the 15th, all were in position. The reserve divisions which were to relieve them later were in readiness in rear. The left division (126th) was to penetrate the German position only 500 meters, the other to penetrate up to about 3000 meters. At 12 o'clock (10 o'clock French time) the penetration, without increasing the artillery preparation, was to start either in skirmish lines or small assault columns. The surprise succeeded, so that the German barrage came too late, and men in the deep shelters were taken completely by surprise. The turning off by the penetrating troops to the flanks proved correct. Special units had been placed opposite the division sector limits and in depressions, as the least resistance was expected there, with the mission of advancing against the flanks and rear of hostile units still holding out. It was left to the initiative of all subordinate commanders to exploit the success should the troops encounter little or no resistance. General Nivelle undoubtedly gained a great victory. The main cause of the failure of the defense was probably the lack of proper advance preparation of the intermediate terrain, and of preparation for co-operation between infantry and artillery in the event of the loss of the leading observation positions. In addition the defense was conducted completely passive, though four divisions were in readiness behind the front. It was shown plainly that a single fortified line was not sufficient to stop an attack formed in depth. Fortified areas in great depth have to be arranged which will enable us to hold the terrain even if separate portions are lost. In this organization the different field works must support each other, and we must also be able to prevent the enemy from extending towards the flanks after he has penetrated.

In December, 1916, Nivelle was appointed commander-in-chief of the troops in France. His instructions for attack dated December 16, 1916, were captured two months later by German troops in the successful operation against the heights south of Ripont on February 15, 1917.

Position Warfare in the West, 1914-1917 87

* * *

The XVI Army Corps had become engaged in stubborn battles in the Argonnes. Mountainous, broken forest terrain and a tenacious enemy, superior in numbers, allowed but slow progress so that even mine warfare was again resorted to and minenwerfers played a great role. Attacks with limited objective started. The smaller attacks proved less successful than attacks on a larger scale. Thus, positions could be taken only after thorough preparation by artillery and minenwerfers. Requirements were that the positions for departure of attacks should be as close to the enemy as would permit firing on the trenches by minenwerfers without at the same time firing on our own. A charge across 30 to 40 meters ground in open terrain was accompanied by extraordinary high losses. In most instances, the time for the assault was chosen so that the hostile trenches could be taken before dark in order that the troops organizing the position for occupation and defense might be hidden from the hostile fire. Preceding the attack, the assault detachments of infantry and pioneers underwent careful practice behind the front, in position and open warfare, which included accurate synchronization of watches. If the enemy had been thoroughly shaken the assault generally succeeded easily and quickly. If we allowed even a few minutes for the enemy to recover, the hope of success faded; and even if the attack succeeded, it was only at too great a cost. The assault itself demanded accurate co-operation between infantry and artillery. The assaulting troops must not deviate from the procedure agreed upon. Otherwise they would run into our own artillery fire. The main weapon of the assault was the hand grenade. The troops were to pay no attention to connection with neighboring troops. They were to charge through to the designated objective and then seek to help the less fortunate neighbor. The assault against the hidden pillbox was very difficult. Their resistance was most quickly overcome by the use of flame throwers.

Utilizing the Experiences Gained

On November 18, 1916, the Battle of the Somme was concluded with a final British attack; the battle had lasted four and a half months. The *Training Regulations for Foot Troops* (German) of January, 1917, published the experiences of all for the benefit of all. General introduction of hand grenades, automatic rifles and steel helmets, facilitated the command in the infantry. Light minenwerfers, flame and grenade throwers were assigned as auxiliary weapons. The winter battles in the Champagne demanded well trained men to handle these weapons.

For support in specially heavy attacks, and also for use as shock troops, special assault battalions were formed which, armed with the auxiliary weapons (machine guns, flame throwers and infantry guns), were attached by groups or platoons to the infantry. These shock battalions were basically different from the Russian Scout Detachments which were formed from the best men of the companies. These scout detachments in consequence of their special training, performed valuable services. They operated under the direct orders of the regimental commander. There can be no doubt of their usefulness in difficult terrain and occasionally in minor warfare; but in large battles, there was a lack of the necessary maneuvering space for their employment. Combining the best elements of a company into a special detachment appears always dangerous, for the troops cannot do without their best men to replace fallen leaders and to serve as the backbone of the company in difficult situations. In the Boer war the battle value of the British infantry decreased rapidly through the continual detachment of the best men for duty with mounted infantry. A well trained infantry unit should be able, under its own commanders to perform the same services as a scout detachment. On the other hand, the assault troops remained with their companies where they were useful as leaders in the fight, and for particular missions they may also be temporarily employed away from their companies. The "assault" battalions were complete units, which get their recruits from all arms and are about equal to Jäger battalions. In France also, about January, 1917, assault groups were organized (*groupes francs* or *grenadiers d'elite*). In the Russian army (August 24,

1917), a shock battalion of four companies (each of 3 platoons) was formed in each division and formed into a technical unit. The shock squads (1 noncommissioned officer and 6 to 8 men) "lead the infantry at difficult points to open the points of entry into the hostile position, roll up hostile trenches, capture hostile machine guns and pill boxes and support the infantry in consolidating the captured position." (Field Training Regulations, I, 389.) The method of the trench fighting taught progressively on the training ground should be participated in also by the infantry shock squads. "The company possesses in its assault squads, composed of the best men, suitable leaders in the fight who should be placed at points where the strongest hostile resistance is expected" (244). Arrangements should be made for the participation of auxiliary weapons where artillery is lacking for strong fire preparation. Assault squads advance during an assault with the leading wave which is to penetrate to the farthest objective.

Machine guns are attached to the assaulting infantry, and also distributed to the waves in rear, for taking strong points, for flank protection and to neutralize hostile machine guns. In the defense, the automatic rifles form the main weapon of defense against the assault, while the machine guns will find their most effective employment in rear of the front line and are placed in the front line only, in numbers absolutely necessary, to furnish harassing and barrage fire. Defiladed and concealed positions are essential for their effective employment. As "weapons of the intervening terrain" they facilitate stubborn resistance and also find employment in defense against airplanes.

The needs of the defense govern the dispositions of troops for the first line. The regiments are placed abreast and are generally divided into position battalions, reserve battalions, and rest battalions. The first are the front line battalions with attached auxiliary arms and artillery observers. The second are the battalions which, reinforced by security detachments, support the front line battalions in their most important task, by emergency garrisons and "joint" detachments reinforced by machine guns; and which independently eject the enemy from the leading trenches he may have taken.

The Regulations gave special attention to the offensive defense. The trench garrison must hold out at all costs, even though in danger of being surrounded by the attacker. "The holding of the position then depends on the success of counter-attacks. Until the latter start, every man of the garrison and every gun must hold his or its place" (227). Counter-attacks should be made at once and without awaiting orders, not alone in our own but also into a lost adjacent sector.

Based on subsequent experiences and after the lapse of one year, the Regulations for Field Training II appeared.

"Thorough training in the use of the rifle and machine gun as well as efficient handling of hand grenades enable the infantry to successfully carry out its task. The rifle and hand grenade, however, can only achieve their very best effect by supplementing each other" (177). The last sentence is of special importance, as the troops were inclined (and even our opponents complained of it) to neglect the rifle in favor of the hand grenade. The first thing to do is to stop the enemy with the rifle and to resort to the hand grenade only when the enemy is within throwing distance or when he can no longer be fired on with the rifle (192). A new note in these regulations was the demand that "all noncommissioned officers and men must be trained in the shock-squad procedure' and that shock squads for special tasks be formed "from specially suited men from time to time" (226).

The directions for fighting against tanks (416-419) and against low flying battle airplanes (420-429) were also new. Each machine gun, that is not occupied in the battle against ground targets, must direct its fire on low flying airplanes (423).

The general directions for the conduct of position battles were proven correct throughout. The machine guns had been specially useful as arms in the intermediate terrain, especially in nests of one to three guns under infantry protection. These nests were again combined under one leader into defense groups, to which dispersed men were to hasten. Skillfully nested in, and hidden from hostile terrestrial and air observation, the machine guns opened fire, only at the moment of the first hostile assault, by surprise, and with flanking effect whenever possible (406) .

The battalion commander of the front line battalion was the

"fighting troops" commander. Heavier emphasis than in the first Regulations was laid on the offensive defense and the necessity of cutting out security detachments. For the counter-attack the commander of the battalions in readiness must not await request for counterattack. To his companies battle tasks and definite battle sectors can be assigned before the start, in which they are responsible for timely and independent counter-attacks (445). The battalion commander was responsible that the counter-attack hit the enemy before he has had a chance to consolidate the captured position.

The Battles in 1917

In the Spring of 1917 the German command reckoned on a repetition of larger attacks in the Champagne and in Picardy. Valuable basis for the conduct of the defense was furnished by Nivelle's Regulations in conjunction with the experience gained at Verdun. It was seen that the best counter-means for the new attack procedure was a weak garrison of, and even temporary abandonment, of unfavorably situated first lines. Absolute abandonment of the foremost trenches had given the usual French strong reconnaissance shocks prior to the attack a new point for starting the assault, and had not made it necessary to insert stronger forces. If the penetration succeeded, then the assaulting troops were to be attacked by the garrison holding the intermediate terrain from all sides with fire and held, so that the French infantry would lose the protection of the automatically advancing fire wave, and that was the prerequisite for the subsequent offensive defense by all arms from the depth, and by reserves brought up. The method of the French fire distribution left no attentive defender in doubt concerning the selected point of entry, so that the reserves could be placed in position in time. The immediately started counter-shock — into the uncertain — was the finger mark of the new leadership. Thus was created the elastic defense, temporary evasion of the annihilation fire to the front — which however found its limits at the obstacles — and then the assault-shock of the reserves. This method required also special artillery preparation: locating the observation positions in direct proximity to the batteries, and special arrangements for communication. Of importance were the directions that pauses in the hostile fire must not lead the defensive artillery into inactivity, as those very pauses allowed the enemy to bring up ammunition, to complete his attack preparations and to bring up his assault troops. From these facts we can now judge why the German army leadership decided, in the face of the progressing attack of the enemy, to evacuate a large projecting arc of the West front, and to go back to the "Siegfried Position," under the protection of independent detachments which had been left behind, and after the execution of extensive destructions. The object had been attained, time had been gained, and the enemy had been compelled to abandon his plan of attack. The Allies were forced to far separated attacks at Arras, on the Aisne and in the Champagne.

Possession of the terrain plays a very minor role, though it had long been considered, especially at home, as the means of determining whether a situation is favorable or a little less favorable, and though the enemy credited himself with success in taking possession of a piece of terrain that had been voluntarily abandoned by his opponent. Thereafter the German command husbanded its strength and held terrain only as long as it was warranted by the means that had to be used therefor.

On the side of the Allies also no time was lost in withdrawing their attack divisions temporarily to the rear in order to practice in the open terrain the attack against the German trench system (4 to 5 kilometers depth). This practice began with the platoon. In addition to the battle and march practice proper and to training in the service of special arms, rifle firing and physical training was carried on, with and without packs. To hasten the advance, movement across country as well as by approach trenches was directed, thus minimizing the effect of the German machine gun fire. Intervals between skirmishers were 4 to 5 paces (3 to 3.75 meters). In terrain devoid of trenches all column of fours were to be discarded, the platoons to advance in open order, as units or in lozenge formation (see plate), to lessen the effect of hostile artillery fire.

COMPANY IN LOZENGE FORMATION

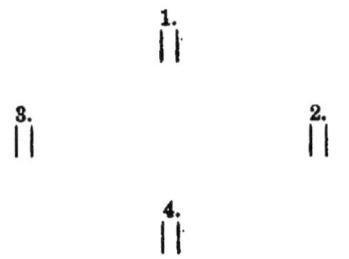

In forests the troops assumed single formation. Capture of villages was left to the tanks. Woods were entered only after the artillery had fired upon them for at least 20 minutes.

In the attack within the division, 1 regiment was generally placed as a shock-detachment with 3 battalions (each 750 meters, companies 250 meters front) abreast on a front of 2400 meters. 2 regiments followed in reserve. The company was formed into 2 waves, following each other at 30 meters distance. The distance of the battalion reserve was 400 meters.

The preparations of the British Army for the Battle of Arras were made in the same manner; it appears that special weight was attached to increasing the artillery materiel. In a sector north of Arras on a 5-kilometer front 456 light, 240 heavy and heaviest guns and 68 minenwerfers were counted. On April 9, 1917, after an enormous expenditure of ammunition, the British infantry forced its way into the German position under protection of a rolling barrage and tanks on a front of 17 kilometers. Between Gavrelle and Roeux (5 kilometers) a depth of penetration of 6 kilometers was attained. By the well laid and exceedingly heavy barrage portions of the German garrisons in the front trenches were completely cut off from their reinforcements. Through the loss of dominating ridges in the leading line, which had been boxed in by the British artillery, the hostile fire compelled a withdrawal at some points of 4 kilometers. Gas was employed on a very large scale. The guns that had to be abandoned to the advancing enemy were made unserviceable and blown up. A British attempt to penetrate at Roeux with a strong force of cavalry was defeated by strong fire. On the 23d the front of the penetration was increased to 34 kilometers; any further increase or advance was made impossible by the energetic counter-attacks of the German reserves.

After artillery preparation lasting for days the British divisions attacked with the assistance of tanks along a division front of 1500 to 2000 meters, mostly with 2 brigades (4 battalions) in four waves. These were to pass through each other in such manner that the leading wave halted on the first objective, where the second wave passed through the first wave to the second objective; and similarly followed by the third and fourth wave ("leap-frog system"). In this manner an organized front was always to be offered to the German counter-shock. (See plate.)

FORMATION OF A BATTALION
(1917)

| Of the 9th Inf. Div. | | | Of the 31st Inf. Div | | |
B	A		C	B	A
———	———	2 platoons	———	———	———
50 m					35 m
———	———	1 platoon	———	———	———
50 m					45 m
		1 platoon			
C ———			———	———	———
50 m					90 m
				D ———	
———				50 m	
				———	
50 m D					
———					

NOTE:—In England the companies are designated by letters.

The infantry was formed into waves or followed in narrow, short columns, which were preferred, in order to avoid losses, from the creeping barrage closely preceding the troops, from shorts or from fragments thrown back. Everything had been very minutely arranged in orders and nothing was left to chance or to the initiative of the commanders. In order to avoid the standing barrage of the defender, the first two lines (the first in very open skirmish line, 4 to 5 meters intervals between skirmishers, the second often in short narrow single columns) were sent before the assault beyond the leading trench, while the third line occupied that trench and the fourth immediately formed in rear of it. At the start of the assault the artillery laid its fire on the front to be penetrated and moved it forward slowly (for instance 90 meters in four minutes) first the heavy calibers, followed by the field artillery with the machine guns between the two. In many cases advance was made under protection of smoke clouds. The assaulting infantry followed the creeping barrage immediately. Losses by its own artillery fire had to be reckoned with. Halts were made to prevent the creeping barrage running away from the infantry. The barrage was then designated a standing barrage. It was intended to produce an effect on any counter-attack and gave the infantry the opportunity to entrench in expectation of a counter-attack and to reorganize. The first wave remained in that position, while the rest continued the advance in the rear of the creeping barrage. It is true that the necessity of taking advantage of the initial success was theoretically acknowledged, but exploiting the success was left to the subordinate commanders up to the battalion commander, who, being insufficiently trained, completely failed. In every instance it was proven a mistake to put in cavalry masses without attaching infantry to them as "pace-makers" (to clear the way). Employing divisions to gather the fruits of the victory, was not resorted to for reasons which may probably be accounted for by insufficient training of officers and men. Thus, in the Arras battle an entrance into the position was made, which, however, was not followed up by a penetration because the British command did not exploit initial successes. The attacking troops were prematurely relieved while they still possessed sufficient fighting power. The troops were trained entirely too theoretically or according to a hard and fast scheme for the attack, and everything depended on the success of the creeping barrage. They reasoned that any attack that came to a halt had better be at once discontinued, and tried at some other point. In that case we must hope to strike some portion of the front that is weaker, or occupied with more or less worn out troops.

PLATOON IN FORMATION UNDER HOSTILE ARTILLERY FIRE

1 squad hand grenade throwers (HG); 1 squad automatic rifles (AR); 1 squad riflemen (RM); 1 squad rifle grenade throwers (RG); total 10 officers, 40 men.

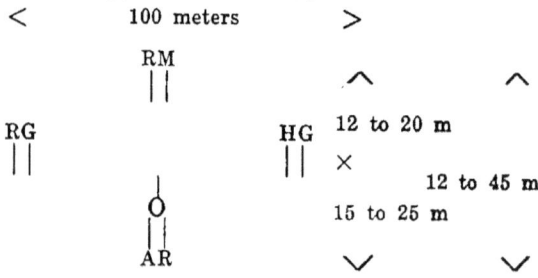

Platoon commander with 4 messengers.

PLATOON IN TWO WAVES

Trench moppers-up, 12 m distance.

The extensive French preparations for attack in the Western Champagne could not be hidden from the German airplanes, and had been materially corroborated by statements of prisoners. Nivelle's main idea of avoiding portions of the front lines that were difficult to attack and taking them subsequently by flank and rear attacks, was to be carried out on a large scale. Such portions, or supporting points, were the Brimont and Berry sectors in the Western Champagne. An army was to attack beyond the Aisne against Laon, to secure the left flank of the main attack and then to take up the pursuit. The main attack, in the Champagne, was planned so that a stretch of 20 kilometers was to be left free in the center at and east of Reims between Bethany and Prouvais. On the left the 5th Army (as had been gleaned from an order captured April 4, 1917, at Sapigneul) with the 32d Corps was to push forward towards Brienne and Prouvais; with the next division (37th), to Suippe; and with the next division (14th), supported by the Russians, to the Brimont. On the right wing a corresponding advance was then to be made by way of Auberive. As strong forces were also concentrated around Chalons, it is not improbable that here a strong group was placed in readiness for attack, probably in the direction of Vouziers and for furnishing flank protection. If the German center made a stand, its fate would be sealed, provided the wings succeeded. Thus it was a Cannae battle in position warfare!

According to the captured orders, prematurely issued, the attack of the 20th Corps, to be started at 6:00 A.M., April 16th, was to reach the village of Lierval situated about 16 kilometers north of the Aisne and to occupy the flats west thereof as far as the canal in the vicinity of the village of Uzel. Thus the rear of the new Siegfried position would be gained and the attack would work towards the British. The 6th Corps had the task of working its way up west of the 20th (on the Soissons — Laon road) and to occupy that village as well as the terrain to the west. Then the pursuing army was to push through this gap. This order assigned to the 39th Infantry Division of the 20th Corps for its first objective the German position on the Chemin des Dames; for its second, the Aillette; for its third, Lierval and the flats to the Aisne — Oise Canal. In this operation the 153d Regiment of the 39th Infantry Division had the task of advancing to the attack in column of battalions. The 3d Battalion was to take the first objective; the 2d Battalion, the second objective; and the 1st Battalion, the third objective. The orders contained similar instructions concerning the adjoining regiments (146th and 156th). The 132d and 106th Regiments of the 56th Infantry Division of the 6th Army Corps were ordered to advance as far as Chavignon. The 132d Regiment was to advance alongside the canal, the 106th Regiment to ascend the Bovette Hill through the Bois des Comites d'Or and then push forward in the direction of La Croix-sans-Tete,

Nivelle intended to overrun three or four German positions and expected an advance of 10 kilometers in 8 hours, taking the Brimont the first forenoon and Laon the morning of the second day. On the second and third day of the attack the advance was to be more rapid and was to be made in the direction of Sedan and Namur to the southern corner of Holland. Nivelle held the view that the penetration of the German front could be made within 24 hours, or at the most 48 hours. Otherwise the battle could not be won.

The opening of the battle was fixed for the British on April 9th, for the French left wing at first on the 15th (later on the 16th), and for the French right wing on the 17th. The blowing up of the Aisne — Champagne front line sector and the accompanying fan-like rolling up to the east and north showed a plan, well thought out and on large lines, which, however, would be successful only if the penetration could be accomplished on the first day, or not later than the second day and to the depth ordered. If the attacks did not succeed one after the other in rapid succession, the plan had to fall to pieces of itself. It was unfortunate for the attack that at the very start the above mentioned attack orders for the infantry of the 6th Army Corps in minute detail should fall into German hands. Though this fact was known to the French headquarters, the preparations for the attack were not changed. Thus the advantage of surprise was lost.

On the German side. Headquarters of the 1st Army (General of Infantry — Fritz von Below) was placed between the 7th and 3d Armies. These headquarters had been able to gather valuable experience on the defensive in the battle of the Somme. As each army (the 7th and 3d) detached the corps on its interior wing continuity in the issuance of orders was assured on the battlefield. Nevertheless disadvantages were connected therewith. Headquarters of the 1st Army assumed command over the two corps while the attack preparations of the French were in full swing; and conduct of the defense was made more difficult by the later insertion of fresh divisions. It was found inadvisable to decrease division fronts by putting new divisions into the line. It would have been better to attach a fourth regiment to the divisions already in line and to retain the remainder of the new divisions as interference divisions (in reserve). Besides it was incorrect to make the division sectors too small, as then it became difficult to post the artillery and facilitate changes in its position. One division with an interference (reserve) division in its rear could perfectly well hold a sector of 4 to 5 kilometers front, although the front of a division should not be extended beyond 3 kilometers.

The attack was commenced by heavy artillery fire reaching far into the hostile rear. Towards evening of April 6th, near Reims, an attack by artillery fire on a large scale, against the German captive balloons and planes, was started; but was unsuccessful, presumably on account of gassing by German defensive guns.

Differing from the Somme battle, in the "Easter" battle the Germans had a superiority in the air even prior to the French attack, which fact became of special use to the artillery counter-preparation by enabling the defense to adjust its fire on the hostile batteries and other targets far into the hostile rear. If a destructive fire was specially directed against any part of the German line, the hostile line opposite was immediately taken under a destructive fire.

In the French 5th Army, the course of the attack was about as follows: April 6th to 11th an artillery preparation including, on the first day, attack against the German air forces. On the 12th, a decrease of the artillery fire, which in the evening again increased to "drum" fire. On the 12th and 13th, reconnaissance attacks (raids). On the 13th, a diminution of the fire, presumably assault troops going into position. On the 14th and 15th resumption of heavy fire preparation, directed methodically on the second position. Night firing on the routes of approach and shelters, preparations for bringing up artillery. Early on the 16th "drum" fire again. At 7:00 A.M., the assault.

The German trenches, that could in most cases be easily observed, had been changed into a stretch of shell-holes by the strong artillery fire. Attempts to repair trenches under this fire, merely increased the losses. On the other hand, it was possible to construct in the shell-hole terrain in rear of the selected line of resistance a continuous trench, which in daytime had the effect of a false position, and which at night offered shelter from the bad weather, to the garrison of the front trenches. Now the advantages and disadvantages of advanced elements of the position came into consideration; and emphasis was laid on the necessity of declining to hold or recapture unfavorable portions of the terrain in place of accepting the heavy losses necessary to hold them. The German conduct of the defense was well known to General Nivelle. It was mainly: weak occupation of the first line; contending for the first trenches by automatic counter-attack of the troops in readiness, thus delaying the assault while the creeping barrage continued on its way; defense of the intermediate terrain by machine guns; and then decisive counter-attack by the reserves starting at the same time the attack commenced. General Nivelle demanded raids on a broad front, prior to the commencement of the assault, in order to induce the machine guns in the intermediate terrain to open fire prematurely and to cause the reserves to be committed to the counter-attack. Captured trenches were to be held as positions of departure for the further advance. Special weight was laid on the prompt forward displacement of the artillery immediately after the initial success. "If we require two months to prepare a new attack, thus permitting the enemy to dig in on a new front, we simply play into his hands. The time of preparation must be limited to the time necessary to bring forward the artillery. The period of two months must be diminished to but a few days, even if the question is one of attack against fortified positions." The battle confirmed the correctness of this German conception concerning the conduct of defense; but also showed its weakness which lay at the junction of two sectors. Only too easily could differences in the estimate of the situation concerning the main defensive position arise in the different sectors; and in that case cooperation in conducting the counter-attacks was not assured and liaison with the neighboring artillery was likely to be interrupted. "Joint" (meaning junction, where sectors adjoin) detachments could offset these disadvantages only in part. The danger of occupying large tunnels immediately in rear of the leading line came into prominence. This procedure of course held the large garrison thereof firmly in the hands of the commander; but on the other hand the garrison was in danger of being shut in by a caving-in and of falling helplessly into the enemy's hands. According to French reports, in the Cornillet Tunnel the garrison, numbering several hundred men, was killed by gases of explosions. Permanent evacuation of portions of the position was made only by direct orders from higher headquarters. This was of great importance in the conduct of counter-attacks.

Position Warfare in the West, 1914-1917   101

Instructions that portions of rifle trenches should be prepared so as to provide all round defense appeared necessary. The known French method of conducting the attack insisted that each unit assure itself of connection on its flanks. The commander was not merely to ascertain that troops were there but he had also to ascertain how and in what line those troops were to fight. The battle confirmed the frequent previous experiences: that portions of the position which had been observed by the enemy were quickly annihilated; that routes of approach observed in quiet periods very soon became unserviceable during battle; that troops in the open suffered less losses than those remaining in known trenches, which, after evacuation, served well as false positions. Counter-attacks conducted by even weak detachments had surprising success if they were started immediately after the enemy's entry. The enemy must be counter-attacked as long as he has not overcome the resistance of the position, and as long as he has not reorganized; and therefore the counter-attack must be started under entirely unknown conditions even under the danger of being started too early. The new conception of the counter-attack gained more and more in value; it was not only to offset a local defeat but the intention was to destroy the enemy. This required the introduction of larger infantry forces; and, as we could not absolutely count on the co-operation of the artillery, light horse-drawn batteries had to be attached to the infantry. The "interference" (reserve) divisions were designated for independent counter-attack. This employment of the reserves made it necessary to keep positions in rear garrisoned by weak security detachments. But if counter-attack could not take place within a short time after the penetration, it became necessary to make specially careful preparation for a systematic counter-attack. Great difficulties were encountered in taking up a position under cover close to the attack objective. Reorganization of the formation in depth after success also presented difficulties. The more time the troops were given, the more certain was success.

Early on April 18, 1917, the 5th and 6th Infantry Divisions with weak artillery arrived about 8 kilometers north of the ridge from Comillet to Hochberk and Pöhlberg, which since the 17th had been in French hands; they moved forward on the 19th in conjunction with a detachment of the 145th Infantry Regiment on their right and with the 23d Infantry Division on their left. They intrenched themselves on the ridge, but did not recapture the Fichtel hills and the first positions at that time, as the enemy was ready for defense in a prepared position and had brought up his artillery. A counter-attack started on May 27th against the Pöhlberg was successful at first but the captured terrain could not be held. A few days later the Hochberg was also recaptured. Lack of forces prevented a simultaneous attack along the entire front, which surely would have had more success, than several partial attacks following each other, repeating the same attack procedure.

The French main attack had gone to pieces with bloody loss. The tanks had not measured up at all to what had been expected from them. For political reasons Nivelle's resignation was demanded; and in his place stepped General Petain, who had come into prominence. The main causes for the defeat lay principally in that surprise was not attained — which is easily explained in such a large attack; that the German artillery had shown a tenacity and power beyond what had been expected, and that the very elastic defense was doubtless a great surprise. The French command renounced large attacks for the present. During the subsequent battles of the year the French satisfied themselves, as the British did also, with limiting the objectives in breadth and depth, and in most cases the object of the attack was merely the capture of a single position by strong forces with great formation in depth (the division on a 1200-meter front). After thorough artillery preparation — including strong gas concentrations on the attack objective and after arrangements had been made for the employment of tanks, the dense skirmish lines started. If they succeeded in their attack, everything was prepared to meet the counter-attack. As the attacks were of shallow depth such counter-attacks were successful only when they struck the enemy while still moving. The attack could be carried beyond the objective only by direct approval of the army commander. A position of departure for the attack 500 meters from the enemy, and never closer than 200 meters, was recommended. The assault was to advance under protection of a creeping barrage; and if the target objective was distant, intermediate halts were to be made. If intermediate objectives were designated frequently a change would be made in the assaulting troops for the subsequent continuation of the attack. The attack was composed of a series of successive offensive-shocks, which finally led to a penetration.

The attack against the Laffaux Corner (October 23, 1917) the base line of which was closed by the Aisne Canal, was a specially good example of the new French tactics. The 7th Army had no doubts whatever of the coming attack. Even the day and hour had become known. As the attack had to be accepted under conditions very favorable to the defense, it had to be decided whether it would be more desirable to consider the Laffaux Corner as a foreground zone and to execute the defense proper north of the Canal. Army headquarters, however, insisted on stubborn defense of the leading positions in front of the Canal contrary to the wishes of the troops and to the views of Imperial headquarters. The French intended to penetrate at Pinon and Fort Malmaison with the support of tanks, then to turn in rear of the German position and to cut off the projecting corner. October 16, 1917, the artillery preparation commenced with greatly superior artillery (for instance, in the 14th Infantry Division 125 against 32 German batteries), which very soon reduced the effectiveness of the German artillery. The creation of a strong gas barrage in the canal lowland of such extent and density that bringing up supplies and reserves to the front line was absolutely impossible was employed for the first time. The interference divisions posted in rear were distributed by battalions to the troops in the first line of the defense. Shelters that had been located from aerial photos were systematically destroyed. The French were satisfied with the line they reached on October 23d, and did not even interfere with the German retreat across the canal. The simultaneous battles at Verdun show similar events. It was specially noticeable that the French understood how to overcome garrisons by attacking them from flank and rear. The advance of the assault troops, delayed by the defense of the intermediate terrain, was very slow. In many instances two hours were consumed in covering one kilometer. The movements of the defenders under artillery fire were not much quicker, when gassed spaces under heavy fire had to be crossed. There were no more attempts at united shocks by entire interference divisions. The difficulties of bringing the troops through the shell-torn and covered terrain were great but where counter-attacks succeeded, they always had fine results.

The British Army attached more weight than the French to the change in the conduct of the attack.

The British attack was marked by careful preparation and utilization of the different offensive means. Against the Wytschaete Arc, the extension of which projected about 15 kilometers beyond the line Double Hill 60 at Zillebeke and Warneton, the attack preparations had so far progressed that by the end of April we had to reckon with an attack. In the beginning of May the artillery preparations commenced, then a pause occurred from May 16 to 21, 1917, on the 22d of May a second preparation, increasing continually in volume, commenced so that there was no doubt whatever (without considering the numerous raids and statements of a flyer, captured on June 6th) that the assault was imminent. On the German side, the means were insufficient for bringing up to the defensive troops (35th, 2d, 40th Infantry Divisions) reinforcements in troops and materiel. In addition, the defensive line was situated on the front slope of the hill. This, the British engineers had skillfully taken advantage of since 1914. The statements of infantry that the noise of mining could be heard, were said by our pioneers to be incorrect. The standing barrage of the defense was too weak. The heavy batteries brought up a few days before had been destroyed, except a few guns. Field artillery, that had arrived shortly before the attack, had gone into position in rear of the third position and remained there unmolested by the hostile artillery. The infantry had also suffered so much, that the battalions kept in readiness and resting had already been drawn up into the first line.

On June 7th, at 4:00 A.M., enormous explosions occurred, followed again by heavy "drum" fire, gassing of the terrain in rear and employment of a new kind of burning mine. At 5:40 A.M. 11 British Divisions of the 2d Army (Plummer) started on a front of 15 kilometers. They contented themselves mainly with reaching an assault position in front of the German "Sehne" position. The resisting power of the defender was broken when the assault began, but everyone that could possibly fight, held out. The remnants of the 2d Infantry Division retreated only when they were enveloped on both wings. A counter-attack against Messines started with portions of the Bavarian 3d and the 1st Guard Reserve Division, made good progress at first, but was attacked in the right flank. Naturally the German losses were very heavy. As in all these battles probably a renewed attack with fresh forces would have encountered but little resistance. Apparently the British did not think of a prompt exploitation of the success. Their reserves were used for relieving the troops in the first line, but not for increasing the entry to a penetration.

Even the subsequent battles show the same: Destroying by "drum" fire a relatively small sector of the front line through enormous artillery effect; the attacking infantry satisfied with assaults of minor depth; the advantages of surprise, not utilized.

The attack at Cambrai on November 20, 1917, against a quiet, weakly held front to a depth of 12 kilometers: against the 20th Landwehr Division and the 54th Infantry Division brought from Russia, shows an entirely different picture. It seems this conduct of attack can be used only against such a front. Everything was based on surprise, which was rendered more probable on account of the bad flying weather. The broad field of obstacles, undestroyed, 30 meters and at some points 100 meters broad, made it appear that any immediate attack was impossible.

In this instance the obstacles were not to be destroyed by a long protracted artillery fire but were to be broken down by tanks followed by the infantry. The position had been excellently constructed and had not suffered in any manner whatever. Statements of prisoners on November 19th about the impending attack, were not believed. The British orders for secrecy had been strictly complied with. Large movements of troops and vehicles were permitted only at night and without lights. The attacking troops did not come into any contact with the front line troops already known to us, so that prisoners taken by us were only from the latter troops, who naturally could not know or report anything about the attack. Strict orders were issued not to fire from new positions of the front line artillery prior to the opening of the assault. The front line artillery kept up its normal fire. As late as the 17th the 2d German Army reported that hostile attacks on a large scale were probably not to be expected and that there were no indications thereof on the northern half of the army zone as indicated by railroad traffic observed. A dense fog, artificially reinforced, hid the position in readiness. Bursts of destructive fire drowned the noise of the tanks, so that when the waves of tanks appeared the German security detachments were completely surprised. After an immediately inserted standing barrage they disappeared in the fog and appeared by surprise in front of the German batteries.

The penetration was made by 6 divisions on a front of 6 kilometers in a first and a second line. 4 cavalry divisions were to work through the German position and, turning off to the north, to cut off the sectors north of the front. To each British division 1 tank battalion had been attached, consisting of 3 companies, each of 4 platoons, each of 4 tanks. The attack was preceded by 6 tanks to ride down the obstacles. These were followed by 2 lines, of 18 and 12 tanks respectively, with 30 and 50 meters distance and a rate of advance of 3.2 kilometers per hour. The infantry followed at 100 to 300 meters distance. The attack was preceded as every other attack by a creeping barrage. Thanks to the surprise and the new method of fighting, the penetration succeeded the first day to a depth of 3.5 kilometers; but had sufficient artillery of the defense been at hand, the attack would have gone to pieces.

Tanks probably can take a position, but cannot hold it. They take the place of accompanying batteries and produce an effect on the morale of the defenders who feel so helpless. A difference is made, according to armament, between male and female tanks, the former having 2 light field guns and 4 automatic rifles, the latter 6 machine guns. Older tanks are used for carrying supplies. Tanks are to open a road for the infantry, destroying the obstacles or by direct support of the infantry in beating down machine gun nests and supporting points. In attacking villages tanks were frequently used. Considering their limited height and slow velocity, the employment of tanks against artillery is precluded. The capacity of tanks is small. Infantry carriers can haul 20 to 30 men and 5 machine guns. Mobility in the terrain is very good, the tanks can traverse slopes of 1 to 2, and can cross ditches 2.5 meters wide. Serious obstacles are offered to tanks by swampy ground, brooks, and watercourses about 60-cm. deep. The "passive defense" against tanks consists in such obstacles, construction of automatic mines, which will permit passage of individuals, but will explode on the passage of heavy weight vehicles. Bridges of great bearing capacity had better be destroyed. "Tank traps" on roads are of minor value, as the tanks can run across country. As the garrison within the tanks is deafened by the noise of the tank in motion, and as the narrow loopholes permit only a very limited view of the battlefield, it is necessary to assign men to accompany the tanks to inform the garrison of the tank where the enemy still holds out. In any case the tanks never fight individually but always in mass; and never unaccompanied; but, like the accompanying batteries, whose place they take, in close conjunction with infantry. The tanks rapidly use up their power. Therefore relief and formation in depth are absolutely required.

The gun remains the best defensive weapon against tanks. If the troops of the defense have once become used to the effect and impression created by tanks, then light tanks can be disposed of by machine guns using armor-piercing bullets; the heavy tanks by use of increased charges, or by direct flat trajectory fire of the light minenwerfers or by the fire of specially constructed anti-tank guns. Even larger caliber (13-mm.) rifles with special ammunition has been found effective. The more the fire of the different arms of the defense is concentrated on the assaulting tanks, the greater will be the losses to the accompanying infantry, and the more will that infantry lose the desire to accompany such attacks. We cannot deny that the tanks, at first underestimated, have proven themselves to be a very effective means of attack. The success must not be accredited to the new tactics proper, but only to the change in the conduct of the attack, and thus must be credited to surprise. But if the defender is once prepared for this change in tactics and if he has abundant defensive means, the hopes of success diminish.

Before the end of the year, November 30th, the German position, lost on the 20th, was recaptured by a brilliant counter-attack on a large scale, based on surprise, against the enemy's flank and rear. It was a good example of the importance of surprise as the enemy did not expect any attack. We succeeded in guarding the secret, so that the enemy did not observe the artillery and minenwerfers going into position. In one division sector, 33 batteries had to be placed in position in 7 days; and in 3 days, 60 heavy and medium minenwerfers. For the first time, accompanying batteries were assigned to the infantry, and to each of these batteries 1 platoon of pioneers and 1 automatic rifle was attached. The success justified this measure. After an artillery preparation lasting only one hour, the infantry broke into the hostile position with ease. The initial penetration was made without loss. The second wave and the attached accompanying guns finished the British machine guns. It was found of great use to signal the progress of the infantry across each line by light signals of different kind and color agreed upon in advance. All participants emphasized the importance of keeping the advance moving or avoiding any halt under any circumstances. It was believed that rapidity of advance was of more importance than formation, which latter would soon be lost in the maze of trenches. It was shown again, that the advance in a number of waves corresponding to the lines of resistance was advantageous and that the leading and strongest wave should be assigned the most distant objective. Differing from this, the British have their single waves pass through each other, which takes more time. Skirmish lines have not always been found best, but a wave consisting of shock squads was proven the best formation in working through a position system. Shock squads were inserted against points where they could, presumably, make the best progress. In any case this experience brought forward the idea of forming flexible battle lines. Fighting in the intermediate terrain was specially bloody. Fighting machine gun nests consumed very much time, as co-operation of the different auxiliary arms had to be arranged first. This took much time and thus the infantry lost the help of the creeping barrage, which kept moving on. A suggestion was made that assault groups be organized, for such tasks in each battalion and regiment, consisting of infantry, light minenwerfers and machine guns accompanied by artillery which, for thorough co-operation, were to be trained in advance for the capture of supporting points and machine gun nests. The light minenwerfers were indispensable in the assault preparation; but were at that time still too heavy to accompany the infantry attack. Here a change had to be made. The

Position Warfare in the West, 1914-1917

depth of the penetration did not suffice. Most of the divisions penetrated not more than four kilometers into the British position system. This was mainly due to the fact that the reserves were not close enough. "The deep penetration," reports a division that had participated in the attack, "would not have succeeded, had not the artillery followed the infantry directly. In the afternoon of the first day and especially on the second day, counter-attacks by tank battalions would not have been defeated with such success had not the artillery been immediately in rear of the infantry..... Two cavalry charges were defeated, in which a portion of the batteries had to face about. Unfortunately the loss in officers in the division in the first line were specially high, which influenced the conduct of battle." But in any event the command had gained the conviction that a penetration on the West front was possible, especially against the British. Thus, after a long period, a brilliant attack had succeeded, an excellent omen for the future!

Chapter IV – The War in the East and in Italy

Russia

The Russian army entered the thoroughly popular World War excellently equipped. The Regulations published in 1912 were complete in all respects; they prescribed the attack in accordance with Russian war intentions, but had paid little attention to the peculiarities of the Russian people; they had not yet become the very life of the troops when war opened with the Central Powers. The leaders had their men firmly in hand. The higher officers were the weakest part, they were too much inclined to wait and be guided by events as they arose. The high command sank into inactivity when its own measures were met by the firm will of its opponent; in attack it endeavored to reach its objective by brute force and an inconsiderate sacrifice of men. The general staff was theoretically well trained and worked better in the execution of this war than in prior ones. There was more seriousness, more critical supervision, more self-restraint in the staffs, more understanding of minor tactical work on the part of subordinates and troops, than ever before. The infantry — the Siberian troops were especially good — was brave in attack and tenacious in defense, but was handicapped by insufficient fire training (it was inclined to long range fire), poor marching ability, and also by a mass-training which had done away with all independence. The conduct of rear guard fighting was brilliant, the troops were skillful in gaining positions and in constructing field fortifications. The cavalry was very aggressive; it performed excellent service in reconnaissance and in dismounted fighting; and sought opportunities to attack the hostile infantry. Though the artillery preferred firing at long ranges it had made great progress in technical firing and training, in comparison with the other arms since the Russo-Japanese war, and it formed the backbone of the army in the first months of the war.

Taken as a whole, the Russian was superior to our allies, and was also a menace by reason of his numerical strength. "We can fight down the Russian only if we energetically utilize all the advantages caused by our better armament, our excellent human material and our iron discipline, and if we train each individual to a sense of absolute superiority over his opponent; increasing his military knowledge and aptitude, and steeling his firm and unshakable will to gain victory."

During the course of the campaign the experiences in actual war were found advantageous in the training and the conduct of the Russian troops, but the great losses in men and material had a retarding influence on their battle activity.

In a handbook compiled by Captain Ignatowitsch of the General Staff, based on experiences gained in war, it was recommended that the attack, adhere as long as practicable to close formation, from which deployment in depth and breadth, or in half companies could be made, and to take up the battle formation only at 1500 paces (1065 meters). The advance was then to be made in long and broad rushes, from firing position to firing position, under fire protection of neighboring detachments, and without firing from intermediate positions. Intrenching during attacks was no longer mentioned. The closer the troops came to the enemy, the shorter became the rushes. Charging distance was to be 50 to 100 paces (35 to 70 meters). Entry of the position was to be facilitated by grenade throwers. Very effective was a simultaneous charge against flank and rear, even if conducted by only a few men. In night attacks the rifle should also be used; and the advance made in close order formation with increased intervals between ranks.

Prior to contact hand grenades were to be used. Should the troops encounter an undestroyed obstacle, they were to lie down at 100 to 200 paces in front of it, fire rapidly for 3 to 5 minutes, and allow two wire cutting squads to cut two roads through for each company. It was not stated if the charge was to be made with or without shouting.

In the construction of positions, narrow and deep trenches similar to our reinforced ones, which in most cases were to be covered with shrapnel proof roofs, were recommended; defensive fire through loopholes. Shelter for about 10 men each were to be constructed in rear at a distance not more than one-half of the distance between the leading trenches and the enemy. Defense by rifle fire with regulation sight elevation (600 paces — 420 meters) and by advancing to the counter-attack up to 50 paces (30 meters) distance was advocated. The counter-attack was not recommended if the enemy had already made a penetration. At night the troops protected themselves by cossack posts, which were advanced 200 to 400 paces, each company of the leading line securing itself by 2 double posts sent out 30 to 70 paces, and for 2 companies 1 field picket also to be sent out. One part of the defensive force remained in reserve; the strength of this post depended on the probability of attack and the discipline of the troops and might amount to two-thirds of the force. The rest of the men were to sleep; distribution of the men should provide that the wakened and sleeping men were equally divided behind the works. Counter-attack was recommended for the defense. "The morale of the troops is more valuable than numerical superiority."

The high losses in men forced the adoption of position warfare in Russia as well as on the west front. In the West, excellent communication arrangements, and a highly developed industry had been able to supply half the world with war implements of all sorts in almost unlimited quantities, while a highly trained people furnished the men to work the machines. In Russia financial difficulties, a limited number of ice-free harbors and greater distances prevented the utilization of these auxiliary means. Thus, in Russia machines had to be replaced by men, which we endeavored to save in the West. The Central Powers could not compete with the Russians in numbers of troops, any more than the

The War in the East and in Italy 113

Western Powers could compete in the matter of material and ammunition; therefore, in the East, the divisions scantily supplied with artillery, had to be assigned to relatively broad fronts (in the Winter of 1916-17 sectors of from 20 to 30 kilometers), in which two-thirds of the troops were placed in the front lines. The disadvantage of broad stationary barrage fire had to be taken into consideration, and less depth in formation was possible.

In contrast with the West, a minor warfare resulted in which we learned that the Russian was our equal and frequently our superior. It was supported by a brilliantly carried out espionage system, but the German infantry knew how to get the best of that. After 1916 the Russians employed the "drum" fire, but this did not reach the same development as on the Western front, so that only in exceptional cases did the front trenches become a shell-holed terrain. This naturally led to a stronger occupation of the front line trenches. The artillery fire also was not strong enough to destroy the wire entanglements, and the hostile charges went to pieces on it. Important places were covered by strongly constructed supporting points in the front line, surrounded by obstacles. The reckless Russian high command sought to gain an entrance by a mass attack. It is true, in some instances that the enormous masses succeeded in entering a position at some points, but they were ejected by the counter-attack of fresh troops.

The Russian tactics were strongly dominated by Joffre's views, but the Russians were unable to obtain the enormous artillery effect used in the West, and which was a material factor in the success of the French method of attack. In the Spring of 1916 the difficult situation of the French troops in front of Verdun forced the Russian Allies to a partial offensive by the Ewert Army Group, though the Russian Army had not yet completed its preparations. This probably also was the reason the Army Group of Brussilow did not simultaneously start the attack between the Polish and Rumanian frontier.

In an order issued by General Ewert, Wilna and the Wilna-Dunaberg railroad were designated as the main objective. Points of entry were to be gained by the weight of a crushing mass. Minute details concerning their tasks were prescribed for the troops and for headquarters. The assaulting troops had been made to believe that the artillery alone would perform all the work. At the same time it was thought necessary to portray to the troops the horrible tortures they would suffer if taken prisoners. "After capturing the trenches of the enemy, the attackers must not allow themselves to be stopped. The penetration must suffer no interruption...The artillery must take all measures to avoid firing on its own troops. Herein lies the real strength of co-operation of infantry with artillery." This was a peculiar confession of lack of tactical co-operation and conception of the principles of fighting of both arms. Peculiar for the reason that paragraph 7 of the order almost demanded certain preparations for firing on its own troops: "It must be drilled into the troops that the reserves and the artillery will open fire on them in case the attackers show any inclination to let themselves be captured." Cossacks also were detailed to drive forward with knouts troops that vacillated in the charge.

The Summer offensive undertaken by General Brussilow was also without success; it started about the time the Somme battles began in the West, and had some hope of success in the beginning. Officers and men had been trained during a long rest. Shock troops had been formed from picked men, artillery and ammunition had been brought up in plenty; and thus nothing seemed forgotten that could achieve success. The orders issued by Brussilow for the battle are of special interest, as the Russians also perceived the correctness of the view that attacks had to be made on a broad front to make it impossible for the enemy to shift his reserves. "The simultaneous attack on all fronts must be conducted so that in each army, and in each corps a persevering attack is made against a definite sector of the hostile position. At a few points along the line the attack will be made, and for that purpose I shall concentrate reserves from the other fronts of the armies." The attack was to be conducted in such breadth that the defender could not fire on the troops from the flanks. This would require a breadth of penetration of at least 10 kilometers and of not more than 30. In a normal 15 kilometers attacking front of an army two corps were to be employed, each reinforced by one brigade, which then attacked with one-half of their force in four waves — skirmish interval of 2 paces — while the other half formed the shock-reserve. For a division of 16 battalions the Russians reckoned on an attacking

The War in the East and in Italy 115

extension of 2 kilometers. Brussilow was opposed to the extensive use of "drum" fire and did not mention gassing.

Co-operation of the artillery with the infantry was deemed a prerequisite of any success. For this purpose the batteries under the orders of the commander of attacking infantry went within 2 kilometers, the heavy batteries within 3 to 4 kilometers of the enemy. Stress was laid on the opening of "roads" through the wire obstacles — several roads required, so that no crowding would ensue — on firing on machine guns and on flanking works. The infantry attack immediately followed the artillery preparation. On the other hand, the infantry was not to demand endless firing on the sectors to be attacked. The infantry attack was to be made in not less than 3 to 4 waves, following each other at 150 to 200 paces distance, machine guns with the third and fourth wave. Squad columns were to be in rear of the wings for flank protection, reserves in rear of the shock troops for immediate repetition of unsuccessful attacks. Assault distance about 300 paces from the line to be attacked; arrangement of the starting point as with the Joffre attack procedure — one wave for each hostile trench. Capture of the first position by one attack with reliable flank protection was demanded. The German counterattack was to be defeated by fire; if that succeeded then a trial was to be made immediately to take the next positions by following attacks. "After successful penetrations, a promising field of activity opens to the cavalry, supported by its riflemen and its artillery. I order that our numerous cavalry be made as much use of as possible."

Emphasis was laid on the fact that by means of continuous insertion of strong infantry forces the entrance could be forced even if the first troops had no success. This led to mass attacks, in which the troops — being cautioned that in case they stopped they would be fired on by Russian machine guns and field guns — were driven forward even under the knout. In consequence of this lack of consideration and the tactical inefficiency of the subordinate commanders the charges were executed in even denser and more vulnerable formation than had been planned by the leaders. Lying down during pauses was even forbidden. The losses were enormously increased. In working up to the assault position, the infantry showed itself very adept and seldom more than two or three men could be seen; but the extensive earthworks and the systematic "road-firing" of the artillery swept away all doubts concerning the points to be attacked. When the attack did not succeed in gaining a foothold at assault distances, attacks were made at longer distances, 300 to 1100 meters, on the run with interspersed walking periods. Large losses resulted in crowding through the "roads" the artillery had opened in the wire entanglements, and which could not be made sufficiently wide. Whatever was lacking in artillery preparation (for time for preparation was between 2 and 5 hours, and 10 to 15 rounds were reckoned for the running meter of the position) was attained by the mass insertion of troops. The German artillery positions were bombarded only when their location had been accurately ascertained. The artillery often deployed in 2 and 3 lines in rear of each other and plentiful use was made of false works and development of smoke clouds. Special weight was attached to flanking fire, there was no hesitation in bringing batteries forward into positions where they were not at all expected (for instance in the sand dunes in the swampy terrain) and which had been considered impassable even for the infantry. Single field pieces were brought into the most advanced lines to fight the machine guns. The Russian attached little importance to surprise; it expected to be victorious by force of numbers; terrain obstacles had no terror for Russian troops in attack; the Russian infantry even attacked going through swamp and water up to the neck. The activity of the artillery was excellent; however, lack of materiel and ammunition prevented it from displaying its power to the fullest extent.

In 1917 the German high command calculated on a continuation of the Russian offensive taking advantage of the experiences in the West. In May the signs became more numerous that an offensive was about to start against the South Army, with minor attacks in the direction of Sloczow and Stanislau, and then against Krewo-Smorgen and Dunaburg. Everything pointed to the fact that this time the Russian offensive would assume the character of a "materiel battle," which was the more required as the disinclination of the Russian troops for a repetition of Brussilow's bloody attacks had resulted in open mutiny. After the strongest artillery preparation, which swept obstacles away, which changed the front battle positions into shell-holes, the attack commenced on June 30, 1917, against the South Army and against the Sloczow sector; on July 6th also against the Austrian 3d Army at Stanislau. This latter attack, originally considered a minor one, had an unhoped-for success (loss of the heights on the Bystrzyca and the Lomnica position in rear and capture of Halusch), which was skillfully utilized by the Russian high command in bringing up fresh forces. At Koniuchy the position of the Austrian 9th Corps was also entered to an extent of an area 20 kilometers broad and 4.8 kilometers deep. In expectation that forces had been taken from the fronts that had not yet been attacked and brought into Galicia, an attack was made on July 21st at Krewo-Smorgon, and on the 23d at Dunaburg. The Russian high command prepared the first part of the attack most excellently. All plans had been prepared to insure a successful attack, if only the tools had corresponded to the demands of the commander. One main cause for its non-success was the inefficiency of the subordinate leaders, whose power of decision and independence did not meet expectations. The attack went to pieces on the firm stand of the German infantry, which was supported by an inferior artillery; the Russian batteries knew how to prepare the attack but not how to support it. Lack of ammunition compelled firing to cease altogether at night and the fire did not reach as far into the terrain in rear as it did in the West. Differing from the attack in 1916 the artillery also was fired on, but without effect due to lack of artillery airplanes. The scheduled gassing had no success. Tanks, inserted in insufficient numbers, had no effect. The Russian infantry attacked, after heavy "drum" fire, in dense skirmish lines by divisions with their brigades alongside each other, and at an extension of 1.5 kilometers. In the brigade the regiments were formed in rear of each other, 3 battalions with 550 men each in first line, battalions with 4 companies divided into half -companies and formed in depth with 50 paces distance. The newly organized regimental pioneer companies were distributed to the battalions. The 4th Battalion followed at 100 paces, then followed at the same distance, the 2d Regiment of the brigade. In the assault the officers were in front. Accompanying cannon and trench guns that had kept silent up to the assault fired over the heads of the infantry. The attack was to be carried within the German artillery position.

The German high command had early pointed to a possibility of a "materiel" battle, so that as a matter of course the same changes were made here that were made in the West. In place of a defense by a densely garrisoned front line, the infantry was organized into weaker garrisons of the front trenches with stronger troops in readiness in rear and reserve, which carried on the battle offensively around the front trenches. The counter-attacks immediately started were successful; more power was gained by the defence through strongly fortified but weakly occupied supporting points in the intermediate terrain.

The battle in Eastern Galicia found a brilliant finish in the transition from the defensive to the offensive, which demanded great exertions, especially from the troops of the South Army, which joined the advance of the Group "Sloczow" without preparation.

The penetration executed with 10 divisions on a frontal extension of 39 kilometers, one flank on the Sereth, was a complete success and the Russian lines far into Rumania were terribly shaken, and the Russian offensive was forced to stop. The German attack proved a far better means of relieving the front that had been attacked, than direct support by the Austrian 3d Army could have been. Such a counter offensive is at all times the best means to defeat a penetration attempted at another point, which, starting a short time after the commencement of the infantry attack on a neighboring front, will presumably strike troops weaker and probably already worn out. The German troops proved themselves equal to the demands of battle even if the lack of practice in marching, the difficulties of transportation, and insufficient supplies for headquarters and troops for mobile warfare weighed heavily against them. The troops going from position to mobile warfare had to get used not only to marching, but to other battle conditions; they had to relearn to attack, to advance again without having close touch with comrades, and to conduct attacks without the support of large artillery masses. The insufficient training of the subordinate commanders, who in most instances knew mobile warfare only theoretically, was sorely felt. The experience gained at this time was especially valuable to us in the subsequent battles on the Western theater of war.

A brilliantly prepared penetration of the bridgehead at Jakobstadt took place on September 21, 1917. In the early morning hours of September 1st a crossing of the Duna was accomplished. The troops then turned along the roads leading from Riga northeastward, which caused the immediate evacuation of the bridgehead on the left bank of the river. The Russian high command firmly believed in an impending attack against the southeast front of the bridgehead and did not believe the reports coming in concerning preparations for a crossing above Riga. This is a good example of the value of so-called "reliable reports."

In all battles the Russian infantry showed an enviable skill in overcoming difficult terrain, considered by us in most cases as impassable.

Battles in Northern Italy

May 23, 1915, the Italian Army joined our enemies, after it had adopted as early as 1911, contrary to its prior custom, a gun of French manufacture (Deport, same caliber as the French field gun) and modeled its Regulations for the Higher Command and Staff on the French Regulations. In Austria they had well learned the method of battle peculiar to the Italians.

The Italian commander-in-chief. General Cadorna, had neglected at the opening of the war to bring the superiority of his army into immediate account by an offensive against the weak Austrian frontier guard troops; and as the latter could not count for the present on reinforcements, a position warfare resulted on the Isonzo that shows the same characteristics as the one in France. Not until June 29, 1915, was commenced the first "Isonzo Battle," which was without result; and the subsequent battles (the tenth fought from May 5, to June 7, 1917, after Joffre's methods), showed only a minor gain in territory, in spite of strong artillery preparation and mass insertion of Italian infantry. Based on the experiences of the tenth Isonzo battle, General Capello, commander-in-chief of the Second Army, issued a general

"Maxims for the Employment of Infantry and Artillery in Attack."

The infantry was not to carry the special training too far; attack was to be executed in waves with great depth (double-barreled Fiat-Revelli pistols — corresponding to the light minenwerfers — in the first wave, machine guns in the succeeding waves) and up to the final attack objectives. The importance of machine guns for flanking fire was pointed out; the troops were to endeavor to avoid the trench warfare proper, which consumed too much time. Similar to the methods in Eastern Galicia, on October 24, 1917 — after the 11th Isonzo battle — the counter-attack of the 14th Army (Otto von Below) with the adjoining Austrian 1st Isonzo Army was started against superior Italian forces. The attack, oblique to the Italian front, conducted from about the line Flitch-Tolmein in the general direction of Cividale turned into a penetration. Through this penetration the adjoining south front was drawn into the defeat of the Italian Second Army. The direction of the attack across the Bainsizza plateau and by Flitch-Tolmein had become known to the Italians as well as the time the attack was to be made. The unfavorable condition of our forces did not permit us at this time to utilize the favorable situation in Southern Tyrol.

On September 8, 1917, the first orders for the offensive were issued. The attacking troops of the 14th Army had been assembled in the basin of Krainburg and north of the Karwanken. There the preparations for the war in the mountains were completed. The "Tolmein Group" had to be concentrated in the narrow spaces of the basin near Flitch and Tolmein, Along two narrow mountain passes, 60 kilometers distance, with heavy grades, several divisions had to be brought forward behind each other (as well as half the artillery and minenwerfer groups) in the face of dominating hostile positions allowing an extensive view. This was accomplished in such manner, that the Groups Flitch and Tolmein stood in readiness with 5 divisions in the first line, and 3 divisions in each of the second and third lines. In spite of the unfavorable weather the march proceeded without friction. The concentration of the artillery and minenwerfers took from September 27th to October 17th.

The experiences of the Carpathian mountains, of the Vosges, and Alpine battles, pointed out the road to the offensive tactics;

The War in the East and in Italy

rapid advance in uninterrupted attack across the connecting land bridges from height to height, utilization of the valley roads to bring up the artillery reserves and supplies; forcing dominating ridge positions by enveloping attack in flank and rear, and by marching around them; and mutual support between the frontal and enveloping groups.

With this in mind, the following operations were started with a view to the simultaneous penetration at several points: The Group Krauss as right wing of the 14th Army by Saga towards the Stol ridge; a strong left column was to open, after the capture of the Vrsik, the basin of Karfreit by taking direction on Ravna — Karfreit and roll up the Stol ridge from the East. The Groups Stein was started against Mt. Matajur. The capture of this area opened the Karfreit basin from the Southeast and thus supported the simultaneous operation of the Group Krauss having the same mission. The Group Berrer was started against the Humand for simultaneous advance via Drenchia against the San Martino in conjunction with the Group Stein. The Group Scotti received the task of assisting the Isonzo Army in its crossing of the Isonzo by attacking with the objective Globocak — Kostanjewitza. By the middle of October the offensive preparations had make such progress that the general attack could be ordered to start the third week in October.

The plan had been worked out down to the minutest details. After a gas bombardment from 2 to 6 A.M., general fire was to be opened at daybreak. After a short but steadily increasing bombardment the entry was to be made into the positions along the entire Flitch-Selo front. However, unfavorable weather delayed the attack till the morning of October 24, 1917. This day was foggy, which was favorable to the advancing troops.

The Italian 2d Army under Lieutenant General Capello awaited the shock of the Allies in strong, apparently invincible mountain positions in the Julian Alps. The preparations for the attack, the filtering through of our divisions along the narrow, distant but visible valley roads, and the attack formations could not remain hidden. Inexplicable seems the small efforts put forth by the enemy during the final days prior to the attack. In the district from Rombon to the Krn the Italian 4th Corps (50th, 43d and 45th

Infantry Divisions) blocked the valley road of Saga and the basin of Karfreit. Forces from the 17th Army Corps could keep the Tolmein basin under fire from the line Kolovrat Ridge to vicinity of the Auzza Canal. The narrow frontal sector of the plateau of Bainsizza — Heiligegeist was defended by the 25th, 60th and 30th Infantry Divisions (14th Army Corps) in strong positions. North of the Monte San Gabriele the line was prolonged by the 2d Corps (23d, 53d and 8th Infantry Divisions). At, and north of Gorz, stood the 4th Army Corps (68th, 24th and 48th Infantry Divisions) as the south wing of the Second Army joining the Third Army under the Duke of Aosta. Not less than 56 brigades and 4 Alpine groups, a total of possibly 350 battalions of the Second Army were to stop the attack.

Cadorna was fully confident and reported: "The opponent, strongly supported by German troops and war munitions, has assembled material forces for an offensive on our front. The hostile attack finds us firm and well prepared." At 2:00 A.M., October 24th, the gas cannonade opened against the hostile batteries. At daylight, an annihilating fire for effect was started by the entire artillery and minenwerfers. Instructions for the forward displacement of artillery for adjustment, and for fire for effect were conformed to and the roads were opened to the infantry for the attack. At 8:00 A.M. the infantry started the attack between Tolmein and Flitch. By 2:00 P.M. the Group Krauss had stormed the positions on the Rombon upon the right wing of the army. In an intrepid charge Austrian infantry advanced from the right wing of the Group Stein and took the positions on the line Krn — western slope of the Mrzli. In the meantime the German Division Lequis pushed forward along the valley road of Tolmein. It is true that the enemy held on the left and right the dominating hill positions. But fog banks prevented a view to the far horizon and into the valley. The Italians did not suppose that deep below German infantry had pushed its way through to Karfreit, that already El Kammo, and shortly after 2 P.M., Ideersko on the Isonzo was reached. The left wing of the Group Stein, after overrunning the front valley position southwest of Tolmein, attacked in conjunction with the Group Berrer, the hostile main position on the Kolovrat ridge. Attacking infantry, under hostile fire, crept up the steep slopes from the valley for more than 1000 meters. The crest of the Kolovrat formed the key point of the entire system in the strongly fortified position on Hill 1114. In the afternoon the attack against Hill 1114 and the neighboring massive Hafnik could be started. Farther south the position on the Jeza block went to pieces under the attack of the Group Berrer. Without stopping, the south wing of the army (Group Scotti) pushed its way across the Hrad Vrh against the Blobocak chain.

By the evening of October 24th, the Flitch basin was opened to immediately east of Saga. The southern slopes of the Km had been stormed. Karfreit in the Isonzo valley and the ridges west and southwest of Tolmein had been taken. No addition to or change in the army orders was made. The attack proceeded.

The gas bombardment shortly before the attack undoubtedly played a great role in its success, as the Italian gas masks did not offer any protection against it. The infantry, though well trained for fighting in the higher mountains, up to this time was acquainted with only the lowland and the intermediate mountains, yet performed its very best. The superiority of troops equipped for and trained in high mountain warfare, was plainly discernible. The Italian infantry could not cope with such troops. Up to the evening of the 26th the Furttemberg Mountain Battalion captured over 100 officers, among them 2 regimental commanders, 4500 men, 60 machine guns, 20 guns, and 25 caissons. Its own losses were but 7 killed and 28 wounded. The skill of our riflemen in moving in the mountains, and the skill of the subordinate commanders saved the battalion from heavier losses. Another thing had its influence; the Italian infantry had no experience in defense; till then it had always attacked; its front trenches were densely occupied; active defense of the intermediate terrain had not been prepared in advance. The Italians had correctly perceived that in the mountains, possession of a certain ridge line depends on the holding of a few dominating points. These points, against which the fire of the attacker was principally directed, were occupied by the Italians entirely too strongly, when they should have attempted to hold them from the side. The attacker's fire had an annihilating effect. No plans had been made for using the reserves, their place should have been immediately in rear of the dominating points which the attacker was forced to take; the roads the attacker had to take were also well defined, and a thorough study of the terrain should have furnished exact knowledge where to employ the reserves. The Italian artillery occupied positions from which it could have well supported an attack, but from which it could hardly carry on the defense; positions for defense should have been selected which commanded the ascent on both slopes of a mountain ridge. Flanking fire is most effective and can be employed almost everywhere; frontal defense had best be left to the minenwerfers.

The penetration was immediately followed by a brilliant pursuit by the German troops to across the Tagliamento; the fleeing masses and their army impedimenta were congested at the crossings of Codroipo and Latisana, and only the delay of the slowly following Isonzo army prevented a greater capture of prisoners and supplies. An attempt to take possession of the Tagliamento crossing at Dignano by infantry carried on auto-trucks miscarried.

Mountain Warfare

No one could have foreseen in time of peace that German troops would ever be called on for mountain warfare; we shared the opinion of our neighbors that it required special training for mountain warfare, that recruits, natives of the lowlands, would take a long time to get accustomed to mountains. Only well trained mountain troops who in their sports do not forget the objects of war, are suited for this special work. We will point out that fostering snow-sports and "Alpinism" is the best foundation for carrying on war in mountains, as was the case in the Alps, in the Carpathians and in the ice and snow covered lower mountain warfare, but troops that had no such training met the requirements after some time. The German troops received aid from their Allies, who had gathered rich experiences concerning equipment, march capacities, and methods of fighting. In the ignorance of high mountains, every inexperience must be paid for bitterly; the first adverse effects will be noticed on the pack animals, and through them the supply of ammunition and subsistence will suffer.

The War in the East and in Italy

Tactical measures must conform to the peculiarities of the terrain, high mountains (Alps) clear of forests, demand different measures than snow or forest covered lower mountains (Vosges, Carpathians). Terrains with and without glaciers, summer and winter conditions, continually confront the leader with changing situations. During the winter battles in the mountains demand the greatest possible exertions. Losses by frost bite and death by freezing can assume the same proportion as the hostile effect of arms. "The main thing for troops in the mountains is mobility and endurance. Troops will then have the best success if they overcome more and greater difficulties than the enemy believed possible, and when they know how to work their way through apparently impassable terrain." (Training Regulations for the Austrian Army, 1911.) The accomplishment of these demands presupposes special training.

The battle of man against nature becomes more pronounced in mountain warfare. Troops must become accustomed to the impressions and dangers of fog, of the breaking off of projections, of snowslides. Fortunately service in the mountains also offers moments that increase the capacity of the troops and have a favorable effect on their spirit and morale. First comes the danger, which undoubtedly has a high educational value. The troops find themselves not only in difficult, but also in dangerous situations, in which it becomes clear to every one that only strict obedience and unity of effort will avert the peril. If that succeeds, trust in the leader increases. The spirit of self-preservation drives many a weakling forward on the march who otherwise would have reached the limits of his endurance. The troops have to learn to march and breathe differently, for the rules of the lower altitudes do not apply.

As a general rule, single file will be the method of marching in mountains. This requires special training and an entirely different method of issuing orders. To pass orders through a column of files will frequently be entirely impossible, and even messengers will have difficulty in getting to the rear. The deep column in single file, or in column of twos, increases most surprisingly in length and is beyond any calculation. This is specially annoying when starting the march and when deploying stronger columns for fighting. Keeping the same pace and cadence is very difficult especially when part are ascending and part descending. A battalion of 800 men will occupy a depth of 1.5 to 2 kilometers, which corresponds to about one hour of deployment. Depth formation makes division into single detachments unnecessary, the sending ahead of one reinforced security detachment will generally suffice. Columns of more than 1 battalion can be employed only if the troops are used to mountains, as otherwise they get too clumsy. The change from teams to pack animals, hard to handle, the equipment of the troops with snow spurs and snowshoes requires far reaching changes. Marching difficulties are especially felt in shifting of troops, in counter-attacks, and in bringing up reinforcements; we can count on the troops only that are in, or immediately in rear of the fighting line. In comparison with earlier wars the development of the use of high explosives, the service of communication (wireless stations, visual signal means of all kinds) and methods of bringing up supplies has made the conduct of mountain warfare easier, but all our fights have merely confirmed the old rule that in mountain fighting the value of and not the number of troops is decisive. A decisive, active battle leadership can make for success in mountains even if the enemy is greatly superior in numbers. Fighting in mountains is especially difficult for large bodies of troops. Decisive battles are infrequent, more often the action will result in forcing deployment, or preventing deployment, out of the mountains. Placing light, mobile forces along the roads through passes gives opportunities for gathering the fruits of success in mountain fighting. In the mountains themselves the possession of the highest ridge is decisive; on account of the far view, the domination of the important valley roads that have to be used to bring up supplies, and on account of difficulties of ascent for the attacking army. Considering the limited number of troops available, not every ridge can be occupied, but points on the flanks must be secured from which the domination of the position and connections with the valley is possible. The defender barricades the points he considers passable. Therefore mountain troops must understand how to work up through apparently impassable terrain, in order to strike the enemy's flanks and rear. Frequently the more appearance of minor detachments on heights, difficult of ascent, will produce a great morale effect, to which probably a good fire effect can be added, since good observation is generally available. The Italians had probably considered this point well in the defense on October 24, 1917, but they had occupied the points too strongly on the possession of which depended possession of the crest line, instead of defending them by flanking fire and fire on the two slopes leading up to these points. Good mountain troops will always find a way out of serious difficulties, while troops unused to same easily allow themselves to be taken prisoners when their retreat is endangered. As machine guns display a great fire power in a narrow space, they are an especially preferred arm in mountain warfare when but few troops can be employed. The arm proper in such warfare is the infantry. Cavalry serves mainly for the purpose of message, connection, and security duties, along the pass roads. Employment of airplanes is made more difficult by the frequency of fogs, the difficulties of rapidly gaining military altitudes and of finding suitable landing places. Artillery and minenwerfers may be brought into position almost everywhere, of course it takes time and labor, but the fire efficiency suffers under the difficulties of influence of altitude and weather. Minenwerfers are of especial use because of their curved trajectory.

In defense, possession of heights gives freedom of action and possession of the valley; therefore forward slopes of the valley are kept occupied as long as the troops have the reverse slope securely in hand. There is nothing more unfavorable than to have the troops surprised by fire during the ascent; therefore the advance is made by bounds from crest to crest. Heights dominating the line of march must be taken possession of as early as possible — frequently a day ahead if on the flanks and in front — by detachments sent ahead and largely supplied with mountain artillery. The organization ordered at the commencement of the daily operation remains unchanged for that day, as shifting consumes time. Division into several columns decreases in a desirable manner the march depth, which, however, the defender can take advantage of only under favorable conditions. In starting the attack flank effect and threatening the line of retreat gains greatly in importance as the enemy in most cases can give ground only in a definite direction. The decisions in forces fighting separately will be materially independent of each other, and in the case of larger units will vary greatly in time; frequently the possession of a portion of the position will bring about the final success. It is the task of the highest leader to perceive the key to the position and to utilize the partial success by the pressure of pursuit and by starting more troops against those hostile portions that have not yet been driven off. Caution is necessary in following up a retreating enemy; with systematic leadership he will attempt to find opportunities to gain success by fire surprise and unexpected counter-attacks.

The defender fights under more unfavorable conditions than the attacker, who can select time and place of attack, and does not suffer under the fire of the defender in the same measure as he does in the lowlands, but is restricted in the employment of his reserves by the mountains. On the other hand, the defender aided by the difficulties the attack encounters in the terrain, can delay the attacker for a longer time with but weak forces. The construction of a position presents great difficulties, trenches can be constructed in many cases only by application of explosives; losses through flying stones (against injury from which the steel helmets offer good protection) are frequent. In the foothills and intermediate mountains the conditions are not so bad as in the higher mountains. One of the inherent qualities of mountain warfare is the favorable opportunity which the defender has in starting a counter-attack when the attacker is exhausted by a hard climb and approaches the crest in disorder. It is only necessary that the reserves be present at the decisive point, which can frequently be ascertained from a study of the map. On October 24, 1917, in the Tolmein penetration, the Italians lacked these very reserves at the decisive point. The decision lies in this attack brought by the reserves, which if made by fresh troops — if possible down hill and against the flanks — has excellent chances for success against an attacker who is exhausted by the ascent. Even when the position is lost a stubborn defense, based on rocks and ravines may still promise success. Only troops, well trained and fresh, can achieve permanent success in mountain defense, if they endeavor to weakly occupy long fronts (but with plenty of machine guns), keeping strong reserves available and remaining prepared for aggressive action.

Superior force plays a smaller role than in the rolling country.

All measures are good which prevent the attack of positions from higher points, from the flank or by enveloping, supported by superior artillery. Making the ascent more difficult to the enemy is always advantageous; every opportunity to take the long columns of the enemy under a cross fire must be utilized. This method leads to formation in squads and platoons in the infantry and its auxiliary arms. Utilization of advanced positions on main lines of resistance on the rear edge of a crest with a limited field of fire will offer themselves. We must caution against the danger of covering everything; the defender must block the hostile routes of approach by advanced detachments, must delay the attacker and seek the decision by means of reserves kept concentrated in rear. The terrain difficulties must positively invite the attack; at no place are cordon positions more dangerous than in mountains.

The Austrian defense of the Southern Tyrol in 1866 will always remain an excellent pattern.

As early as the winter of 1914-15 mountain formations were adopted for employment in the Vosges, after the French had forced us to adopting snowshoes in that region. The Bavarian General v. Hoehn demanded that the following be equipped with snowshoes:

> 1. Infantry in strength from patrols to company; suited for reconnaissance, security and fighting, messengers, signal and telephone troops, litter bearers, and machine gun platoons.
> 2. Artillery headquarters, artillery officer's patrols for target reconnaissance, fire control and observation for artillery.
> 3. Commanders, general staff officers, personnel of the staff, telephone squads.

Snowshoe runners can be employed also for tramping down roads for detachments in close order.

The very useful drawing of two to three snowshoe runners by troopers was not adopted; but the transportation of machine guns on snowshoe sleds proved advantageous.

In the Masurian battles snowshoe runners were employed, but thawing weather setting in, their usefulness soon ceased. Snowshoe runners of the German 2d Snowshoe Battalion were used by the German South Army for minor operations successfully, for instance, to gain flanking fire positions.

Chapter V – Technique In War

Utilization of all the peace time technique for purposes of war conforms to the nature of a people's army. Only with the start of the position warfare could the proper basis be secured which this technique required for the full development of its capacity. In time of peace, this is easy but it is very difficult in mobile warfare. Thus, the technique will either accomplish something brilliant, or its tools and implements will become mere ballast. Nothing would be worse than to place our reliance principally on technical means. The moral forces in the breast of the commander and in the soul of the entire people are the qualities which have finally turned the scales in war. "Only the psychically qualified may chain chance to fortune" (Goethe) or, as Moltke expressed it "Only the efficient has fortune permanently." Possibly even more than at the opening of the 19th Century, the words written by Scharnhorst in April, 1806, have importance: "We have started to appraise the art of war higher than military virtues. This has caused the collapse of peoples in all times. Never do the moral qualities rest, they fall, as soon as they cease to strive for improvement."

In a more confined sense the military technique had been

prepared by peace establishments and was gradually increased to the enormous extent demanded by the World War. The utilization of our highly developed industries and chemistry by the military departments was difficult as there was a lack of a central governing authority. Recommendation and control by some bureau was of decisive importance. In addition to the utilization of industrial establishments and raw materials captured in the enemy's country we will merely mention: Concrete construction, light and water supply, etc. In Germany the lack of raw materials was of special importance. It is possible that more could have been achieved, and more rapidly, by the use of digging machines (especially in construction of cable trenches) and with drill machines in the construction of positions. Construction of positions finally demanded a closer study of "war geology." In what follows we will treat only of the war technique in a closer sense.

The principal question was to replace the animal trains by mechanical trains through adoption of auto trucks for more rapid transportation of men, supplies and materiel. In Italy, in France, and finally also with us auto trucks were used on a large scale for shifting reserves, and with success. The disadvantages of disrupting units, the separation of the dismounted men from their horses and vehicles could not be avoided. A further link in the chain was the introduction of "tanks" for traveling across country. The possibility of demolishing obstacles by their means, was a minor result. They were in the first line an attack weapon, underestimated by us at the start, the more so as they, appearing in small number, could be quickly put out of commission; toward the end of the war, however, our defensive means were insufficient to meet the unexpected mass employment. Our defensive measures could not keep pace with the increase of the fighting means, though our industries achieved the almost impossible. "The best arms against tanks are the nerves, discipline and intrepidity. Only with the decline of discipline and weakening of the fighting power of our infantry did the tanks in their mass employment and in conjunction with artificial fog gain a dangerous influence on the course of military events." (Ludendorff.)

The French had heavy tanks (40 to 60-ton) under construction, possessed medium (24 to 30-ton) and light tanks (model Renault,

6.5 ton). Medium tanks were organized by fours, in groups (3 batteries) and sur-groups (3 groups each). Small tanks were formed into platoons (5 tanks), companies (15 tanks) and battalions (45 tanks). Marching on roads was to be avoided because of the tracks left and the damage done to the roads.

For attack each army corps received 1 "tank regiment," consisting of several battalions light tanks and sur-groups of heavy tanks. The light tanks were allotted to the divisions participating in the attack, in general, 1 tank battalion (45 battle tanks) to the division. The heavy tanks, on the other hand, were a unit attached to that attack sector in which the greatest resistance was expected. In order to keep close connection between infantry and tanks, the tank units were placed under direct orders of the commanders of the attacking troops down to the battalion commander.

The medium tanks had to be directly accompanied by special troops in the fight, who helped them across especially difficult obstacles. One infantry company was required for this for each group of medium tanks (12 tanks). That company, which was usually taken from some unit not designated to participate in the battle, received special training for 14 days. It usually was divided into 2 detachments; 1 advanced with the first infantry wave and executed the heaviest repair work (ditch and trench crossings, alleys through entanglements, foot bridges). The other detachment furnished 3 selected men for each tank who followed the tanks directly, furnished connections between the men in the tank and the exterior world and served as supports in possible accidents. Removal of obstacles which can delay the march must be finished at the latest by evening of the day before the battle. The most dangerous enemy of the tank is the artillery, which must be destroyed, or engaged by airplanes. Tanks quickly give out, so depth formation is necessary.

In attack the heavy tanks preceded the infantry and the light tanks, to open the road for the infantry and to cover it during the cleaning up of the hostile position. The light tanks advanced with the infantry. The light tank platoon as a rule fought in close order against definite targets. As soon as success was attained, the platoon was again at the disposal of the infantry commander to whom it reported for orders, and followed the infantry on reconnoitered roads.

The infantry must quickly perceive and utilize the freedom of action given it by the tanks. It must keep close to the tanks; it must be a point of honor with the infantry never to let a tank fall into the enemy's hands. In no case must the infantry retreat if it sees the tanks traveling to the rear, as they have probably turned around only to fight against nests reappearing in rear, or to assemble.

If at some points a block occurs in the forward movement through fire from some trench, or from a machine gun nest, the tanks fight down the resistance. The parts of the infantry not struck by the fire must not let themselves be stopped in the forward movement. If that piece of terrain has been cleaned up, the troops that for a time remained behind advance again with the tanks.

A BRITISH TANK ATTACK, 1918 (POSITION IN READINESS—ADVANCE GUARD)

A second battalion follows in reserve

In England 3 battalions (36 tanks in 3 companies) were formed into a brigade. In addition to the new large battle tank (35-ton) and the light (Whippet) tanks there were transport tanks for infantry (20 to 30 men with 5 machine guns) and for guns (12.7 CM.). Each division had 1 tank battalion (36 tanks), which was formed into 2 waves and its first wave traveled 30 paces in rear of the creeping barrage, which was intensified by smoke and fog shells. Infantry remained with platoons deployed in squads up to 180 meters.

Immediately behind these infantry platoons 1 tank of each tank platoon remained as reserve to fill up resulting gaps in the line and to fight down reappearing resistance. Then followed the mass of the infantry, which overcoming the stationary barrage, closed up and gained the necessary depth in the further advance. The distance of the second tank wave from the first differed. It was the task of the second wave (which also was followed by infantry) to fight down the resistance nests that remained in the intermediate, terrain, and attack any new target. Sometimes a third wave was formed which had the same tasks as the second. If a tank became disabled and could not proceed, the crew had orders to descend with 1 or 2 machine guns and gain a foothold in the terrain until the infantry came up. In crossing watercourses without stable bridges a tank may be used as a bridge tank.

The infantry must fight as if no tanks were present. It must make full use of its auxiliary arms and must in no case halt if tanks fall out or remain stationary.

In fighting for villages the infantry at the start pushed forward to the edge of the village and nested itself there. In the meantime the tanks drove to the side and outer edge of the village and then broke through the houses into the interior.

Because of the enormous demands on the German industry for supplies of all kinds, ammunition, and artillery materiel, we were prevented from introducing tanks in sufficient numbers, as the main point was to keep up our artillery, the aerial fighting forces and the submarines. Only by limiting construction of these essentials could we have manufactured tanks in sufficient numbers. The United States of America has finally adopted the last word in transportation of guns in difficult terrain by introducing "motor mules," which are not limited to the hard surface roads, like the draggers of the heaviest guns. The advantage consists principally in the greater economy (driving power for 80 kilometers at only 25% of the cost of the teams), lessening the train parks, shortening the march columns (in consequence of greater load carriage) and increased capacity.

The necessity of securing to the higher command in position warfare quietness for work, brought about a drawing back of division headquarters from the front lines to about 10 kilometers.

From there, according to the needs, officers were sent forward to the fighting points for observation and as representatives of the commander. As the leader no longer could personally view the terrain, facilities for making reliable maps on a large scale (in the West 1:80,000, 25,000, 10,000 and 5,000) was necessary. These were executed with the assistance of photographs taken from airplanes and reproduced in large quantities in three colors, the different points being designated by numbers.

For connection with the places of commanders, telephone nets were established with other points, with defense guns, infantry and artillery. Up to May, 1917, there were 515,000 kilometers (322,000 miles) of lines in the West and 349,000 (220,000 miles) in the East. The average monthly expenditure on main battle front in the West was in 1917 1.7 kg of 1mm wire, 19 kg of 2mm, 21 kg of 3mm and 20 kg of 4mm wire per kilometer of front (about 250 lbs. per mile of front). The telephone had the advantage of direct personal exchange of thoughts and thereby became an unreplaceable auxiliary means of leadership, even if there was danger of interference of higher headquarters and the danger of attempts to influence the decisions of the higher leader by direct communication between adjutants and general staff officers. In spite of ail efforts we were not able to overcome many disadvantages. The traffic left no visible traces behind like the telegraph instrument with writing attachment. It is true that the efficiency of the wire circuits was influenced by gun fire and by the weather, still we succeeded in keeping the telephone in commission under fire by seeking out stretches where the fire was not so hot, by avoiding places open to direct bombardment, by laying the wires in cables in trenches from 0.5 to 0.8 meters deep and by employing numerous "trouble" squads. The danger of listening-in (by the enemy) was grave; this we at first underestimated; the enemy did listen-in at ranges of 3 kilometers; we tried to overcome that by construction of double lines and by the strictest supervision of conversation, by installing special "centrals" (also by use of code, by limiting conversation in the danger zone to the utmost necessary, using a tone of voice strange to the enemy; and by using a foreign language or dialect). Wireless telephones with a range of 16 kilometers (10 miles) were used by the British toward the end of the war for airplane communication.

As a supplement to, or to take the place of, the telephone, the slow relay chain of messengers or mounted messengers proved reliable under heavy fire. We soon abandoned the very slow wigwag signaling of peace time, while on the other hand, utilization of carrier pigeons found favor (each division sector in the West was allowed about 4 cotes, situated at least 15 kilometers behind the front); these contained 80 to 120 pigeons, which were freed by twos or more. Long changes of location of the cotes should be avoided, but minor changes up to 3 kilometers did no harm; it took about two weeks' training for the pigeons in their new home when the change was longer. The pigeon was little influenced by hostile fire or gas and the altitude at which they are released from airplanes (up to 3500 meters) did not matter; but the pigeons were dependent on clear weather. The flying velocity was about one minute per kilometer. The disadvantage remained that the pigeon should be used only in one flying direction, from the front to the rear. It was a reliable means of information coming from the first line and could be also advantageously employed during the range finding by the artillery.

The war dog (message dog) proved very good up to a distance of 2 kilometers after previous training (12 dogs per regiment) between two well known points occupied by commanders whom the dogs knew and who knew the dogs. The service in such cases was excellent. We will not discuss the sentry dogs the French loved to employ; it is not known if their "attack" hounds were a success. The dogs found their road even in very difficult terrain; but we must avoid demanding anything beyond their abilities. Only a very small percentage of the dogs employed were failures. Some dogs carried more than 30 messages per day. Occasionally their work was decreased by their being fire-shy. To overcome this was a matter of training. Frequently under very heavy fire dogs sought cover in shelters and bombproofs and continued their run carelessly as soon as the fire became weaker. Prerequisite for employment was good treatment by both dog masters, and that no one else interfered with the dog. However, in case of disability of one of the dog masters, the dog was useless. Carrier pigeons and message dogs frequently were the only means of communication between the fighting troops and the commanders.

Technically, the means of information were supplemented by message projectiles, by the message throwing grenade fired from the rifle at a range of 1000 meters and by the light trench mortar with a range of 1300 meters. During the course of the campaign the light signal apparatus, that had been neglected during peace, was improved and information troops were equipped with the large flashlight apparatus. The infantry, artillery, pioneers and minenwerfers were equipped with the medium and small flashlight apparatus. Flash-light No. 17 served for communication with airplanes. The source of light was an electric lamp; communication was by means of the Morse code. Division and regimental headquarters (infantry and artillery), and field artillery battalions had 4 medium signal apparatus, No. 16, and brigade headquarters 2 No. 16, while infantry battalions, and cavalry rifle regiments had eight, and machine gun companies two small signal apparatus No. 16.

Flash-light stations were quickly arranged, but they were dependent on the intermediate terrain and could not be entirely hidden either in the terrain nor on the aerial photograph. They were influenced in their use by unfavorable weather conditions (fog, rain, snow), and the transmission took time, as all messages had to be sent in code as the enemy could also read the signals.

Special progress was made in equipping the divisions with a wireless battalion of two platoons. This battalion had a wheeled wireless station with a range up to 100 kilometers; two large, portable wireless outfits for transmitting 4 to 6 kilometers, five medium for transmitting 2 to 3 kilometers, and 6 smaller portable for transmitting 0.5 to 1 kilometers range. Bullet-proof establishments were required for employment in position warfare. By wireless communication with the airplanes, separated detachments were kept in touch regardless of the terrain, but we had to reckon of course with the fact that the enemy could listen in and so might gain information as to our distribution of forces. The French claim that by such listening-in that they received information of movements of German range-finding airplanes and were able to notify the pursuit squadrons to interfere with the hostile activity. Listening-in was also an aid in the location of hostile artillery. The fact that such listening or cutting in is possible in wire and wireless communication offers the possibility of misleading the enemy. The advantages of wireless are its independence of terrain and fire effect, and that short messages can be rapidly transmitted. Interruptions by traffic occurred to our own and hostile stations, so that placing of many stations in a confined area was impossible. Wireless can be completely cut out by aerial electrical currents.

Of special importance was the ground telegraph, by which we mean the transmission without wire of Morse signals, where geological conditions were favorable, up to 2 kilometers distance, when communication over telephone lines was impossible. As the enemy could listen-in, messages had to be coded; telephone and ground telegraph could not be used simultaneously alongside each other; ground noises, thunder and strong currents interfered. Ground telegraph instruments performed valuable service during advance and in attack, and, at a distance from the message assembly stations, and frequently were the only means of communication with the flanks of the divisions. It proved valuable in solving the communication question from company to battalion; from battalion with ground telegraph, flash-light, or small wireless equipment to division battle observing station and to the division message center; and from the artillery observer to the guide battery to start barrage fire by agreed signals.

False signals sent out and screening of the service of radio communication should in each instance be carefully considered, for measures that are too crude fail in their object. Measures for receipt should be the same in all districts under hostile observation. To screen this service of communication it may become necessary to stop the division in the second line from using wireless. Calls should never be sent out in the clear (for instance, one Italian army called all its units in sequence prior to our offensive in October, 1917). Wireless silence and then a sudden renewed wireless activity are almost always a sure sign of change in the tactical situation and should therefore be avoided.

The fifth arm, the aerial fighting forces owe their remarkable development to the World War. Airships (dirigibles) were replaced by airplanes due to the developments in size and capabilities of the latter.

The primary superiority of the French in the matter of planes did not last long.

At the opening of the World War airplanes were only used for reconnaissance. They were poorly equipped with photographic apparatus and machine guns were not mounted nor wireless equipment.

At the beginning of the war, airships (dirigibles) operated at an altitude of 2400 meters and attained a velocity of from 54 to 87 kilometers per hour. Airplanes operated at an altitude of approximately 1000 meters with a velocity of 70 to 120 kilometers per hour, and an effective range of 350 kilometers. Dropping bombs was still in the incipient stage. At the most, only 4 bombs weighing 10 kg each could be carried. The employment of improved anti-aircraft artillery continually forced the planes to seek higher operating altitudes.

Aerial battles were not thought of at the opening of the war, airplanes avoided each other, unless some fired with revolvers at others. The mounting of machine guns on airplanes was first done by France. This forced all other states to follow suit. An excellent solution of firing from an airplane was found by synchronizing the machine guns to fire through the revolving propellor without interfering with it. The mounting of 37-cm. guns on airplanes interfered with the rate of speed, so that procedure was abandoned. Bomb dropping was consistently developed. The Allies dropped bombs on open cities at the commencement of the war and made no secret of their intentions to attack the hostile capital. Wireless communication from airplanes (adopted by the Allies in December, 1915) proved of incalculable value for transmission of messages and exceeded in reliability all heretofore applied means of communication.

Captive balloons received little attention at the beginning of the war. They were at the mercy of hostile artillery and planes. The gases of the balloons easily caught fire, and the protection afforded by the anti-aircraft defense guns was seldom sufficient. Batteries in action were seen from balloons at distances of 14 kilometers and marching troops and columns at 25 kilometers. Hostile artillery fire forced captive balloons to be kept about 8 kilometers in rear of the front lines. The balloon observer at 1000 meters altitude could see from 30 to 40 kilometers. He also had a stationary position with good permanent ground communication. These advantages were so great that captive balloons were universally employed for observation of artillery fire and the battlefield. By means of the balloon and telephone, headquarters received reliable information on both the hostile and friendly situation.

Dirigibles took a back-seat in the war; they offered too large a target, demanded special arrangements for landing, skillful construction, required an enormous amount of material and took a long time for construction. They also required a large suitable landing place, and an expensive hangar construction which took more time. These disadvantages could not be offset by the fact that the dirigible could carry large quantities of explosives and traffic supplies. Employment of dirigibles was confined to naval warfare.

With the development in the capabilities of airplanes grew the manifoldness of their tasks, which naturally led to dividing the airplane organizations into: pursuit squadrons for attacking hostile aerial fighting forces; protective squadrons for offensive protection for observation airplanes; artillery squadrons for adjusting the fire of the artillery; attack squadrons for fighting ground targets with machine guns; and infantry squadrons for the requirements of the infantry in their battle on the ground. Bomb-dropping was retained. The photographic work of the reconnaissance flights steadily increased in importance. The participation of planes in an attack in best illustrated by the attack on the Chaume forest (Ornes sector in front of Verdun) on September 24, 1917, by the 13th Reserve Division, to which 5 plane detachments, 3 protective and 8 pursuit squadrons were attached. Route of attack and attack objective were photographed. Based on these photographs, maps were reproduced showing the lines to be reached by the attacking troops and the desired route to be taken by the attack squadrons, and these maps were liberally distributed to headquarters, troops, and airplane organizations. At 5:40 A.M. the infantry started the attack, at 5:55 A.M. the first attack squadron with 6 planes appeared and in four attacks fired on hostile reserves from an altitude of 100 to 400 meters; a second squadron repeated the procedure and dropped bombs. Reconnaissance planes that had timely perceived the start

Technique In War   141

of the hostile counter-attack, called for barrage fire and caused a repetition of the attacks by the attack squadrons. Pursuit squadrons prevented hostile planes from attacking during the entire action.

The necessity to sweep away the counter effect and to reach the objective in spite of losses suffered, led to the employment of airplanes in formations; in chains (of 3 to 4), in swarms (2 to 3 chains), or as pursuit echelons. Several of the latter, assigned to a troop unit, formed a pursuit squadron, several squadrons a group. Thus aerial battle units in close formation of 50 to 70 airplanes, had their inception. The unit was under the orders of the commander, who, however, had authority to employ the unit in echelons or squadrons, or as a complete unit. Captain Boelke was the originator of the organization. The third year of the war saw squadron fights in the air. Giant airplanes served for the purpose of dropping bombs on important targets. A prerequisite for the solution of tasks given to all airplane organizations, is, supremacy of the air — by relentless attack, never by defensive tactics. If supremacy of the air is once lost, it is difficult to regain. Screening is possible only after the enemy has been thoroughly frightened.

The airplanes found support in the anti-aircraft guns which compelled the hostile airplanes to use greater caution and to operate at higher altitudes. Toward the end of the war the number of airplanes brought down by anti-aircraft defense guns increased materially. Machine gun fire with some tracer ammunition is the best means of attacking low flying airplanes.

How the fighting conditions developed during the war is shown by the following table:

The following airplanes were lost:

	In September 1915:			In September 1918:	
	German	British	French	German	Allies
In aerial battle	3	4	11	107	652
By firing from ground ..	2	1	4	---	125
Missing	2	3	7	---	136

Airplane defense searchlights proved to be a valuable means

of airplane defense at night for the protection of important works, villages and roads. They forced airplanes to seek higher altitudes and thus abandon the chance of finding the marks on the ground so necessary for correct orientation. Blinding the airplane pilot by the direct rays of the searchlight deprived them of their assurance in the flight, so that they were induced to drop their bombs prematurely or unaimed.

The attack sections, or echelons (6 airplanes), organized in the fourth year of the war from protective echelons, produced a moral effect by diving from high to low altitudes, and participating in the fight with machine guns, bombs and hand grenades at the moment of the assault. Their assault was directed on the leading infantry lines or against the artillery which was laying down a barrage. In the defense, in the pursuit, and also in the retreat (holding up advancing cavalry and artillery) attack sections found far reaching employment.

Infantry, airplanes watched permanently over the battlefield and took over the battle reconnaissance, transmitted signals from the front to the rear, and supplied the front line, when required, by dropping orders, subsistence, ammunition and hand-to-hand fighting means. Details of our, or the enemy's position, were noted on maps or photographed. Of special importance was the information, whether or not the hostile trenches were filled, where the reserves were and location of hostile tanks. To be able to perceive all positions in readiness in hostile trenches, the airplane had to descend to an altitude of 300 meters. Infantry airplanes could solve their task only if the infantry, on demand, showed the location of its advance line with either white or red cloths, according to the color of ground, or by displaying light signals. It took a long time for infantry to lose its fear in thus supporting the airplanes. The infantry airplane frequently was the only means of communication between the fighting troops and headquarters and thus furnished the first basis for battle conduct. The certainty of being recognized by its airplanes strengthened the moral feeling of the infantry and induced it to hold out, even if surrounded by the enemy. Effective firing against the enemy offered the infantry airplane the best protection.

The development of photographic reproduction by airplanes

Technique In War 143

forced troops to pay more attention to the screening of all works because success of the attack was primarily based on surprise. The rule was to construct the works so exact in color and shade effect that they could not be distinguished from the surrounding ground.

Screening the position, which must absolutely begin even before construction of the position, must not only conceal important works from view (for instance gun embrasures, entrances to shelters), but must also not attract attention to the point screened. The point screened must not distinguish itself by any means from its prior appearance and must never appear unusual. On March 11, 1918, the British 5th Army demonstrated that the screening should even be in conformity with the approaching spring colors. For instance, the battery commanders had to state the color and peculiarity of the ground where their batteries stood.

Camouflage was especially improved on by our enemies. "The Frenchman suggests hiding from sight any work on the ground, even before starting it, by cover and to carry on the work under that cover. The Englishman does not recommend that expressly. The Frenchman believes sowing and setting plants on artificial works to be especially effective; and besides this he uses opaque screening or grates covered with sod or painted canvas. The Englishman loves to use nets to the meshes of which colored strips of cloth are attached. The Frenchman hides his batteries preferably in old or not yet completed, infantry works; the Englishman likes to make battery positions unperceivable by avoiding the shadow effect and to then camouflage them on a large scale to correspond to the entire surrounding (deception of square fields, etc.) or to give them a very irregular appearance defying detection. For the rest, both Frenchman and Englishman place the same value on the fact of having the terrain well guarded by airplanes prior to and during the work.

"The French have within their airplane units certain 'camouflage detachments' which are charged with advising other troops concerning the camouflage. The Englishmen, on the other hand, have a special camouflage officer at each corps headquarters. In addition they have special camouflage depots; both showing that they carry on camouflage on a large scale. Even the pioneer parks keep camouflage material in readiness. As such they serve special nets with attached (to the meshes) strips of material made of gunny sack and scrim, which are colored corresponding to the season."

In the last months of the war the airplanes were not only means of reconnaissance to evade battle but they participated in the battle in many ways, such as described in the preceding paragraphs. Aerial fighting was their principal duty. The intention to prevent the enemy from accomplishing its manifold aerial tasks was merely a means to the object. "There can be no doubts whatever, that supremacy of the air will be of decisive importance in future wars. The one that has gained supremacy of the air will see the victory on the ground fall into his lap like a ripe fruit. Wars will be of short duration, if they are not smothered in their inception. That party which gains a complete victory in the air will prevent the hostile mobilization, transportation and concentration, or at least greatly interfere with them. The hostile centers of industry, the hostile capital will be annihilated, no matter how far they are from the frontier. No longer are there protective distances in the face of modern airplanes with their radius of action. Protection by darkness is cut off as well, as parachutes with magnesium lights can change night into day. Even low flying clouds do not interfere with the activity of airplanes, as was proven by the British aerial escadrilles in the September and October days of 1918. All defensive measures such as anti-aircraft, machine guns, searchlights, etc., have been unable to materially interfere with the hostile flying activity, have not prevented the hostile airplanes from successfully dropping their bombs, in diving down to within 10 meters of the ground and attacking march columns and skirmishers with machine guns. If no absolute defense means is found, the aerial arms will become decisive. This knowledge our enemies took into account in the peace conditions, by prohibiting our keeping war airplanes, in place of which they allowed us to keep a relatively strong cavalry."

The Hague Conference of July 21, 1899, prohibited, against the representations of England and the United States, "the employment of projectiles the sole purpose of which is to spread choking and poisonous gases," — this with the intention of preventing the adoption of a form of mass killing which it would be impossible for anyone to evade. Attempts to increase the effect of arms by the use of gas originated with our enemies.

Attempts to use gas weapons were begun in France as early as September, 1914, and, according to the "Pall Mall Gazette," these weapons were employed the same month at the front. A French War Ministry Order, dated May 21, 1915, contained directions concerning deadly gas projectiles (26-mm. rifle grenades). On the steamer "Lusitania," which was sunk on May 7, 1915, there were 2500 hundredweight of tetrachloride intended for the production of poisonous gases. The French began to use stupifying gases March 1, 1915, and subsequently used them in the battles of Suippes (April 10-17, 1915,) and Verdun, and the British at Ypres. We made the first gas attack, according to British reports, on April 22, 1915, in front of Ypres. The effects of this attack were the more marked because of the lack, on the part of the enemy, of gas defense equipment. A gas bombardment of the 9th Army, at Bolimow, on May 2, 1915, was without result.

In view of our lack of raw materials for manufacturing ammunition, we were compelled to follow the example set by our enemies, and the highly developed chemical industry in Germany was called upon to furnish us the preponderance in the production of the new offensive and defensive materials. At first, chlorine and certain gases which, without being poisonous, affected the membranes, were used. These were later replaced by phosgene, and finally, in 1918, an especially effective fighting gas was found in the "Yellow Cross" (called "mustard" gas by the English, and Yperite by the French). Poisonous gases are the more effective the less they can be detected by the eye (i.e. when colorless and invisible) and the nose; and when their effects make themselves felt only after some time. Gases may be made effective through clouds released from gas cylinders or through the use of gas projectiles. The cylinder discharge is dependent on wind, weather, and terrain. Only in rare cases can these prerequisites be brought into consonance with the intentions of the commander. Gas clouds can be employed more effectively for generally damaging the enemy. When the method was first tried out, the disadvantage became evident that in a change of the wind our own troops must be endangered, and frequently the cylinders had to be held in readiness for a long time awaiting favorable winds. Particularly wide gas attacks are required when it is desired to extend the effects so as to nullify hostile flank fire. As a rule the troops underestimate the effects of a gas attack, as shown by later statements of prisoners. In all cases the execution of a general attack as a follow-up of a gas cloud was a matter of chance, dependent on the wind. We therefore followed the lead of the French and British, who utilized gas clouds, not for introducing an attack, but for the general damaging of the enemy, thereby obviating the necessity of assuring the difficult matter of co-operation with the infantry.

More independent of the wind is the employment of minenwerfer and artillery gas shell, which, however, can be used only against reserves and artillery positions, particularly for neutralizing barrage batteries, but not against troops in the front line. Against the use of the heavy minenwerfer shell, there is to be considered the slow rate of fire and the limited range of this weapon, as well as the great weight of the projectile; its advantage lies in independence of the terrain. In case heavy minenwerfers are installed for other purposes, however, they can be utilized for gas bombardments at any time by bringing up the special gas ammunition. The effects of gases depend on the terrain (depressions, cornfields, and low-lying roads are especially favorable) and on the weather (rain during gas firing diminishes its effect); in the matter of time, the first morning hours have proven best. Gas bombardments have effect only when large areas are gassed, with much ammunition and for long periods of time, as otherwise the troops can too easily avoid the bombarded area. If the gas is to be effective, it must appear as a surprise, or else, by its long duration, exhaust the efficiency of the gas-mask canister.

If we fire gas in connection with an attack, the enemy does not know how long this will continue or what kind of gas we are using, and he will be forced to wear his mask. This facilitates the hand-to-hand fighting for us, if our infantry has been fully informed and instructed concerning the gas fire; the small possibility of incidental damage by gas to our own troops must be borne just as is the case with occasional loss from our own high-explosive fire. If it becomes necessary, our infantry can advance with masks on across short stretches where they may happen to encounter any remaining gas.

A particularly valuable improvement was brought about by the introduction of gas projectors. These were used first by the British (April, 1917, in front of the Sixth Army), and were afterwards employed by us with advantage. They were dug in, in the style of earth mortars, in a number of rows, one behind the other. Fired by electricity, a burst of 900 projectors could be fired with a range up to 1800 meters (time of flight, 25 seconds). Each projectile contained 13.5 kgs., of liquid phosgene or chlorpicrin, so that a great concentration of gas could be produced on a limited area. Projector emplacements could be detected on airplane photographs, so that by timely bombardments the emplacements could be destroyed. Detection of the projector discharge could not be prevented, but the sudden mass strike of the projectiles nevertheless came as such a surprise as to be effective before the men could put on their masks. All regularity in the employment of projectors was avoided. A projector bombardment was accompanied by a burst of other fire, or was made independently, or simultaneously with an attack, thereby befogging the point of penetration. With gas projectors one can attain a far greater gas density than with cylinders, and, in addition, the gas is released directly at the target.

The matter of gas protection became one of particular importance. Each unit had its gas defense officers and noncommissioned officers, who were charged with the maintenance and careful fitting of masks in the gas chamber, under the full responsibility of their commanders. Gas masks were also used for horses and messenger dogs. Rapid adjustment of masks; removal of the same only by order of an officer; regulation of the gas alarm; practice in carrying the mask at rest and while in motion; and training in wearing the mask at exercises, trench work, and ammunition work, are necessary to avoid losses. Practice with masks should include passing orders from mouth to mouth, giving commands, estimating distances, aiming, and target practice, throwing of hand grenades, serving the telephone, repair of telephone lines, and first aid to wounded. In addition to the ordinary mask, certain self-contained oxygen breathing sets were used for protection against mine gases, for which the regular gas mask offered no protection. Toward the end of the war the use of gas increased continually, so that gas defense appliances became equally as important as the battle weapons themselves.

Of other projectiles, there are still to be mentioned hand grenades (filled with irritating and smoke charges), and incendiary and smoke shell. The British were the first to make use of smoke materials, for the purpose of protecting the flanks of advancing infantry; to obscure the view of an observation station or machine gun; for deception, to divert the attention from important points; to simulate a gas attack; to screen troop assemblies in the open, movements along roads and the flash of guns; and, finally for the purpose of hiding troop concentrations and movements, batteries, and the flash of guns from the view of airplane observers. Batteries were completely helpless in the presence of smoke. One could not see 10 meters. Progress could therefore be made from gun to gun only by clinging to guide ropes. Registration points could not be seen. Security sentries sent out could not find their way back. An enemy attacking from the flank would not be noticed until he reached the flank piece. Terrain and troops in rear of our own smoke screen were in general poorly protected against aerial observation. In the interior of the smoke cloud, the men, of course, could not be seen, but were, nevertheless, subjected to the fire directed against the smoke cloud. For this reason troops generally kept 400 meters in rear of the smoke cloud. By frequent repetition of the smoke screens, the enemy may be made to believe that he is being deceived, merely to draw his fire. If this has been done a few times an attack following a smoke cloud may have success. Troops advancing through a smoke cloud easily lose direction.

The employment of minenwerfers had been foreseen in Germany in time of peace for use in fortress warfare for the destruction of wire entanglements. In position warfare, the need was soon felt of supplementing the fire of the high angle artillery by some additional means for accurately projecting high-explosive bombs at the shorter ranges. Auxiliary weapons were thus introduced in the form of "Ladungswerfer" and smooth-bore minenwerfers. Even if minenwerfers could not compete with artillery in the matter of range, improvements nevertheless seemed desirable in order to assure greater freedom in the selection of emplacements.

Minenwerfers were set up on base plates, which did not become firmly emplaced, however, until after the first few rounds were fired. The light minenwerfer bomb had the explosive force of the field artillery shell, but, naturally, with less force of impact, due to the smaller initial velocity.

With like weight projectile, the propellant charge was less, the explosive charge larger, and the dispersion smaller than is the case with artillery. The construction was simpler and the weight of the barrel smaller than for guns of the same caliber; consequently it was possible to produce a larger material and moral effect with less weapons and ammunition. But the gun had the advantage of a wider field of utilization; it was also difficult to conceal the fire of the minenwerfer, the bringing up of ammunition was difficult, and the rate of fire was far less than that of field guns. Minenwerfers took the place of and augmented the use of field guns, and in their method of employment conformed to that laid down in artillery regulations.

The problem as to which arm of the service the minenwerfers — which are placed in position and served by pioneers; intended to augment the fire of the artillery, and for larger battle control assigned tactically the same; and which must be employed in co-operation with and emplaced in the area on the infantry — were to be assigned, was a much-mooted question that was not answered conclusively in the World War. Probably it would have been the simplest thing to have assigned them from the beginning to the infantry.

At first each division was furnished a minenwerfer company by the pioneers, in which all 3 kinds of minenwerfers (3 heavy, 6 medium, and 12 light) were united, and which was under the orders of the pioneer commander. Finally these companies included 4 heavy and 8 medium minenwerfers. This arrangement was not satisfactory. Then each battalion during the position warfare, until May, 1917, was equipped with 4 light minenwerfers, which were served by the infantry, and which were employed, in defense, for barrage fire and against trenches; in attack they were employed especially against machine guns. The instructions which were issued to combine the minenwerfers of a regiment for the purpose of securing uniformity of training and employment, prepared the way for the organization of regimental minenwerfer companies. Distributing the minenwerfers to companies in the battalion was forbidden. The difficulties of ammunition transport by means of infantry carrying parties necessitated the adoption of minenwerfer carts. With the introduction of a wheeled, flat-trajectory mount, the possibility of employing minenwerfers against tanks and machine guns was very much increased. Later, the High Command held a large number of minenwerfer units at its disposition. On September 1, 1918, the division minenwerfer companies were disbarided and their place taken by regimental minenwerfer companies, with 9 light minenwerfers, horse-drawn (1-horse); and with 3 medium minenwerfers, unhorsed, to serve as reserve material. The order to organize a company consisting of medium and heavy minenwerfers came to naught because of the difficulties of the draft replacement situation.

In large battles, the tactical employment of minenwerfers was in accordance with the orders of the artillery commander. The minenwerfers adopted the methods of fire of the artillery (destruction, harassing, annihilation and barrage fire) . This was especially applicable to the minenwerfer battalions of General Headquarters. But as the minenwerfer companies were integral units of the infantry regiments, they had of course to revert to the regiments at the proper time. Heavy and medium minenwerfers were unsuited for barrage fire, because of their low rate of fire. They found employment, however, in destruction fire and also in gas bombardments. They were quite effective against obstacles. When equipped with flat-trajectory mount, the light minenwerfers were employed especially against live targets, against machine gun nests, and in flat-trajectory fire against tanks. They performed valuable services also in mountain warfare. To facilitate fire control, the minenwerfers were formed in groups according to target and terrain. It was estimated that, for assault preparation, 2 medium or 1 heavy minenwerfer bombs were required for each meter of front of the hostile position, so that in order not to extend the duration of the preparation too much, 1 medium or heavy and 1 light minenwerfer were employed for every 50 meters of front.

Chapter VI – The Defensive Battle in Position Warfare

The battles during the year 1917 had brought opinion concerning the defense to a final conclusion. All battles confirmed the experience, that any penetration of a position can be stopped only by a properly prepared depth zone; this of course demanded enormous labor of the troops. No matter how desirable it was to have the troops construct the position in its entire extent of breadth and depth the necessity of having the troops enjoy complete rest at times operated against this. A division front in tranquil sectors could be 6 kilometers and more, but in an active sector that breadth could not be more than 3 to 4 kilometers. It was difficult to determine the exact time when the division sectors could be reduced by the insertion of fresh divisions; if reinforcements came too late, the fresh troops did not have time to get accustomed to their new surroundings. As knowledge of the terrain is one of the principal advantages the defender has over the attacker, it is better to hold the fresh troops back than to insert them too late. Even the strongest construction went to pieces in the course of time under heavy concentrated fire. The trench system was changed into a shell-torn field. Obstacles were swept away, well known points or targets destroyed or obliterated in a very short time, while inconspicuous works, that did not betray themselves on the airplane photographs by tracks and shadows, had an unusually long life. Artillery positions in the open protected from aerial observation lost far less than well entrenched batteries. Artillery effect can be diminished only by extending the targets in breadth and depth. The greater is the distribution of works, the less they are perceived by the enemy, and the more difficult it will be from a question of ammunition supply, to destroy them.

It is important to have the main line of resistance and observation posts withdrawn from direct terrestrial observation. Of less importance is the extent of the field of fire, which is frequently best met by a "Rear-slope position" with direct observation. On nearly all parts of the front, hostile attack preparations were easily perceived. Surprise, as a prerequisite for success, gained increased importance.

In tranquil times, earthworks, with shelters and obstacles, are important principally as they force the attacker to start extensive preparations. His artillery fire will aid in penetration, and therefore will be directed mainly upon the front line trenches; these must be weakly occupied as "security" trenches and equipped with only a few small shelters. In the 2d and 3d line trenches the rest of the garrison is distributed with their light minenwerfers, while the heavy minenwerfers are imbedded, under infantry protection, in the shape of a checkerboard, and as inconspicuously as practicable, to serve as "strong points" in the intermediate terrain. It is the task of the troops in readiness behind the first line to eject the enemy by an immediate counter-shock. More and more did the importance of a deeply formed gallery system become evident. There was a lack of labor to meet this demand. Skillfully constructed approach trenches, arranged for fire preparation, proved especially suited to "lock-in" an enemy that had entered.

Battle zones must extend sufficiently in depth to force the attacker to move his artillery forward. Every opportunity for defense between the lines and fighting zones must be utilized for strong points.

Looking back we will once more emphasize, that, at the beginning of the position warfare, the front lines (without regard to the terrain) were where our attacks had stopped. For reasons of morale abandonment of terrain was rejected; the battle was conducted on a single line with the resisting power increased by all possible means (Autumn battle in the Champagne). Even in favorable cases hostile entry into our positions was prevented only with heavy losses. In the Somme battle the attackers succeeded in smashing with their artillery our front line, so that the troops in readiness could not start the counter-attack. That had to be left to troops farther in rear. The smashed trenches in front could have been temporarily abandoned, if, at the conclusion of the battle, the terrain was still in our hands. We fought for the possession of the front trench at a heavy loss. The necessity to camouflage all works from air and ground reconnaissance, in order to deceive the hostile observer by color and form, assumed prime importance both to us and our enemies. It was shown in 1917 that in the face of the increased artillery preparation the leading trenches were always lost. The more the defense insisted on holding the leading trenches, the more severe was the loss in men and materiel besides the loss of terrain. Loss of men could be avoided only by a distribution in depth. Difficulty of replacing our losses demanded husbanding our men. "The object of defensive battle is no longer clinging to possession of the terrain, but rather the utmost infliction of damage to the enemy while preserving our own forces." If possible, unfavorable terrain should be left in the hands of the enemy. It is better to voluntarily abandon unfavorable, shell plowed and torn positions and to lose terrain only, not men and valuable materiel in addition. "The defender is not rigidly bound to his place, he is far rather justified to fight mobile on the battlefield, that is to advance or give way according to need. But the maxim, that at the conclusion of the battle the entire battle terrain shall be in possession of the defender unless direct orders are received to the contrary must be at heavy cost in men." The defender gave way under the hostile fire, the battle line responded to the pressure and laid itself like an elastic band around the attacker. For the support of this mobile defense "strong points" were created in the intermediate terrain interspersed with machine guns and infantry groups. Through skillful adaption to the terrain these were hidden from view, and could not be annihilated by the artillery preparation. It was their task to stop the flood that rolled forward after the shattering of the front trenches, and to disorganize it prior to its reaching our rear. Only with the introduction of tanks was it possible to hold down our machine gun fire during the attack. Mobility of the reserves was increased, regular mobile battles ensued within a position, in which horse artillery participated.

That was the substance of the elastic defense. Thus, from the battle for possession of the front trench, developed a battle in a depth zone.

By the fact that the opposing positions were very close to each other, frequently considerably less than 100 meters (believed impossible prior to the war), it happened that the front line was exposed to hostile minenwerfers. This proximity of front lines enabled the attacker to quickly pass the stationary barrage, and be in the hostile trenches, before the garrison could leave its shelters. Almost without exception the weak defender, working gradually out of his shelters, fought against superior numbers. This fact accounts for the large number of prisoners taken. Creating more favorable conditions for the defender could be obtained only by avoiding crowding the front trenches, and prolonging the distances the attacker had to cover. This led to the establishment of the zone defense. Troops in the front line in the zone defense are charged with the same tasks that in the mobile war, falls to the outposts.

The outpost position is for the purpose of preventing the enemy gaining, without great losses, a point of attack in the immediate vicinity of our main line of resistance. Resistance should increase the deeper the enemy penetrates. Deceiving the enemy concerning the location of our main line of resistance and creating time for the troops in rear to be ready for action, is the duty of the outpost position. Whether the main battle runs its course on the outpost line, or in rear is the business of the highest commander, and not of the troops. The troops offer a stubborn resistance at the point designated, until different orders are received. The outpost position is occupied in force only by direct orders of the commander when the attack has been perceived. In tranquil times, the outpost position is held lightly but with sufficient force to drive off hostile patrols, or eject at once a hostile raid. The effort to establish two fortified positions, keep them up, and supply them with means of information and communication,

The Defensive Battle in Position Warfare

requires too many troops for the labor purposes.

In tranquil times, we will frequently quarter a portion of the garrison in the outpost position, and withdraw them at the opening of the artillery duel, or at other unmistakable signs that an attack is about to commence. To deceive the enemy as to strength of garrison is difficult at all times. Diminution of troops and the traffic as well as the up-keep of the position will soon leave traces on aerial photographs. The method of conducting the battle cannot be kept away from the troops, and may be brought to the knowledge of the enemy by prisoners. In any case the outpost position must have sufficient troops to compel the attacker to deploy his full force, so that they can hold the hostile advanced troops with the means at hand and give way, according to plan only when it is clearly seen that the main attack is imminent, and our main defensive forces have been alarmed. Only when we strictly insist on the outpost position not being evacuated without orders, can we overcome the disadvantages connected with giving way to the rear. The outpost position may also be given the mission of offering as much resistance as possible to the attack, in order to create favorable conditions for the counter-attack. It is better to sacrifice the garrison than to abandon the original battle plan. If the attacker succeeds with his surprise, then the foreground will become a false position. In such case we can count on a decrease of the hostile artillery fire. But if the defender himself intends to carry out extensive artillery fire on the hostile back areas, there is nothing left for him but to leave a portion of his guns in the foreground; it will be questionable in case of a heavy attack if the guns can be brought back in time. The outpost battle when conducted with small detachments with many machine guns firing from all sides will delay the attacker. Infantry in the outpost acts primarily as security detachments for machine guns and advanced artillery. Reduction of the infantry force in a sector leaves no doubt in the minds of the troops concerning the intention of our high command, and naturally does not increase the feeling of security of the garrison. Consideration of plans for artillery in defense requires a decision as to whether the falling-back to its final position is to be made in one move or whether a temporary halt will first be made in the intermediate terrain. The longer we delay the enemy in front of our main battle position the better, but this should never lead to the outpost troops being cut off. Frequently the necessity of keeping possession of important observation posts leads to the decision to hold the outpost line. In this case the main line of resistance would coincide with the outpost defensive line, unless terrain in front could be gained by an attack. The primary mission of artillery is protection of the main battle position and it must in certain cases decline the important artillery duel during the hostile attack preparation. Some artillery must be in advanced positions, and stationary barrage and annihilating fire must be assured in front of the main line. Detached pieces (advanced guns) which can deceive the enemy as to their number by rapid fire from several different positions are efficacious. As we learned, bringing back the artillery was successful beyond all expectations. The main target for the artillery will always be the hostile infantry. It must be beaten down before it reaches the main battle position. This requires powerful and accurate fire concentration from the artillery's own and neighboring sectors against definite points of the foreground. The different tasks of the artillery in the fight for possession of the outpost zone of the main battle position can be in most cases solved only from many different positions. The most careful preparatory work in tranquil times covering supply of ammunition, arranging observation posts, laying lines of communication, etc., is essential. Regard for secrecy must never mislead the highest commander to abandon range finding for the primary barrages and the annihilating fire directed in front of our main battle position. Normal fire in tranquil times may be laid on zones far in rear of the enemy. With increasing activity of the hostile artillery there arises increased difficulties in distinguishing between our and the enemy's hits, a temporary evacuation of portions of our positions may be ordered, and firing data carefully collected in quiet times must be available. The main point is to hide the range-finding from the attention of the enemy by proper distribution over a period of time. For the purpose of deception it was found well to use for range-finding shells with time-fuses, or fire by salvos of three pieces against the enemy, while the fourth piece found the desired range. A few trial shots sufficed for the necessary firing data.

The Defensive Battle in Position Warfare 157

Theoretically, the idea is that the outpost should be evacuated only at a well understood signal of the commander of the troops, but errors in this are very easy. How is this order or signal to be made known to neighboring and our own troops? If the departure is to be made without friction, the subordinate commanders and troops must have a clear idea concerning the course of the retreat fight, and this knowledge will betray the intention of the commander. Probably the first intimation given to the subordinate commanders that the position will be evacuated will be when the artillery is drawn back, which requires at least one or two nights. The later the orders are issued, the more difficult will it be to transmit them through the increased hostile fire. Before evacuation begins the enemy should at least be compelled to resort to extensive enveloping work, heavy losses, and expenditure of a large amount of ammunition. There are no rules governing the exact time these orders should be issued; to properly determine that time is one of the most difficult tasks of leadership. Raids, increased gassing, and the arrival of deserters, are sure signs an attack is imminent. The right to order the evacuation had best be left to the Army or Corps, not to the different division commanders. There may be cases when the commander of the outpost troops should have authority to independently order the evacuation. Orders for covering fire should be issued by the same headquarters at the same time evacuation orders are issued. The possibility of fully utilizing the advantages of the outpost terrain depends above all else on the efficiency of the means of communication, which must assure battle control. Increased means of information are necessary. As a last means there remains communication by simple signals with our airplanes. Communication between troops on the ground with airplanes is difficult. It is probably too much to demand the troops keep one eye on the enemy and one in the air. Every lull in the hostile fire should be taken advantage of to move troops.

In general the depth of an outpost zone will be about 500 meters and never more than 1000. In greater depth, means of communication are insecure. Barrage fire to the flank on portions of the position which are holding out become ineffective and personal observation which the commander should have is difficult. If any foreground is less than 100 meters, the advantage of compelling the opponent to cross a fire swept zone is lost. In any case, the weaker our artillery is, and the less time available to prepare the position, the greater will be its depth. A prime requisite for success is concealment.

After an attack has been stopped the troops, by counter-attack, at once regain possession of the foreground. If this is not done, we will finally be forced to evacuate our position. But the danger that the decisive battle may take place too far in advance must be called to attention; if we desire to hazard that, it must be done with firm decision and not left to the subordinate commanders.

The strength of the outpost garrison is generally fixed at 1 to 2 infantry squads and one machine gun squad for each company; this is in general better than to place an entire company on a broad sector. We generally disliked to do without the light minenwerfers of the infantry; medium and heavy minenwerfers, considering their limited range, have to be placed far to the front. These can hardly be brought back in time because of their poor mobility, but they are excellent means of misleading the enemy, and if they succeed in deceiving and inflicting loss on the enemy their own loss has been weir paid for. The outpost zone has proved its value in the battles in Flanders. The events at Verdun speak less in its favor.

The infantry soon felt that strong occupation of the front trenches, unnecessarily increased the losses. When the Allies concentrated their heavy fire more and more on the trenches in rear, it was quite natural that all eluded the fire by moving forward and thus again made more dense the occupation of the front trenches (October, 1917, in Flanders); large losses were the result.

The demand came from the troops themselves not to occupy the front trenches systematically. This procedure undoubtedly would have been advantageous at the time of the hostile artillery preparation in attacks on a large scale.

There must be sufficient troops to stop an attack and the individual must have a neighbor in his vicinity to increase his self-confidence.

The losses among the defenders of the front line can not be avoided; the commander however, must refrain from continually reinforcing that line, for the losses then would be unjustifiable. The reserves must seek the decision. The general rule within the division was to place the infantry regiments abreast with battalions in column. These were known as fighting, readiness, and rest battalions, and were changed about every two weeks. In the matter of formation it was advised that from the front line battalion of 4 companies to every 200 meters front there should be one-half of each company occupying the main position, one-sixth of each company with their automatic rifles 200 meters in advance for security purposes and to resist weak attacks by raiding parties, about one-third of each company with 2 automatic rifles forward as a support. Before a threatened attack the support was withdrawn to the main line of resistance. The supporting battalion deployed on a depth of 500 meters was brought up to within 200 meters, and in case of an attack the 2 companies automatically took the place vacated by the support while the 2 rear companies take the place of the 2 front companies. The regiment had a front of 800 meters with both its forward battalions having a depth of about 1000 meters. Proper consideration was given to holding only weakly the front line, only 80 men with 12 automatic rifles, while in the main line of resistance were 240 men with 12 automatic rifles and 8 machine guns, which were reinforced by 160 men with 4 machine guns, while for a counter-attack 240 men with 12 automatic rifles and the Machine Gun company were in readiness. This was the arrangement made for strong counter-attacks. Against hostile attacks, artillery counteroffensive preparation fire proved specially effective, whereas barrage fire was always a makeshift as in most cases it came too late, and on account of the intensive artillery counter preparation was undertaken by fewer guns than had originally been intended. The "stationary barrage" required material augmentation by light minenwerfers and by the fire of machine guns withheld until the moment of the assault. It was intended to stop the hostile reinforcement by placing barrage fire on critical points, to delay by tenacious resistance within the position the progress of the hostile infantry, at least enough to prevent their having the protection of the creeping barrage. Only artillery which co-operates fully with infantry and which observes every nook and corner of the battlefield is equal to the demands of the defensive battle. In the forces held in readiness in rear lies the decision.

In the penetration planned by General Nivelle certain troops held in readiness were to be thrown in if the attack had passed over the trench system. It was realized that the deeper the penetration the weaker would be the leading detachments, the more insufficient the artillery support and the deeper the flank. To counteract the effect of the penetration that might cross our trench system, an "interference"* division was placed in readiness behind the trench system. This division could be used if the attacker endeavored to reach far off objectives beyond the main position. But when General Petain perceived the German method of defense he contented himself with limited objectives at close range aided by a systematic barrage of shell and gas. Nothing therefore remained for us but to execute the counter-attack with troops consisting of all arms in the position system. If the counter-attack is not launched immediately the reserve troops remain inactive and are finally destroyed by fire. The commander of the defense has to reckon with a deep penetration and also with an attack against a limited objective. The task of the interference troops is difficult; they must be at the proper point and beyond hostile artillery fire. They must not be frittered away by piece-meal, but must be thrown as a unit into the counter-attack.

The local counter-attack and the general counter-attack differ only in point of time when they become effective. The local counter-attack acts automatically, immediately when the enemy enters. The disorder among the hostile troops, the impossibility of support by artillery facilitate the counter-attack and explain the success achieved by even weak, but well led detachments.

The general counter-attack is a systematic attack, made after thorough artillery preparation unless the situation permits surprise. "Local counter-attacks launched too late do not differ from overhasty general counter-attacks; they are useless and must be prohibited."

In the general counter-attack preparations can be made only after a definite decision has been reached. The time element is

---

* Interference troops are those held in readiness for counter-attack.

immaterial. General counter-attacks have been successful when the leadership understood how to wait and not endeavor to recover every loss of ground. It is an error to be led into making any attack insufficiently prepared. Frequently the measures taken by the enemy are insufficient to retain what he has gained.

In the local counter-attack all preparations must have been completed beforehand. If the enemy has entered, that is the signal for starting the local counter-attack; if we delay all hopes of success will fade. In tranquil times local and general reserves must utilize the available time for practicing counter-attacks. Any counter-attack comes too late if the enemy has succeeded in arranging his defense, that is, if he has regulated his depth formation, issued his orders and prepared artillery barrage, and counter preparation fire. The better we have prepared our defensive zone the more effectively our machine guns can participate from all sides, the more decisive the counterattack will be executed, and the more stubborn will strong points hold out. The more time leading waves can be held up in overcoming strong points and machine guns the less will the attacker profit from the protection of his steadily advancing barrage. Only in this manner can we account for the surprising success gained by small detachments. If, however, the troops hesitate only a short time and allow the attacker to reorganize the terrain it is not improbable that the shock of even a prepared detachment will not be successful.

A prime requirement for success is that the commander of the troops in readiness carefully observes conditions of the front line, that he does not allow himself to be drawn into making a jump in the dark, or an uncertain start. Interference troops held in rear of the defensive zone are reserves in the hands of the higher commander. They form a support to the fighting front. They may relieve front line divisions by furnishing security detachments, connecting groups and finally, battle reserves, so that the divisions in the front line can insert their last man without fear in holding the position. When the battle reserves of the division in the front line are inserted, portions of the interference division may take their place as battle reserves, their own places being then taken by troops from the rear. Through this systematic closing up of the reserves, the sharp and rapid counter-attack is assured. Places of readiness for troops depend on the task and the possibility of shelter. In tranquil times it will be advisable to advance from each division, what is called an *interference* third (3 battalions, 3 batteries, pioneer company and telephone detachment), to the edge of the zone of hostile fire. Attaching labor parties to the interference third to construct covered trenches is desirable. The remainder of the troops of the interference division remain in their quarters in rear and in their sectors complete their training. For bringing up troops and supplies, horses are useful in tranquil times. The message service performed by troopers, proved very satisfactory in Flanders and at Verdun. Only thus can we avoid the regimental units becoming lost or losing touch with their commanders. From the base of attack forward, the employment of horses, however, will be impracticable, from there on the message dog and above all the efficient battle runner, starts his work.

Reinforcing the front line almost always proceeds under the pressure of events and under heavy hostile fire. Only prior knowledge of the battle terrain, of its shelter, communication, organization, and plan of defense, may procure favorable conditions for the success of the interfering troops. It is necessary that the plan be so completely prepared that it can be started at a given work or signal.

As a matter of experience, the division in the front line had best keep control of its interference troops; that division knows the progress of the battle information conditions, and the terrain, and has the greatest interest in holding its fighting zone. Only in this way may we assure unity in battle action. For the same reason it is advisable to have the headquarters of the division in the front line and the interference division at one and the same command post. If the interference division covers several division sectors, then personal conferences should take place prior to the battle and it will be advisable to send liaison officers to the divisions in the front line. In the same manner, connection between the interference regiments and the regiments in the front line will be required. Headquarters should be at one and the same point if for nothing else than mutual exchange of experiences and utilizing the shelter facilities that have already been prepared.

Rank of the commanders must not be allowed to interfere. By

placing the interference division under the orders of the division in the front line, there is danger that the latter will absorb gradually the battalions of the former for mere defensive purposes. This absorption has no bearing on the final result of the battle, and is absolutely dangerous. In nearly all battles, portions, sometimes strong forces, of the interference division remain immobile. In most cases the commanders of the troops in the front position have, without good reason, requested that units should remain in a certain place in order to reinforce some endangered part of the position. No attention must be paid to such requests. The commander who declines will take the responsibility for declining. Orders for starting local counter-attacks can be given only by the headquarters of the division in the front line. Headquarters of interference divisions knows too little about the situation, and its orders in any case would arrive too late. The commander of the interfering troops had better orient himself with his own means at hand, concerning the situation, and independently order the general counter-attack. Army Headquarters ordered, and not without justification: "It is strictly forbidden to delay local counter-attacks while permission of next higher headquarters is requested." That is indeed very correct: such a question merely shows that the commander is lacking in decision and energy, and in waiting for an answer so much time is lost that the shock would come too late. This holds good equally for small and large engagements. The question, when the division counter-attack shall be started, is of very great importance. At Verdun it took in favorable cases, from 1½ to 2 hours after the division orders were issued until the troops started. In heavily shelled terrain we can count, in favorable cases, on 45 minutes for covering 1 kilometer, and frequently it is even more than double that time. Not only the hostile fire, but the difficult passage over the shell-torn terrain, obstacles, and the necessity of making detours to avoid being seen, increase the period of time. Haste can be made only by an indomitable will and by the example of the leaders. A premature start is, in any case, a lesser fault than to wait too long. The main point is not to come too late! A premature start may result in a jump in the dark, but delayed too long, the counter-attack leads to a costly defeat, or in the most favorable case, to a mere densifying of the troops in the front line. It is wrong, therefore, to wait for the results of reconnaissance. Considering the incalculable slowness of the service of communication, and the march, we will surely come too late and lose the best opportunity. Therefore, without question, we must start without the usual battle reconnaissance.

The lack of reconnaissance also increases the difficulties of the flanking counter-attack, which presupposes that the commander knows the exact location of the enemy. It is wrong to move forward and then change direction to gain a favorable attack position. Great losses will be the consequence, troops will be used up before they gain contact and will probably arrive too late. Such an attack had therefore best be executed by troops in a neighboring sector. It would be unjustifiable independence unless a very favorable opportunity offered, to push a flanking attack into a neighboring sector without orders from higher headquarters, which can see the whole situation. Only commanders of connecting groups may act in this manner.

Flaking counter-attacks demand reconnaissance of the terrain, so that obstacles will not be encountered unexpectedly. They further require special protection on the flank towards the enemy. The attacking troops should not be bothered with their own flank protection. Flanking counter-attacks have the advantage of forcing the enemy to execute a change of front and further of avoiding the hostile box barrage. Finally, in the flanking counter-attack the occupation of the captured position is by no means simple, but if the attack succeeds, the prize in prisoners and supplies is large.

Carrying the counter-attack rapidly forward, is the surest guarantee for success and for lessening the losses. But an attack can be carried through rapidly only if it is supported by the necessary fire. This is not the business of the assaulting troops, but of the attached automatic rifle, machine guns, light minenwerfers, infantry guns, and artillery. If we must transfer the fire preparation to the infantry, we must then form strong firing lines at long ranges, and not employ open skirmish waves, and thus suffer greater losses. The open skirmish waves are not for fighting but a movement formation. The advance without firing can be made as soon as the hostile infantry is held in their shelters by our machine gun, and artillery fire. Only when that has not been accomplished

The Defensive Battle in Position Warfare 165

must our infantry work itself up to the hostile position under protection of its own fire. Only the skill of the subordinate commanders and the efficiency of the troops can find the right road to success. We may say, in general, that in such cases our old attack, conforming to the drill regulations, promises the best success. Working up by rushes, with fire support by all available machine guns and with sufficient support by the accompanying artillery using direct fire against the hostile machine guns.

The general rule, to close rapidly with the enemy, is frequently influenced by the endeavor to keep the proper direction. The direction is the enemy. Therefore it is the general maxim never to wait for one's neighbor; if we wait, there is no assurance that the troops will get to the enemy. The less open the terrain, the more depressions and woods prevent a view on the points of direction, the more necessary is it that a "leading" company precede with carefully sought out intermediate points, straight along the compass direction. Companies following in echelon may utilize without hesitancy any cover the terrain affords if they always regain their proper position in regard to the "leading" company.

Whenever possible, our old line of trenches must be retaken in the counter-attack. If that is not done, absolute connection with the artillery must be arranged so that the latter can regulate its fire accurately. It is advisable to attach liaison officers from supporting artillery to the attacking troops. Frequently at the most important moments reconnaissance to the flanks and connection with the rear is neglected. If the line is reached all available weapons must be fully utilized in pursuing fire, and steps taken at once to reorganize the position. Of importance is depth formation. Rapid re-establishment of depth formation must therefore be practiced in advance, like the counterattack itself. In most cases establishment of depth formation can be done only at night. Immediate withdrawing of detachments may be considered by weak minds as a sign of an intended retreat.

In taking the measures for the counter-attack, the high command must always consider that the troops may lack the necessary material for constructing and holding the position after their success. To lay out panels is possible only after the action has been brought to a close and this had best be done by selected detachments, when requested by the infantry airplanes. Fog and smoke increase the difficulties of observation, the position has been changed into a shell-torn terrain and infantry airplanes have to descend very low to distinguish by its uniforms their own infantry.

Co-operation of artillery and infantry has been mentioned several times. Generally one artillery battalion of two gun and two howitzer batteries is attached to each infantry regiment as accompanying artillery. It has the task of sweeping obstacles out of the path of the infantry, and especially of destroying hostile machine guns. After the assault, the accompanying artillery gives the necessary stability to the victorious infantry, and supports it during the first critical hours. This is impossible from positions far off and under cover. Accompanying the infantry attack is necessary also for moral reasons. It is said that the artillery loses time in moving forward but that is much better than to keep silent in positions in rear, because in critical situations it may fear to fire on its own infantry.

The fire of the defense artillery must stop the enemy who has entered, then annihilate him. During a hostile attack with limited objectives the artillery in defense is uncertain as to what is taking place behind the rolling barrage. The questions: How far did the attacker push forward? Do our troops hold out? Are local counter-attacks being made? cannot be answered with any degree of certainty. One of the duties of defense artillery is "locking-in the enemy that has entered," that is cutting off by fire hostile reinforcements as well as keeping up the artillery protection for the neighboring sector. Only where the enemy can be absolutely distinguished in our position can he be immediately fired on. Systematic locking-in to the rear prepares in the best way our counter-attack. Counter preparation fire which should be laid by all available batteries on the space in rear of the barrage can then be of decisive effect. When the enemy steps into the open, under the protection of his creeping barrage, moving slowly to the front, the task becomes easier. The situation is then clear and locking-in takes a back seat.

The aerial fighting forces are of great importance in the execution of the counter-attack. Infantry airplanes should not be given too many tasks. The commander must be moderate. He should demand only:

1. Where is our front line infantry?
2. Where is the point of entry?
3. Conduct of the enemy (advancing in what direction, rolling up, etc.?).

Pursuit squadrons did excellent service; their appearance at low altitude over the battlefield and their participation with machine guns and bomb never failed to create a deep impression on friend and foe. Especially effective is their participation at the moment of the assault. In counter-attack the leading hostile infantry is the most important objective. The main point is to confuse it, to hold it down, and to defeat it. Hostile machine guns, minenwerfer positions, as well as batteries firing on our infantry's advance are proper targets for our machine gun fire. By the help of panels staked out at the headquarters it is possible to give the battle airplanes information of the direction of the hostile penetration and to demand a repetition of flights and complete reports.

When well prepared counter-attacks did not have good results as at Verdun and in Flanders, the reason always lay in the piecemeal manner of making the attacks, generally too late. Giving missions that are not clear, insufficient co-operation between troops in the front line and supporting artillery, and transfer of reserve to various commanders should be avoided.

Chapter VII – German Attacks with Limited Objectives

Attacks with limited objectives occurred along the entire front for the purpose of securing local advantages such as observation positions. These generally succeeded after artillery preparation with relatively small loss. Frequently more material losses occurred in holding what had been gained. These operations proved to be effective means of increasing the morale of the troops. The desire for the execution of such operations was expressed by the troops themselves and they were encouraged even though the expenditure of ammunition and the losses suffered were not always commensurate with the success attained. The narrower the attacking front, the easier can the defender concentrate his artillery fire on it. In the winter of 1916-1917 a large number of operations took place on the Somme (9th Army Corps Maisonnette, October 29, 1916; Pierre Vaast Forest, November 20, 1916), in the Champagne (Hill 185, south of Ripont, February 15, 1917) and around Verdun (13th Infantry Division on Hill 304, January 15, 1917) and others, which offered valuable lessons in attacks with limited objectives. The selection of the places to be entered and of the attack objective has to be made so that a sector shall be captured in the hostile trench system which cannot be easily

German Attacks with Limited Objectives 169

flanked by the enemy himself and which can be easily incorporated into our trench system. Through mining and entrenching, flank protection and routes of approach must be prepared in advance.

Conditions of the ground also have to be considered. Heavy rains frequently render the assault terrain too slippery and soft. Progress across No Man's Land will be very slow. Under certain conditions the operation may have to be delayed.

The plan for the attack, made by division headquarters, is submitted to the Corps. It is important in such matters that Corps Headquarters should not discourage the initiative of the division commanders by unimportant objections. Any order that is sound is better than a technically correct order that is carelessly carried out. Battalion and company commanders issue their orders in the form of sketches and tables which should include position in readiness, attack objectives, roads, formations, composition of the waves, time and place of issue of equipment, etc. The artillery commander, assures proper range finding, and in his order covers the artillery fire activity and co-operation with the minenwerfers and the infantry.

An important element for any attack is the correct designation of time and watches must be repeatedly compared. Orders must be in the hands of the troops at least 24 hours prior to the attack and should be repeated back to assure correctness.

Surprise is one of the decisive elements in the success of the attack. Every repetition of a former method of attack makes success questionable. False operations (inserting flame throwers, exploding mines, sudden artillery fire at different points and cessation after 5 minutes) will mislead the enemy. There should also be pauses in the artillery preparation, increase in the volume of fire, which the enemy will in most cases reply to with stationary barrages, so that at the assault proper the final fire is delivered without increasing the volume and with shells with time fuses. The assault will hardly be noticed by the enemy, and this will make it easier for our infantry closely following the barrage. A slow forward creeping barrage in front of the assaulting troops has been found very effective. The infantry must endeavor to push forward under the hostile barrage in close order and take depth formation subsequently. The less the distance between starting point and final objective the greater the possibilities of success. Lifting of the barrage and the sudden start of the assault is made by watches that have been accurately synchronized.

The time of attack had best be set shortly before dark, so that the troops will have about an hour's daylight to find their way into the position, to strengthen it and to regulate the barrage. The longer it remains light, the more time will the enemy have to direct counter preparation fire on the position; a strong gassing of the hostile batteries after the assault is launched will benefit our infantry, while gassing prior to the assault merely attracts the enemy's attention. Darkness also facilitates the use of more troops for labor, but these must be withdrawn before daylight to lessen the losses.

We must absolutely adhere to the hour and minute fixed for the start of the assault. New troops generally underestimate the time absolutely required for issuing orders and believe that it is possible to change an attack at the last hour. That is impossible and leads only to losses and failure.

The leader must decide whether he can base his success on surprise, or whether a longer artillery preparation will be required. A mixing up of both methods almost always leads to defeat. Along battle fronts troops are on the qui vive and a surprise will be difficult. We select that method, nevertheless, when there is no chance of assembling the assaulting troops under cover. The better the construction of the hostile position, the deeper the attack is to penetrate, the more thorough must be the artillery preparation. This will be more effective the more it is crowded into a short space of time. In about 3 hours a heavy field howitzer battery can batter down a trench of 100 meters with from 400 to 600 rounds. For light howitzers it would take one-half more of that amount of ammunition, and for mortars one-half less. Destruction of hostile obstacles may be an additional artillery task during the preparation, or this mission may be assigned to the minenwerfers during the artillery preparation. It may be best to assign to the artillery the task of counter battery fire and to make the preparation on hostile trenches by minenwerfers, concentrated with maximum fire for about 5 minutes. Heavy and sudden minenwerfer fire, in any case, has a great moral effect. About 20 medium and heavy minenwerfers, per 1000 meters of trench will be needed for this five-minute preparation. The preparation has to be so regulated that, even if no view can be had, the artillery fire runs like clockwork. Besides making the position ripe for assault, our artillery must fire on hostile headquarters and places where it is known reserves are held in readiness as well as on routes of approach. The hostile artillery must be neutralized prior to our attack. As to whether or not the hostile artillery should be gassed during our fire on the trenches depends on available time and whether we are willing to abandon the surprise element. In addition, the artillery must prevent the approach of the hostile reserves and annihilate visible machine gun positions and flanking works. The assault troops had best be placed in readiness during darkness in order to prevent hostile counter preparation fire. Passage through our own obstacles should be made as late as practicable. This is best accomplished by explosives (gas containers, filled with explosives, open passage ways from 4 to 5 meters broad). Air protection is secured by cautious use of airplanes which must not attract the enemy's attention (they should not arrive until 10 minutes prior to H hour) and by taking the necessary defensive means against hostile airplanes.

Assurance of success lies in employing fresh troops that have been trained behind the lines and practiced in the formation to be adopted for the particular assault and who adhere closely to the exact course the attack is to take. These troops should be relieved as soon as possible after their success. A sufficient number is about 3 battalions, 3 minenwerfer companies (each of 4 heavy and 8 light minenwefers), and 2 pioneer companies, per 1000 meters of front. More important than numbers is the quality of the troops!

The assault detachment is divided into attack waves, to which machine guns, pioneers, artillery runners and signal squads are distributed; shock-troops go ahead to be employed against resistance points noted by the leader. Carrier squads with sandbags, quick obstacles, and means for hand-to-hand fighting follow. Whether the attacking waves advance in skirmish lines or in single columns must be considered in each case. Distance to pass beyond the hostile barrage at the same time to prevent the attack from becoming disrupted should be as short as possible. Each wave must

German Attacks with Limited Objectives

FORMATION

of a battalion in attack from trench to trench, piercing depth into the trench system that is to be held about 500 meters. Strength of one infantry company: 3 officers (off. aspirants), 22 squad leaders and MG comdrs. 116 men and 6 automatic machine guns

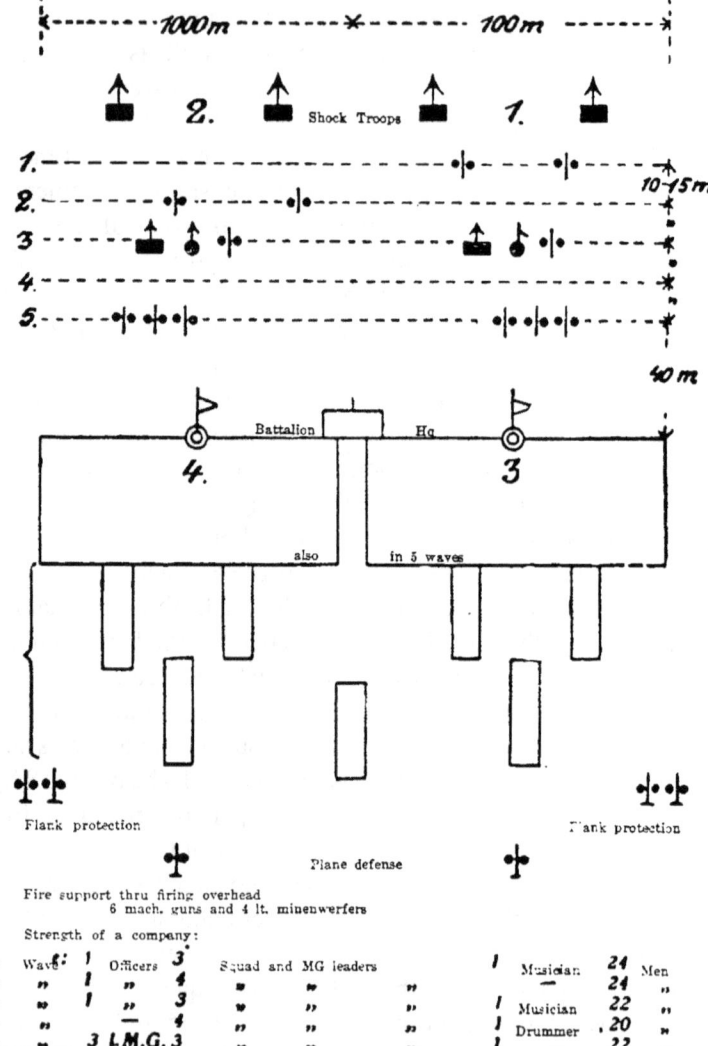

Flank protection

Plane defense

Flank protection

Fire support thru firing overhead
6 mach. guns and 4 lt. minenwerfers

Strength of a company:

	Wave:		Officers		Squad and MG leaders			Musician	24	Men
1.		1		3					24	,,
2.	,,		,,	4	,,	,,	,,	—		
3.	,,	1	,,	3	,,	,,	,,	1 Musician	22	,,
4.	,,		—	4	,,	,,	,,	1 Drummer	20	,,
5.	,,		3 L.M.G. 3		,,	,,	,,	,,	22	,,

6 automatic MG

As a rule companies with less than 120 men are formed into two platoons. 6 automatic mach. guns with 12 men and cartridges for each gun are in 5th Wave.
The necessary 24 litter-bearers have to be furnished by the bearer company considering the small strength of the fighting companies. The grenade thrower squad is also in the 5th Wave.

German Attacks with Limited Objectives 173

reach its designated objective independently and without regard to other waves. The guide is the objective.

If we assign the task of demolishing the hostile front line trenches to the medium and heavy minenwerfers, the artillery has the task of protecting the operation against the hostile works lying further in rear, and throwing a barrage on the hostile routes of approach as well as counter battery fire. Range adjustment must be done without attracting attention and with the aid of balloon observation. Considering the small distance between the opposing lines hostile front line fire by our artillery can hardly be accomplished without endangering our own infantry. Early artillery fire against the hostile artillery betrays the coming assault. The barrage fire of the artillery increased by the fire of the minenwerfers starts simultaneously with the infantry. After the successful assault it remains, gradually lessening, on a spot beyond the objective and thus forms the stationary barrage for the new position.

The entrance of the infantry in the hostile trenches following directly on the bursting of the last shell has always proven comparatively easy; it takes some time before the opponent regains his senses and perceives the situation; that condition the attacker must take full advantage of by rapidly pushing forward. The deeper he pushes his way into the enemy's position the larger is the gain in prisoners and the less will be his own losses.

Success of the attack depends on rapidity and on systematic co-operation between infantry and artillery; this requires that after reaching the objective, the infantry does not advance beyond it; otherwise the infantry will be annihilated by its own artillery fire. Careful arrangements must be made as to the action to be taken in the event that the assault miscarries, or is perceived by the enemy ahead of time. There is no hope of sending orders to the first line; the time consumed is incalculable, and it would only lead to a portion of the troops assaulting without artillery support and they would surely be annihilated.

When the objective has been reached it must be clearly made visible to our artillery and, on demand, to our airplanes, and communication to the rear must be promptly established. The artillery immediately starts range adjustment for barrage.

More difficult than taking, is the holding of hostile trenches. In most cases counter-attacks accompanied by artillery will be started. The subordinate commanders must be prepared to combat the carelessness and the disinclination for labor that so easily takes hold of troops after a success.

Occupation must permit active defense in depth; all crowding is to be avoided; approach and communication trenches towards the enemy must be blocked by fire or otherwise, as the first counter-attacks will come from these. Experience has shown that after a successful assault there generally is a lack of hand grenades and means of illumination.

Raids are undertaken along the same lines; the main question is that of returning to the exit point after a short stay in the hostile trenches. The necessity of these reconnaissances in force is for the capture of prisoners. In these operations also we may achieve much with weak detachments.

Chapter VIII – Machine Guns

Based on the experiences of the Russo-Japanese War all armies had gradually come to about the same number of machine guns, viz., 2 guns per battalion and about 2 guns per cavalry brigade. In Germany and Russia the machine gun platoons had been consolidated into machine gun companies of 8 guns, while France and England preferred the platoon formation and regulated the tactical consolidation of platoons according to requirements. In any case, the company was enabled to more easily cover greater spaces in depth with its 3 platoons than could have been done by single separated platoons. Doubtless all experiences gained in war speak for tactical employment by platoon, while for administration the company formation is better. While Germany had decided to transport the guns on wagons, almost all other countries favored transportation on pack animals (load of pack horse 130 to 150 kg). The latter method enabled the machine guns to follow the troops everywhere and offered smaller targets, but the amount of ammunition that can be carried is limited, and getting into action is retarded as gun and tripod have first to be assembled. Should a pack animal fall the gun may not get into action at all. Saddle sores cannot be avoided no matter what care is taken. And finally the question depends on the number of pack animals available in the country. But in spite of all these obvious disadvantages, on the battlefield it is probably preferable to transport machine guns on pack animals instead of wagons.

In a technical relation, there were differences in the various armies, first in the mounts, second in the manner of cooling the barrel by air, or by enclosing the barrel with a heavy waterjacket and, third, in the manner of ammunition supply either by clip of 25 rounds, or by means of belts holding up to 250 rounds. The endeavor of the manufacturers had been directed to simplify the arm (System Schwarzlose has only one spring, while the breech of the Maxim has 22 parts) and to decrease the weight so much that it would be possible to equip companies and troops with several guns carried by the men. At the opening of the World War experiments had not been completed in use of machine guns in airplanes. The question of employment of bicycles had been sufficiently cleared, for instance in Austria in 1913, the cyclist company of 4 Jäger battalions received a fourth platoon of 4 machine guns. The question of ammunition supply had not been solved; if we did not desire to adopt loading clips, as in France, we had to fall back on the time consuming loading belts with cartridges. It is absolutely necessary that the rifle and the machine gun should fire the same ammunition, and also use the same way of packing, so that the loading clips of the rifle, attached to each other may be readily used by the machine guns. The machine gun gave the opportunity of developing the strongest possible infantry fire effect on a narrow space in the shortest time, especially against upright targets. Considering the possibility of jamming, the rapid expenditure of ammunition, and the difficulties of ammunition supply the arm was considered suited in the first line only for taking advantage of short, momentary periods for flank and defensive fire but by no means for carrying on a long fire fight. The cone of dispersion, itself very narrow, either has no effect at all, or a brilliant moral and material effect. This opinion caused the machine guns to be posted in dominating or flank positions, allowed them to fire through gaps in the fighting front, or under strict limitation, to fire over the heads of the front lines. If placed

MACHINE GUN EQUIPMENT AT THE OUTBREAK OF THE WORLD WAR

	Kind	Attached to Infantry	No. of M.G. of a Division	Attached to Jager Bn.	Attached to Cav. Division
Germany	System Maxim, water-cooled and sled mount gun wagon	Each Inf. reg. one Co. of 6 guns	24	1 M.G. Co. of 6 guns	1 M.G. Det of 6 guns
Austria	System Schwarzlose 07.12, water-cooled, tripod, pack animals	3 M.G. Det. of 2 guns each, Mtn Troops 4 guns each	24	1 plat. of 2 guns	19 Cav. Regts. 1 Det. of 2 plat. of 2 guns each
France	System Puteaux-Hotchkiss, air cooled, tripod, pack animals	3 M.G. Plat. of 2 guns each for each regiment	24	1 M.G. platoon of 2 guns	Each cavalry brigade 1 plat of 2 guns
Great Britain	System Maxim, water-cooled, tripod, pack animals	M.G. Platoon of 2 guns for each Bn.	24	------	Cav. Reg. of 3 sqns., 1 plat. of 2 guns,
Italy	System Maxim, water-cooled, tripod, pack animals	Inf. Regt. 1 platoon of 2 guns	8	------	Cav. Div. 24 guns Cav. Regt. 1 platoon of 2 guns
Russia	System Maxim, water-cooled, tripod, pack wheeled mount	Each Inf. Regt. M.G. Commando of 4 plats., of 2 guns	32	------	Each cavalry Div. 1 M.G. Det. of 8 guns

in the front lines, machine guns required a protective shield to enable them to await the proper time for going into action, but the size and shape of the shield soon drew the hostile artillery fire. Test showed that even on the level ground at a range of 1500 meters, with 100-meter dispersion in depth, it was practicable to fire over our advancing infantry. In firing over the infantry we must remember that in continuous fire dispersion increases and finally, when the barrel gets hot, the bullets no longer maintain the same trajectory. It was an acute disadvantage that the various positions of the machine guns naturally attracted the hostile artillery fire and that information between infantry and machine guns was always difficult. All these conditions were materially simplified when the machine guns were placed in the firing line. In mobile warfare the German machine gun companies adhered to the general rule to "support the infantry fight directly" with all means at hand, and they abandoned the maxim that the arm "is not enabled to carry on a protracted fire fight." They were crowded prematurely into the firing line, where the heavy weight of the sleds was very troublesome when the mission was to keep up with the advancing infantry. Regulations requiring them to keep in place during the assault until the hostile position had been taken was felt to be onerous, the more so as reverses were attributed to their belated arrival.

In France the light mount was fully utilized for the employment of the gun from effective points, for instance, from trees and houses. French tactics did not advocate their use in the firing line, and favored employing the guns as a "nerveless firearm" for defense at close range. Objection to air cooling was emphasized on the ground that the barrel became red hot after only a few hundred rounds, making handling and transportation more difficult; that heat waves rose above the barrel and prevented aiming, and that the dispersion increased continually. We have not heard of any cases where the cartridges exploded of themselves; to prevent that orders were issued that no more than 200 rounds should be fired per minute. The British machine guns proved especially serviceable in all respects and frequently fired over the heads of the troops. In Russia also it appears that the machine guns were in the beginning looked on as a defensive arm at short range;

they found little employment in the offensive, while the regulations in defense were that positions could be held by machine guns alone. However the idea of using them in separated "nests" soon arose.

In position warfare the machine gun soon gained special value as a flanking arm for the purpose of defeating an assault. As it is difficult to hide them in a frontal fight from sight and fire, and as this fact was realized there grew up masked, bullet-proof shelters in checkerboard formation, where machine guns were concealed prepared to fire only when necessity demanded. During the attacks on a large scale by the Allies in 1915, placing the machine guns in well constructed positions in the front line, even in concrete positions, did not prove of advantage, as the guns generally were put out of the fight by heavy artillery drum fire even before the attack actually started. From shelter in deep chambers below the ground the guns could not be rapidly brought into the firing position in time to be of assistance considering the short distance the attack had to cover. After the Autumn battles in the Champagne, the conclusion was reached that machine guns had best not be placed in well constructed positions in the front line — except a few guns designated for flank fire — but should be placed in inconspicuous positions in rear of the front line. The unexpected opening of fire of a single machine gun under efficient leadership, even if served by only a few cool men, has several times been the decisive factor in victory and defeat. Good training must overcome malfunctioning of the gun. No matter how excited the man may be, the constant readiness for fire depends on his training. He should be able to repair stoppages in about 20 seconds as these are annoying and hard to perceive. Only continual practice and training can insure that the men quickly perceive the cause of the trouble and rapidly repair it.

The importance of the machine guns in battle was properly estimated by friend and foe in position warfare. In Germany single machine gun platoons of 3 guns each were organized as early as 1914, and soon combined into companies. In 1915 each infantry regiment received a second, in September 1916, a third machine gun company. Machine gun sharpshooter battalions, used by army headquarters at the most important battle fronts, formed a material reinforcement of the fighting power; they were posted from 1 to 3 kilometers from the front line and principally undertook the protection of the artillery. In the Spring of 1917 the number of guns of a company was increased from 6 to 9 and later to 12; but for mobile warfare, companies of 6 guns proved better.

In France, in 1916, considering the difficulties of bringing up supplies, battalions of 3 infantry companies and 1 machine gun company of 8 guns were formed. In addition each company received a reinforcement of 8 automatic rifles.

In England the machine guns, first attached to the battalions, had been organized into a brigade machine gun company of 16 guns. In its place the battalions received 8 to 12 automatic rifles. The Lewis type gun weighing 12.5 kg. drum magazine, air-cooled, fire rapidity 300 rounds per minute, being materially lighter could accompany the troops on any kind of terrain. A mobile reserve was formed by the machine gun batteries transported on motorcycles. In the battle of the Somme the Allies attempted to gain the decision by an enormous use of material. A new method was the liberal use of the automatic rifles by the Allies. These accompanied the front waves of the attacking troops and offered them a rallying point in counter-attacks. We could have done the same in Germany, had we been willing to do without the sled and utilize the sandbag mount. Numerous automatic rifles were an absolute necessity. Issue of these was delayed for a long time, so that the troops in many cases used the ones that had been captured. At first 2 "Bergmann" guns (model 08.15) were issued to each company, these were gradually increased to 6 per company in the fighting line. The weight was about 15 kg. A disadvantage was that it was impossible to fire over high grain or grass fields. We must not forget that the automatic rifle can perform good service only at ranges from 600 to 800 meters, provided the troops are well drilled in handling the piece, and that the arm is not suited for firing over the heads of our infantry. Firing while in motion may be of advantage.

The infantry found it very annoying in the Battle of the Somme to be exposed to the machine gun fire of the low flying hostile airplanes, against which they were helpless at the beginning. The actual effect was not very material, but the infantry exaggerated it at first and erroneously assumed that each airplane was able to get

Machine Guns 181

its artillery to immediately open fire on any desired target, and that the pilot could observe any movement on the ground even that of an individual. They soon learned their fears were groundless and that they could, with machine guns, fight these airplanes successfully. It was especially beneficial that infantry officers by making trips in the airplane could personally convince themselves that the observer could by no means see everything, much less hit everything. In any case, the danger of attracting the artillery fire was less than giving the hostile airplane the opportunity to carry on its business undisturbed. During the Winter of 1916-17 the airplane defense was materially improved by constructing anti-aircraft mounts and by the construction of a circular front sight for the rifle, which in a very simple manner, indicated the range at the arrival and departure of the airplane from view (arranged for 800 meters range and 150 kilometers per hour airplane velocity). Machine gun fire is especially annoying to airplanes. They cannot evade it. A firing machine gun can be perceived only at a low altitude, and can be heard only at 400 meters, with the airplane motor cut off. The activity of the hostile airplanes forced us to equip batteries and columns with 2 machine guns each; these guns were also for use at short range fighting. The rule for airplane protection is that up to the commencement of the infantry battle proper anti-aircraft machine guns fire on every airplane within range, while the remainder take cover in order not to betray themselves. At the commencement of the infantry fight the number of hostile airplanes will increase, so when each machine gun, not employed against the hostile infantry attack, must take part in the anti-aircraft defense.

According to battle experiences the effectiveness of machine guns in the first line was a failure as the available shelters were unable to withstand the heavy artillery bombardment. Far better service was performed by the machine guns when dispersed in the intermediate terrain, protected by weak infantry; these guns found protection in shell-holes or behind the remnants of destroyed trenches where they could best be hidden from the airplanes. Thus they evaded the systematic artillery fire and had to be destroyed singly by the guns accompanying the infantry of the attackers.

For fighting detached German machine guns the British

Regulations laid down (April 17, 1917): "Cautious advance under protection of covering detachments which locate machine gun nests and call for artillery fire against them. Our own machine guns are to cover the advance of the light mortars and infantry. It will be found advisable frequently to attract the attention of the German machine guns by opening fire with a Lewis gun in a certain direction. Attack from the flanks, especially with rifle and smoke shells usually leads to the desired result."

The employment of machine guns in embrasures required thorough practice in firing over the infantry in the front trenches and then gradually lifting the fire over troops advancing to the attack in depth formation. In peace time the machine gun firing regulations had made this procedure dependent on a number of limitations, but in the face of the enemy we had to proceed with fewer restrictions. Under the conditions of the position warfare, firing over the heads of our infantry could become a very important factor in attack operations. New barrels, that had not yet fired 5000 rounds, must be used and water must be replenished after every 500 rounds. Very close connection with the troops to be fired over has to be maintained, and the wishes of the troops must be rapidly transmitted. Bullets that strike twigs, grass, etc., will be easily deflected and endanger our own men.

Employment of reserve machine guns leads quite naturally to the employment of indirect fire. Machine gunners at first satisfied themselves with the simple means of "hidden rifle fire," with the range ascertained by trial shots, from a position out of view of the enemy. Technique of machine gun fire soon improved; instead of aiming on targets hard to distinguish, we employed auxiliary targets that could easily be seen, thereby simplifying fire control and increasing the effect. As the gun itself was hidden, it was not exposed to the hostile artillery fire.

In the defense it may be advisable to conduct the fight with machine guns with small infantry protection, and to hold the infantry companies back for counter-attacks. "First let machines produce effect, and only then men." If we expected in the defense, heavy hostile artillery preparatory fire, we would decline the defense of lines, and form the machine guns in depth. The battles of 1917 showed the necessity of separating tasks for automatic rifles and machine guns. For the battle in the firing line the automatic rifles were employed as well as for fighting in the intermediate terrain; the machine guns were for firing over the attacking waves against reserves. Depth formation of machine guns is best arranged by machine gun nests, surrounded by obstacles, with infantry guard under specially selected leaders, and in close connection with observation and command stations of the artillery. Distributed generally by platoons, in checkerboard formation, they offer the possibility of keeping the front position and every point in the intermediate terrain under fire. As fire comes from two or more directions the enemy cannot immediately locate it. Special attention must be given points which our artillery cannot reach. Flanking fire was employed as much as possible. When these detached machine guns should open fire the commander alone can decide. Not every attack is planned for a penetration; in many instances reconnaissance attacks on a broad front are undertaken prior to the attack proper in order to draw the fire of the machine guns. The effectiveness of the machine guns depends on remaining unobserved until the main assault. The machine gun nests formed the natural rallying points for the defender and facilitated counter-attacks with their fire. But their participation was effective only if they did not betray themselves on the aerial photographs; attention was attracted to them especially by their obstacles and through tracks left by the daily movements. They are best assumed to be in the proximity of trenches, ditches, and shelters, in single clumps of woods, projecting angles of villages, etc. The more inconspicuous the position, the longer life will the machine gun have. Surprised from all sides by machine gun fire, even well prepared attacks make progress with difficulty after the primary success. In many cases it was found the attacker turned about or threw himself down, and was finally overcome by the counter-attack. The first dangerous enemy to the machine gun was the tank. All machine guns have their definite tasks (barrage, defense of the zone in depth, support of their neighbor, protection of the artillery), which they must solve from several prepared positions.

Machine guns drawn back are by no means to be used for the purpose of serving as replacement for guns disabled in the front line. These latter must be replaced from a reserve held out by the commander from the beginning. We allowed for each machine gun about 3000 cartridges in belts and 2 water jackets; a liberal supply of spare parts and grease, in expectation of a gas attack, decreased the danger of jams. It is very advisable to construct a shelter for the belt filling squad in a position in rear.

The fire of the attacker compels the defender to seek cover so that the latter no longer offers a target for infantry fire. It is therefore well to work up as close as possible to the enemy under the protection of artillery and machine gun fire. Machine guns sweeping across the cover of the defender, keeps him below ground.

According to "Training Regulations for Foot Troops" the automatic rifles were distributed to platoons and bore the brunt of the fire fight. They wore down the enemy. If that was accomplished then, and then only our costly infantry materiel was to be employed for a rapid advance. It was very favorable if the first firing position of the infantry was so close to the enemy that from it the assault could be delivered.

In the offensive battle a certain depth formation cannot be avoided; when the automatic rifles had tasks under 500 meters range, the rifles, model '08, had targets beyond that range. The difficulty in reaching favorable firing positions in open terrain forced the machine guns to be employed at extreme ranges. In many cases nothing remained but to put the guns in action early and let them go forward with the skirmish lines. If a gun was once inserted in the skirmish line, it suffered in changing position in the advance by rushes. If the infantry delayed the rush, for the slower machine guns, favorable moments were lost. In many cases infantry frequently missed the supporting fire of the machine guns at the moment of the rush, and the guns reached the new firing position later than the skirmishers and thus betrayed themselves.

An attack method may consist in the infantry working up, under the fire protection of machine guns, together with automatic rifles to a short distance from the enemy, the latter facilitating that working up from advanced "attack nests."

Frequently from elevated positions in conjunction with the artillery, machine guns facilitate the deployment of the troops, the advance to the first fire position, or the assault. Time for coordination and timely reconnaissance of the next firing positions are necessary. It may be well to send ahead supplies, water jackets and ammunition even during the fire fight. A portion of the guns may be designated antiaircraft defense. In the attack from trench to trench machine guns take over the preparatory fire as soon as the artillery and minenwerfers lift their fire farther to the front. They remain in action as long as possible without endangering their infantry moving forward to the assault. Direct fire is the general rule; indirect fire may be employed against terrain in rear of the enemy. As soon as practicable the machine gun companies follow in platoon echelons and assist with the fire protection of the infantry. From elevated positions, they break up counter-attacks and assist neighboring sectors by rapid flanking fire. "The final purpose of the machine guns remains always the same: To assist the relentless pushing forward of our infantry by the shock power of their fire."

In open warfare the fire of the machine guns assists the infantry, together with the automatic rifles, in reaching the first firing position. "Machine gun squads of 1 gun with 8 men, a very mobile fire power, form the skeleton of the infantry attack." Liaison between squads is necessary for mutual co-operation and increase of fire power. In the attack from trench to trench, automatic rifles are sent ahead during the artillery preparatory fire as "attack nests." At the cessation of the artillery fire, or when that fire lifts, they take over the fire fight and cease only when the first waves of infantry overrun the enemy. There are also automatic rifles in the first wave which fire at short range during the advance. If guns in the leading waves are disabled, they are replaced from the rear.

The advance of infantry under fire protection demands much initiative on the part of all subordinate machine gun commanders. They must understand how to concentrate fire against points where the enemy still offers resistance, and after the successful assault to take over the fire protection of the troops that are reestablishing the position.

In the advance the skirmish squads are in groups or in single file; the gaps resulting can be used to fire through by machine guns in rear. Automatic rifles go with their skirmish squads. The line

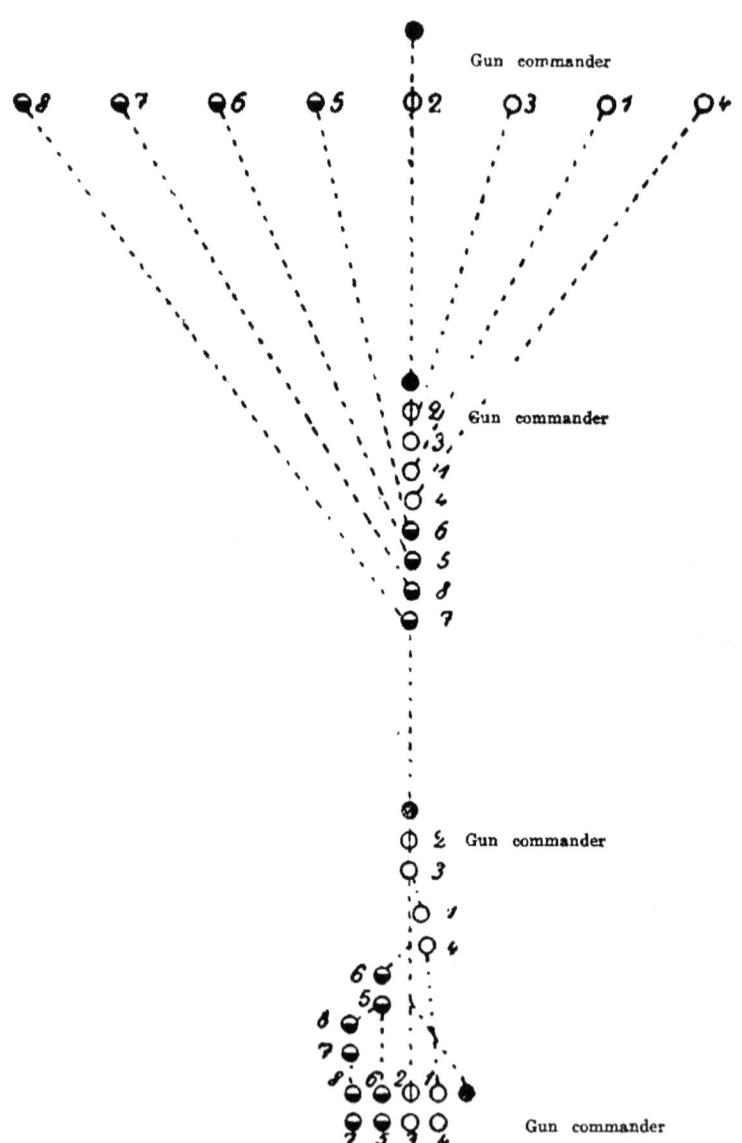

upon which the general fire fight is to be taken up can seldom be designated in advance; if it is known, the machine guns kept back must work up to it.

An important element for success is that the machine guns succeed in reaching the firing position unperceived; machine guns that have been seen are easily annihilated by an alert enemy. In the fire fight the automatic rifles will fire short bursts, say 5 to 10 rounds, and save the duration fire for specially favorable moments. For the assault the fire on the move gains special importance, although the actual effect of this fire was below expectations.

At the time of the large offensive in March, 1918, equipment of divisions in machine guns, were as follows:

> Germany: 9 battalions to the division with 9 machine gun companies of 6 guns (12 guns) a total of 54 (108) machine guns and 144 automatic rifles.
> France: 9 battalions to the division, with 9 machine gun companies of 8 (12) guns, a total of 72 (108) machine guns and 216 automatic rifles, 8 (12) per company.
> Great Britain: 12 battalions to the division; 3 Brigade machine gun companies of 16 guns — 48 and 1 division machine gun company with 16 guns a total of 64 machine guns and 192 automatic rifles, 4 per company,
> Italy: 12 battalions to the division. Each battalion had 1 machine gun company of 6 guns, a total of 72 machine guns (additions had been arranged for), each battalion 1 to 2 platoons, 24 to 48 automatic rifles.
> United States: 3 battalions to the division. Each regiment of infantry, 1 machine gun company of 12 guns; each brigade 1 battalion of 4 machine gun companies and the division, 1 battalion of 2 motorized machine gun companies with 12 guns each. This makes a total of 168 machine guns and 768 automatic rifles. 16 automatic rifles in each company.

Chapter IX – The Infantry Attack in Open Warfare

Requirements

Fighting methods are governed by the technical progress of arms and armament and their resulting moral effect on the troops. Both have to be considered in training troops and in the conduct of battle, if we want to be equal to the demands of war and safeguard ourselves against disappointments. France underestimated the effect of the German infantry and machine gun fire, while we were surprised by the effect of the French field artillery. At the opening of the World War the effect of the flat-trajectory fire of all arms had been increased to its fullest extent, but the development of high-angle fire had been neglected. Only Germany and England had sufficient high-angle fire artillery, while gas projectiles were unknown. At the conclusion of the World War we see the demand that infantry and artillery must be equipped for high-angle and flat-trajectory fire, to force the enemy into his shelters and still reach him at short range.

The French infantry was the first to realize the possibilities of short range, high-angle fire; in 1915 it introduced the automatic rifle and the rifle grenade, but confined the equipment with hand grenades to but a few individuals, while we equipped all our men with both hand and rifle grenades. Since the Franco-Prussian War the number of batteries of an infantry division has at least trebled and the other arms have materially increased, it is clear that the influence of firearms on the fighting of infantry is, at the present time, far different than was the case in the campaign against France in 1870-71. This appeared most plainly during attacks in position warfare. Divisions had more artillery at their disposal than in mobile warfare and the question was not one of covering with fire a wide front, but only of a narrow sector with the fire lifted from trench to trench. When the infantry attacks in mobile warfare, its road is opened by artillery and machine guns which force the enemy to take cover. The result is the attacking infantry sees no target. Prior to the war, this matter had been carefully considered in France; there appeared doubt that fire superiority could be attained as French artillery had no high-angle guns, and the hostile infantry, in trenches, could not of course be reached by rifle and shrapnel. On the other hand it was believed that their field artillery could overcome any halt forced on the troops by hostile fire. It was held that the infantry would not fire except when absolutely necessary; it was to advance under the protection of its artillery without firing a shot, keep on the move and close with the enemy. In Germany, the infantry was cautioned to never wait for our own fire superiority, which as had been learned no one could perceive. The infantry should far rather compel the enemy, by its advance, to occupy his position thereby offering shrapnel targets to our artillery. This did not happen at all times, however, as the main role in defense was not left to the infantry but to the artillery. The attacking artillery must finally lift its fire from the defender so as not to endanger its own advancing infantry. In Germany we attached special importance to "carrying forward the fire to the enemy," in case of need to the closest possible range. Thereby sanguinary hand-to-hand fights resulted before a final decision, in which the German infantry finally gathered the fruits of its thorough training on the rifle range, though under heavy losses. On the other hand, it suffered out of all proportion, if it attempted to gain the assault position without waiting for fire preparation.

The Russian infantry gained the same experiences in the

Russo-Japanese War. The bayonet training preached by Dragomiroff had its roots in the belief of the moral influence of the bayonet, as well as in the knowledge of the poor marksmanship of the troops; thus it came about that (with the intention of getting up to the enemy as rapidly as possible) the infantry pushed forward without proper fire preparation. Fire success attained by infantry and artillery, are due to better target practice, fire control, fire discipline, better cover, and the concentration of a larger number of projectiles on the decisive point. Thus, the enemy's resistance is finally overcome, he no longer dares to raise his head above ground, even if the fire temporarily abates, and our movements are no longer interrupted by fire. With the defender, individual men attempt to escape, followed by entire squads, while with the attacker, active groups encouraged by small losses, attempt by quick rushes to get ahead. We then speak of the fire superiority of the attacker.

The attacker should always feel out the fire superiority when he attempts to advance, and ascertain if the enemy is able to prevent his advance by its fire. Fire superiority can generally be gained only through a costly fire fight lasting for hours. Machine guns hurl, with less guns and less men, the same number of bullets upon the enemy in shorter time and with greater accuracy, while the number of casualties decrease due to fewer men in the firing line. Thus, we can replace the infantry fire at the shortest ranges by automatic rifles, and at mid and long ranges by machine guns. For instance, one infantry regiment could insert on a 1,000-meter front 20 automatic rifles and 18 machine guns throwing about 10,000 projectiles per minute. The main fire power of the infantry platoon lies in the automatic rifle, its shock power in the skirmish squads. The endeavor to preserve the power of the skirmish squads as long as possible for the decisive shock, leads to the fire fight being conducted principally by automatic rifles and machine guns. As a general rule we must gain a point as close to the enemy as possible before opening fire. We must demand of well trained troops that they open fire only when special effect can be secured from use of rifle and machine gun. This will be the case in open terrain at ranges less than 1,000 meters. Our new tactics for the attack seeks rapid decision, with a minimum use of shock-tactics. It seeks to

The Infantry Attack in Open Warfare

save men. Maximum use of machines at the start before throwing into the battle the very costly human element, so hard to replace, is the rule. But the decision proper, as always, lies in the hands of the infantry, whose physical endurance and moral power must be increased to the highest possible point by all available means. This battle method has been proved correct. It demands thorough training in the co-operation of all arms.

Besides our own fire effect utilization of the terrain has a special importance in working up to the enemy. Battle reconnaissance must ascertain the difficulties of deployment from any cover in the terrain. Utilization of cover presupposes flexibility of the skirmish line, both at a halt and moving-forward. The whole idea is wrong if the demand is made to cover the entire terrain equally with skirmishers under any and all conditions.

Procedure of Attack

Our training regulations distinguish between rencontre attacks, against an enemy deployed for defense, and against a fortified position. We shall hereafter adhere to these distinctions. Air reconnaissance may be able to procure information as to what degree the defender has made preparation for defense. We may always be sure that trenches, and false works, have been established in a greater or lesser degree of completeness. The construction of extensive obstacles and the presence of numerous sheltering works (which it takes weeks to construct) made a "fortified position," the capture of which demands reinforcement and increase of artillery and technical troops. The German Army has always preferred the attack knowing that by the attack alone can a victory be won. Even situations which strategically force defense upon the troops can be solved tactically, in many cases, better by attack than by defense. The decision whether the commander shall attack or defend does not, as is the case so frequently in peace maneuvers, lie in the relation of strength of the two forces. We hardly ever know at the moment of having to make a decision, anything but the general situation and the mission. The enemy is in the same uncertainty as we. A sharp quick attack may convince him that we are stronger. Frederick the Great cautioned his troops, which in almost all instances had to fight against superior numbers: "*Attaquez donc toujours.*"*

Troops trained in the will to attack will always be able to attack. Not the number of rifles is necessary for the success, but the fighting power gained in training, the equipment, the skill of leaders and troops, the co-operation of the arms, the utilization of the terrain, and rapidity and decision in the fight. Attacks, without fire support, are useful only in surprise situations or occasionally at night. The normal method consists in combining fire and movement. It is the task of regulations to point out the correct relation between fire tactics and shock tactics. Infantry regulations state: "The best means for working up to the enemy is by securing fire superiority," which is made known by the decrease of the hostile fire or the enemy's bullets flying high and wild. Field Training Regulations presents another viewpoint based on experiences in war. "Rifles and machine guns bear the brunt of the fire fight; the decision is brought about by the shock power of the infantry," and "Opening and carrying on the fire fight will generally be left to machine guns; they must make the enemy take cover, and then only will our infantry appear in the intrepid attack." First, the effect of machines, then insert men.

Par. 324, I. D. R.: "The attack consists in carrying forward the fire." It is demanded of well trained troops that they open fire, even in terrain devoid of cover, only at mid range (800 to 1200 meters). Today, when all means of fire have been improved and augmented, we must demand more. The infantry must work up without firing a shot so close to the enemy that the fire will be opened as late as possible — in any case less than 1,000 meters. The time to open fire is when the troops can work forward under the hostile fire only with great loss. The front of a division sector will hardly ever be less than 2 kilometers, which will, of course, not be covered equally by skirmishers. Infantrymen may be replaced without loss of fire power by machines (guns, machine guns), etc. An attack that is to be carried deep into the enemy requires formation in

---

* "Always attack."

The Infantry Attack in Open Warfare   193

depth. This cannot be secured if the front is too wide. If too wide nothing remains but to make a portion of the division sector strong, place the center of gravity there and penetrate deep into the enemy, while other portions of the sector have to be satisfied with near objectives. The enemy which was threatened only, and not directly attacked, will later on fall upon the flanks of the penetrating attack.

Near Reconnaissance

Troops approach in march column the effective zone of the hostile fire, and without having to face long range batteries, we must count on the route being fired upon when within 10 kilometers of the front. This requires the forming of the march column into separate elements, "Deployment." In view of the modern long range guns it may easily happen that the enemy's projectiles will arrive sooner than the first reports of the reconnoitering units; thus, the infantry will have to feel its way after it reaches the fighting zone. In no case must troops enter the hostile zone of fire in close order.

All arms participate in battle reconnaissance. As shown by experience, after the first reports have been received concerning the enemy, there will be for a time a lack of information which may be explained by the cavalry giving way towards a wing in the face of the enemy, and by the other arms pushing out reconnoitering parties. We must also not forget that a column marching along a road is more easily distinguished than troops advancing deployed. While patrols can overlook entire hostile columns advancing along roads, they are when observing deployed troops confined to only small portions, and this observation will be made more difficult by the opponent's cavalry which after deployment, can protect his flanks more thoroughly than was possible with the long march column. Should the patrols nevertheless succeed in getting through the opponent's cavalry to their infantry they will in most cases only be able to make a hasty long range reconnaissance as they will now be afraid of the hostile infantry and of being discovered in a precarious situation. What happens between the wings of the opponent they can neither see nor report. Natural cover will increase the difficulties of view. Observation of the immediate front can of course furnish local information only. Patrols may ride far enough to the front to be fired on, and report that fire, but what hostile troops fired and the exact direction from which the fire came they will, in most cases, be unable to correctly ascertain, as the troops firing are hidden and the smokeless powder conceals the direction from which the shots came.

There must be no interruption in the reconnaissance, and it must be carried on with great care: not however, to excess so that it may delay the battle action, and thus render questionable the final success. Only cavalry can determine the position of the enemy along extensive lines, ascertain extension of wings, location and movement of reserves, and approach of probable reinforcements. This while important lacks the details so necessary for the conduct of the infantry battle. Details of the hostile position can be gained only if the enemy is careless or unskillful; false and advanced positions can be discovered only during the course of the battle. Terrain reconnaissance will include the following points: Up to what point may the troops move under cover and in what formation? Where does the terrain allow cover for portions of the troops only? Where will be the first firing position and what is its nature? Where are the supporting points for the attack located? Where are dead angles in front of the line to be attacked? What are the difficulties to be encountered in passing over the field of battle?

A simple sketch showing the above points will help the leader to think himself into the situation. Concerning the actual view of the hostile position a good sketch will be valuable. Airplanes will generally have much other work to do to meet the requirements of the high command. Artillery patrols, usually sent out only when definite reports have been received of the presence or advance of the enemy, must ascertain what is necessary to know for the artillery. Strength, deployment and location of the hostile artillery, as was demanded at the opening of the war, they will be able to ascertain only in exceptional cases. This had best be left to aerial reconnaissance. Location of hostile observation positions is especially valuable. It is not correct to charge artillery patrols with reconnoitering roads and firing positions; these patrols must not allow themselves to be diverted into such general reconnoitering tasks, or to help other arms. On the other hand, artillery patrols must establish connection with the reconnoitering units of the other arms and exchange information with them.

The infantry must be called on in good time for near reconnaissance, as well as for the usual battle reconnaissance. The main difficulty for the infantry lies in the fact that their cyclists are bound to the roads, that the mounted officers must be temporarily withdrawn from their proper duties, and that there is a lack of men to accompany the officer's patrols to send back messages. But this should not preclude (it must even be demanded) that officers ride to points permitting a good view and observe through field glasses. But if they personally ride back to report, the reconnaissance is interrupted, a great disadvantage. Infantry patrols move slowly and send in their reports more slowly which, before reaching the desired point, may have been overtaken by events. But, on the other hand, with correct use of cover they can get very close to the enemy unobserved. At the same time they possess a certain fighting power especially when machine guns are attached.

Near reconnaissance at the present time is of more importance than ever before. Changes of front with deployed lines is impossible and troops coming under hostile fire in close order, suffer losses amounting almost to annihilation. The reconnaissance becomes more difficult as we have to reckon with the enemy's covering forces and we may be sure he will not voluntarily permit us to get a view from high points. Weak infantry can neither break the hostile covering forces nor force them back sufficiently for the leader to reconnoiter personally. In many cases strong forces will be required. From these reconnaissance patrols we come to the reconnaissances in force. Unless we threaten an attack, the defender will not uncover his positions. Reconnaissances in force must be resorted to, because we can immediately make use of its results.

Infantry reconnaissance must be carried on with great care, proper arrangements must be made during the march, distribution of tasks, and plans for sending messages back must be thought out. If we for instance send infantry patrols with automatic rifles along the march route and along neighboring roads as soon as the first cavalry reports of the enemy are received, these patrols will offer a certain stability to our cavalry patrols, while they increase the enemy's difficulties of reconnaissance. The leader had best reconnoiter personally and not rely entirely on the tactical knowledge of his subordinates. He must, under infantry protection, see for himself and then he can the better use his troops. Sending out company commanders for reconnaissance which is much done in peace maneuvers, should be avoided. Exaggerated thoroughness, especially on short winter days, may delay the reconnaissance so much that the success of the attack will become questionable. It would be entirely wrong and our attacking power would be weakened if we delayed the decision for the attack until we have full knowledge concerning the enemy's strength and grouping. Clearness in this regard can be attained only after the battle. The general situation in the first line decides the question of attack. The situation may force immediate action without awaiting the results of the reconnaissance. Conditions of the terrain and degree of known preparations of the enemy will govern the leader in deciding whether to attack at once, to await darkness to bring up the troops, or to maneuver the opponent out of his position.

Deployment and Development

The near reconnaissance is supplemented by systematic observation. From favorable observation points, by means of good field glasses, the distribution of the enemy and his routes of approach can often be observed. The results of such observations are collected first at the regiments and form the basis for battle orders.

Within the division regiments receive a battle sector of from 600 to 1000 meters. The regimental commander equally divides his sector into battalion sectors of about 300 to 500 meters. Each battalion receives with its battle sector its fighting mission. Regimental orders cover, connection with the artillery, arrangement of means of information, orders for the combat train, and for the regimental aid station.

Generally the battalion will assign 2 companies for the front line, each on a 200 meters front, the other 2 follow in the second

The Infantry Attack in Open Warfare 197

line. The machine gun company remains, as a general rule, with the battalion, but may temporarily be employed otherwise: "As support for special tasks, flank protection, independent support of the firing line from dominating positions, etc."

In addition the regiment disposes of its minenwerfer company and its information detachment. The liberal supply of means of information furnished during the World War permitted telephone connection from division headquarters to the division artillery commander, from there to the artillery battalions, and from division headquarters via brigade headquarters to the infantry regiments and from the latter to their battalions. The possibility of division headquarters conversing directly with different battalions must never lead to its interference with the detailed conduct of the same.

The *development of the attacker* must be made under the assumption that heavy artillery fire may start at any moment, and the larger his force the sooner will the enemy open fire. The utilization of the cover offered by terrain, assuming formations calculated to lessen the effect of fire, timely removal of all vehicles from the column, and their movement from cover to cover, are the best means of avoiding the hostile artillery fire. Of course, this covered approach takes time, but it saves loss. In a rencontre battle such a loss of time may be fatal, but something will have to be hazarded. In the attack against an enemy deployed for defense, time consumed has not the same importance as loss in men.

Narrow formations — (the French even reject march column of fours on the battlefield) — of little depth, irregularly dispersed over the terrain, have proved best in crossing ground swept by the hostile fire. French and British almost always divided their platoons into 4 separate squads and lessened the losses. In general we adhere to division of platoons into half-platoons. However, when the hostile fire becomes effective a further division should be made, with due consideration of loss of time and control. But if the advance is not to be completely disrupted, a line has to be designated. This line should be under cover and at close range. The class of artillery fire will in each case demand a special procedure. If the hostile artillery seeks to find the range to a unit with some short or over shorts, that unit will at once, lessen the effect of the expected fire by deploying into smaller and narrower units, dispersing over the terrain, or by rapid backward or forward movements. In many cases the enemy artillery will find the range to some point in the terrain, one task of the near reconnaissance is to locate those points and warn troops not to stop near them, but pass quickly by without offering large targets. Sweeping fire is best avoided after exact observation of the spaces that are comparatively free from the fire, and those spaces crossed in close order, the commander keeping his troops well in hand. Much depends on luck. It is far more difficult to move forward and so observe counter preparation fire; a battalion that is struck by such fire can do nothing better than to lie down and wait, fail to give the enemy any guide for regulating his fire and avoiding conspicuous appearances such as horses, standing officers, etc. Meanwhile units more favorably situated continue the forward movement. Assuming that the hostile batteries are ready for action and awaiting the appearance of favorable targets, we must never offer large targets but attempt to gain ground by squads or individuals. Detours are frequently correct. While in the next cover the troops are reassembled and an attempt made to continue the movement. By paying due regard to these experiences we have been able to pass through heavy artillery fire without material losses.

Artillery of the Attack

Simultaneously with the infantry advance the attacking artillery from covered positions fire at a range of about 3000 to 4000 meters. Its fire no longer comes from long, inflexible lines, which make the firing comparatively easy, but from groups, hugging the conformation of the ground which can be located by airplanes only. This echelonment of guns has an advantage for infantry and artillery in that infantry no longer crosses the line of its artillery support at one time. A consequence of the old method of lines of batteries was that the defender succeeded in a very short time in ascertaining the position of the hostile artillery, and could apply sweeping fire within relatively small zones thus effectively carrying on the artillery duel. One saw from the point where noise of cannon came, that thunder suddenly cease, and at the same time skirmishers appeared working forward by rushes, or several columns with exact intervals came over the rise and the hostile artillery again resumed the fire.

Even though valuable time may be lost and another unit's battle zone temporarily invaded it is better to go round than to cross a fire swept zone.

A portion of the artillery will hold down the hostile artillery, while as many guns as possible direct their fire on the hostile infantry. The danger must never be underestimated that at long ranges there is doubt concerning the situation of the hostile position, which can be cleared up gradually only by infantry observers and the artillery liaison officers who have gone ahead with the infantry.

Defensive artillery should not reply to the guns of the attack. Its target is the hostile attacking infantry; only when that target cannot be fired on will it fire on the hostile batteries.

Whether the attacking artillery succeed in holding down the defender's artillery depends on how exactly the batteries of the defender have been located. The outcome of the artillery duel is doubtful, but it is absolutely necessary for the success of the battle. Thus, the underlying teachings of earlier regulations to seek with all means at hand to gain the fire superiority, before starting the infantry to the attack could not be discarded. Even if the artillery duel has not been absolutely decided in our favor, the infantry must not decline the execution of the attack as an impossibility.

How many batteries of the attacker may fire on the defensive artillery depends upon the effect of the latter. K the defender's artillery can materially increase the difficulties of advance for the attacker, then he must place a portion of his guns, which have heretofore fired on the enemy's infantry, against the artillery; the task of such guns may be then taken over by machine guns. It cannot be avoided at times that a portion of the defensive artillery is not fired on and can direct its fire on the advancing skirmishers.

Working Up to the Enemy

We must lay down the following maxims for the attack:

    1. The attacking infantry advances under the protection of its artillery and machine gun fire as close to the enemy as the hostile fire permits; it would be simpler if the assault could be taken up from the first halt, as was laid down in Troop Training, but which was found to be not always feasible.

    2. The defensive artillery attempts to drive off the skirmishers of the attack; the attacking artillery fires on the defensive artillery only with as many guns as is necessary to hold down effectively the latter's fire.

    3. Attacking artillery will finally be forced to enter into a time and ammunition consuming artillery duel (to relieve the attacking infantry from the defender's artillery fire) and the attacking infantry will be forced into an infantry fire fight.

The main fire power of the infantry platoon lies in the light minenwerfers. We have thoroughly proven during the war that the machine gun is an excellent arm of opportunity but not suited for a long continued fire fight. The increase of machine guns in all armies, has made movements in long, regular, dense skirmish lines impossible; thereby finally and definitely answering the question whether it is correct to make long and broad or short and narrow rushes. The former are far too costly under machine gun fire, not even considering the fact that a platoon in a thin skirmish line cannot be controlled any longer by its commander. It is different in situations where we are not directly under machine gun fire, for if the troops can get rapidly forward, long and broad rushes are in order. Short rushes by no means shorten the time during which troops are visible; they only increase the enemy's difficulties in directing a well aimed fire on the skirmishers. Under protection of our own effective fire we can make each rush long, provided we do not prefer to advance at the walk. For training reasons we will generally adhere to long rushes with great breadth; they are executed as soon as the effect of the fire permits.

We, as well as our enemies, saw ourselves in the World War forced to make our skirmish lines thinner and thinner. The 176th

Infantry Regiment adopted the interval between skirmishers at two meters, while, based on experiences of the Boer War, the British adopted in the fire deployment an interval ranging between 5 and 15 meters, which shortly before the assault could be diminished to 0.90 meters. In Russia, based on the experiences of the Russo-Japanese War, it was thought that one rifle to every 4 meters (2.5 to 3 meters interval) was sufficient. Training Regulations required an interval of 6 paces, which could be diminished according to need to one pace. France permanently favored the formation of dense skirmish lines.

The more the intervals were enlarged, the more difficult became control, as the individual skirmishers were left more to themselves. But even the thin skirmish lines were exposed to heavy loss when under machine gun fire, and the machine gun carriers in the skirmish lines could be easily distinguished. It was therefore found advisable to make the lines irregular especially shortly before the opening of fire. Advance by squads in single file with intervals or by skirmish squads with little intervals, but with gaps between them and neighboring squads, offer many advantages. The squad leader can make his influence felt on his men from the time fire is opened. Gaps between squads permits machine guns to fire through them, disruption of squads in joining the line is avoided, and the squad leader fights with the men whom he has trained for battle. Small, irregular targets permit the infantry to get forward without material loss.

We should not demand regular formations within the platoon: One portion is more favored, the other less. The formation must be such that it will not unnecessarily increase the losses if hostile fire is suddenly encountered. To take up the desired formation only at that moment is entirely too late and will lead to annihilation. In terrain where a good view cannot be had, scouts must be sent ahead, and even in open terrain it will often be advantageous for the platoon commander to go far to the front with a few acouts. The advance is made at the walk as long as practicable, with the firm will to open fire as late as possible. If broad stretches, without cover, have to be crossed the hostile fire effect may compel formation into the smallest units (squads), which gain ground either by thin skirmish lines following each other in waves, or

EXAMPLE OF THE FORMATION OF ONE COMPANY AT OPENING OF THE FIRE

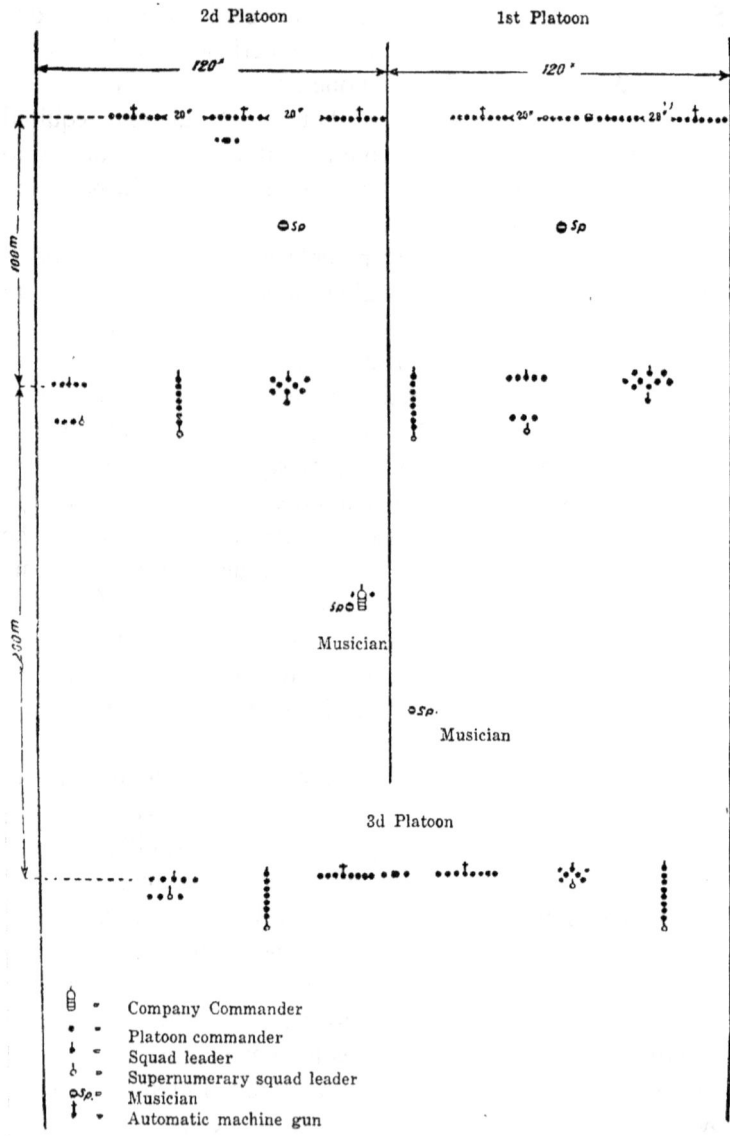

(1) The interval may be materially larger or smaller.

The Infantry Attack in Open Warfare 203

single file formation abreast with large intervals. This formation must however not interfere with combined leadership. In addition, direction of attack and guide must be definitely laid down by the platoon commander and strictly adhered to by all units. Formation and method of movement are left to the discretion of the squad leaders. Only effective hostile fire must induce the individual soldier to work forward from cover to cover. The troops do not like to crawl for longer stretches and the expenditure of energy is not commensurate with the lessening of losses, as the crawling skirmisher offers a larger target than the man lying down. To cover by crawling 100 meters in favorable terrain will take 2½ minutes, and in addition, it is difficult to preserve order and cohesion and to keep to the general march direction. Entirely different is the occasional use of crawling, for instance, in entering a position. The advance will be aided if we succeed in getting a portion of the machine guns into favorable, inconspicuous firing positions, "attack nests" from which they facilitate the advance at the start and then support it by firing over the heads of the troops. The infantry should never lack the support of machine guns, and nothing must be allowed to interfere with bringing the machine guns forward. It is therefore advisable to let a portion of the machine guns at the very start follow the infantry for fire support at short range and to move the other part up from position to position. Closely hugging the ground, appearing suddenly, skillfully evading the hostile artillery fire, they follow the fighting line in echelon. They also keep in mind the task of facilitating the advance of the skirmishers and automatic rifles. We must avoid, as long as possible, placing machine guns in the skirmish line. They crowd that line badly, and increase the losses and in addition, it is a great disadvantage to have to take much time to get ready for a rush. Guns must be unloaded first, and as the carriers cannot rush forward like the skirmishers; they remain behind and as a result draw the hostile fire on this most important fighting arm.

 The fire fight is conducted by the skirmish line according to well known rules. The opening of fire will be ordered by the platoon commander only when there is no other way to get forward. Target and sight elevation will be designated by the platoon commander as long as possible, but under heavy fire the control will slip from his hands and then the squad leader takes his place and finally the individual soldier. Loss of fire control does not matter very much at short range if through training the skirmisher carefully observes his fire effect, husbands his ammunition, increases his rate of fire, when the target is favorable, decreases it when the target becomes unfavorable or entirely stops firing when the target disappears. The command "fire faster," or "fire slower," only emphasizes the inattention or bad training of skirmishers.

Light minenwerfers must work their way forward in the same independent manner as machine guns. Positions should be selected within 600 meters of the hostile position, so that they can use their short range weapons effectively during the assault. Prematurely taking up a position is correct only in a reverse; support had best be left to the artillery. Their mission is annihilation of observed machine guns or guns placed in readiness to defeat the assault. It will almost always be advisable to attach them by pairs to the leading companies. When going into position and when ammunition is being brought up for them they offer large targets; therefore cover for them gains in importance.

Co-operation between infantry and artillery previously arranged for is put to the test on the demand of the infantry when entering battle. Machine guns seen by the infantry are best and more quickly annihilated by artillery, but it will not be easy to designate the target to the artillery in rear. If the advance of the infantry is delayed or prevented by hostile fire, it can be resumed best by waves. The infantry must be trained to immediately utilize fire support of the sister arm, which means infantry must immediately advance when it sees our shells bursting on the enemy. The advance is not to be made in rushes but at a walk, when the enemy is blinded by dust, smoke or iron. The infantry has often been able to push on when single guns or artillery platoons came up close and supported its advance, paying no attention to losses. There is no reason to expect especial danger to these accompanying guns, as the opponent in defeating an assault has more important things to attend to than to bother about them. Accompanying guns should always be under the orders of the infantry commander. Artillery follows up the infantry after the capture of the position, and secure its possession. A well planned, energetic counter-attack made after the capture of the position will hardly go to pieces under artillery fire which comes from far in rear, and the observation of which by the advance troops is very difficult, especially in close country. The artillery at long range, limbering up at that very moment leaves to the infantry the entire difficulties of meeting the counter-attack. Retreating infantry finds stability only at its first guns and is enabled to make a stand there. We must not underestimate the moral effect which is made on the infantry by guns following up close on its heels.

The infantry guns either by piece or by platoon, support the troops directly at an effective range of 1200 to 1800 meters. These guns fire point blank which demands that every shot be observed; the difficulty of observation requires employment of single guns. The battery is merely the unit for supply, discipline, etc.

During the entire war the question of employing the spade in the attack was hotly discussed. During the Russo-Japanese War, the Japanese as a general rule fortified their first fire position, and resorted to the spade again in the subsequent advance. The cause is probably to be found in the fact that the Russian fire was of little account of itself, that the Japanese probably could have advanced further, but their disinclination to suffer loss caused them to advance slower. The Russians did not follow the Japanese example. In the first regulations, based on the experiences of the war, the Russians demanded intrenching in every firing position, even in the assault position, while the Japanese army was warned against the too frequent use of the spade. The German infantry never relished the use of the spade, realizing that gaining time is more advantageous to the defender than to the attacker. The difficulty of bringing a skirmish line that has just dug itself in under effective fire by hard labor, to again resume the advance is very difficult, hence caution is necessary in the use of the spade. Never must construction of cover weaken the will to attack. Troops that entrench during an attack must lay aside one-half of their rifles; even fire superiority, difficult to attain, cannot offset this loss. The man at work entrenching offers a larger target, the freshly turned ground is an easy aiming mark, and the cover obtained is insufficient. If the cover is such as to provide actual protection, much time is required, which the opponent will use to good advantage. Thus a fire superiority that has been gained with difficulty, can easily be lost. We must not forget that the steel helmet offers protection at long range against rifle fire and thus lessens losses better than earthwork. If the hostile fire is actually so powerful that there can be no thought of a further advance, it is, in any case, better for the troops to defend themselves at all hazards with their rifles, than to endeavor to intrench. On the other hand if the enemy is so shaken that the loss of half the rifles is of no moment, we do not need to remain lying, but can, in most cases, close with him. Filled sandbags will, in most instances, give better protection than hastily constructed trenches. Carrying along filled sandbags, which retard all movements may be justifiable in position warfare, when the ground is rocky, or when it is frozen hard.

The spade is used in attack only when the question is to hold captured terrain, when diminishing hostile fire permits labor and when the situation or the available fighting means do not permit an immediate continuation of the advance. Thus in former times as now, the use of the spade in an attack was a makeshift, which delayed the course of the battle in order to offset the lack of sufficient fire support. Troops that have fought successfully will decline the use of the spade, while troops, insufficiently supported by artillery, which have worked themselves up to the enemy, will employ the spade in situations in which it does not appear at all necessary. We must absolutely discountenance a general use of the spade in every attack, as the best protection against the hostile fire lies always in our own fire.

The Assault

The World War has shown clearly that the assault is by no means the spectacular performance of times gone by. Now as ever "the assault with cold steel seals the defeat of the opponent." The skirmish line is made denser, the fire of rifles and machine guns increased. Of the greatest importance is fire protection, in advancing to the charge, few orders can be issued then; much must

The Infantry Attack in Open Warfare 207

be left to the initiative of the subordinate commanders, who must be thoroughly imbued with the importance of fire protection.

Charging distance cannot be laid down by regulations; in peace time we calculated it to be 100 meters. In any case we must, with one breath and one rush, enter the hostile position. In the last Russian Regulations before the World War it was recommended that the start of the assault was the length of a bayonet — this of course was figurative only. In war it has been shown only too often that assaults started at long range broke down under the hostile fire. The shorter our charging distance, the surer the success. On the other hand, however, infantry desirous of attacking will start the charge at long distances when there are clear indications that the enemy will completely abandon resistance.

The decision for the assault either originates in the firing line with the subordinate commanders, or the commander of the attack gives the impetus by engaging his reserves. The latter without doubt is the better way. "If the decision to assault has its origin with the leader in rear, the signal 'fix bayonet' is hoisted as a sign for the assault, which must be obeyed by all troops concerned. At this signal all skirmishers increase their fire to the utmost limit; the portions of the firing line farther back work up as rapidly as possible to close distance; all reinforcements in rear hasten straight to the front. As soon as the leading line is to start the charge, all trumpeters sound 'charge,' all drummers beat the general, and all portions of the line throw themselves with the utmost decision upon the enemy. It is a matter of honor on the part of the skirmishers never to let the supports overtake them before they have reached the hostile position. Immediately in front of the enemy pieces are brought to the 'charge bayonet' and the position entered under loud shouts of 'hurrah!'" Thus it read in the old Regulations. In the future also we shall not be able to do without "fix bayonets."

It is very difficult for the commander of the attack to determine the correct time for starting the assault as he is forced, especially in the case of larger units, to remain far from the attacking line, so that he can follow the course of the attack only along general lines. Whether the fire power of the enemy is entirely broken or not he can determine only by the progress made in the advance of his own lines. Still more seldom can he correctly perceive when the resistance of the enemy breaks at some one point, and he may be entirely unable to issue orders in time to take prompt advantage of such an event.

For these reasons the firing line will have to give the impetus for the assault, probably in every instance. It is especially necessary, when the enemy vacates his position, that the firing line, quickly taking advantage of that opportunity, proceeds to the charge. If it were to wait, in this event, until the reserves come up, much valuable time would be lost, the opponent might recover from his temporary unfavorable situation and again face about, and even receive reinforcements. If the impetus for the charge originates with the firing line, there is danger that instead of a general attack only a partial attack will take place. It is impossible for the entire skirmish line to judge simultaneously that the proper time for the assault has arrived, only a portion can do this. Such partial attacks are dangerous and have a chance of success only in covered terrain. In most cases such an attack, made by a single battalion or even by one company, will draw upon itself the fire of a large portion of the hostile line and naturally go to pieces under it. Even if a bold charging detachment is fortunate enough to enter the hostile position at some one point, it will be at once attacked by the defender with superior forces and forced to flee under heavy loss. Usually the defeat is not confined to a single detachment for the troops on the right and left will as soon as they see the others charging start forward on the run without having gotten close enough to the enemy in their front to have sufficiently shaken him. Thus, in most cases the decision for the charge, arrived at in the skirmish line, will turn into a series of defeats but, will, nevertheless, bring fresh troops closer and closer to the enemy until finally the great moment of the preponderance of men and fire is attained.

The execution of the assault portrayed above demands still another special preparation, namely advancing the artillery and minenwerfer fire. As long as that stays in one position, any assault is impossible. If telephone or flash light connection still exists between the artillery liaison officer and the batteries, it is possible of execution, otherwise it will be necessary to come to an agreement prior to starting the assault, to the effect that when the "artillery signal flags" are waved from side to side, or when light pistols are fired with certain colored lights, that signal is to be understood by the artillery to indicate the commencement of the charge. But if this decision is confined to but a portion of the line, errors are unavoidable, which will probably be paid for in blood. A more favorable way is the execution of the forward advance of the fire of the artillery, when the commander decides to assault. The signal "fix bayonet" acts like a preparatory warning, and then, by a previously agreed-on signal, the fire can be advanced.

In many instances our enemies met us with a counterattack in our assault. In such an emergency the assaulting troops must throw themselves down and defeat the counterattack by fire, and resume the forward movement as soon as possible. The guiding thought in an assault must always be: to reach the designated objective, regardless of whether that consists in breaking the resistance or irresistible pursuit.

In preparing the assault we generally favored the employment of hand grenades in such manner that shortly before the closing 3 hand grenades were thrown by the men lying down, who then charged with loud shouts. The rule, that in a charge in daytime rifles must be loaded appears not to be superfluous as the bullet is the most effective attacking means at close range, although our infantry, as well as our enemies, overestimated the effect of the hand grenade as compared with the rifle. The charge requires special training, in which the hand to hand struggle with pickax, sharpened spades, rifle with bayonet fixed, or even with bare hands must be practiced. Shouting hurrahs shortly before closing in, and shouted with full lung power, hurts the morale of the enemy, however premature shouting prevents surprise. In exceptional cases it may be well to charge without shouting so as not to attract the attention of neighboring forces of the enemy. "As soon as the shout is taken up, all trumpeters sound the 'charge'." The platoon commander charges ahead of his men; his example is of decisive importance; a charge once started must lead into the midst of the enemy. Every hesitancy spells annihilation. The charge must find the commanders of the machine guns in the front line. The minenwerfer fire can be of great use at short ranges. The main point is that the machine gun squad leader gives to the best of his abilities such fire support that the skirmish squads reach the enemy with as little loss as possible. If the entrance succeeds only at a few points, those points are to be immediately changed into machine gun nests from which the hostile machine gun fire is held down, and from which the enemy can be enfiladed.

If the intention is to penetrate the position, we must avoid stopping within the position. The charging troops must not pay any attention to either taking prisoners or materiel and attempts by the hostile supports in the matter of counter-attacks are to be smothered in their inception by relentless pushing forward. The retreating enemy must be kept on the run, thus preventing his lines in rear from firing and causing them to vacillate. When the attack objective has been reached, a moment of weakness sets in, which must be quickly overcome to avoid reverses. The control, lost by pushing into the position, must be at once reestablished with severity. Detachments no matter how small, are to be cut out as reserves. These troops in "readiness" with their machine guns must at all times be able to defeat counter or flank attacks. Machine guns and light minenwerfers held in rear must come up quickly, but the highest commander must at once prevent excessive crowding in the position, on which the hostile artillery fire will soon be directed. The importance of the quick arrival of all commanders, from the regiment up, cannot be emphasized enough.

The inclination to pursue the enemy along the entire line with the bayonet instead of halting and utilizing the fire power of the rifle has shown itself in all battles. The measures the attacker has to take after a successful attack are, to use the victorious infantry for pursuing fire as soon as a field of fire presents itself, under protection of which fire, fresh detachments start from the wings in pursuit. In selecting the points from which the pursuing fire is to be delivered due attention must be paid to the observers who have gone ahead and the batteries that are to arrive shortly. Reconnaissance on the wings is necessary during the pursuing fire, as is also locating our position for the artillery by means of flags and to the airplanes by spreading out panels, as well as bringing up hand to hand fighting material.

If the enemy has fled beyond point blank or short range, all

The Infantry Attack in Open Warfare 211

subordinate commanders will independently follow without waiting for orders from above. Assembly of the troops in close order, leading off prisoners, occupying the position, replenishment of ammunition must come after the more important mission of starting the pursuit. Only later when the enemy permits, are units correctly reorganized.

Means for defeating a counter-attack are especially important, and we have to count on counter-attacks in all cases. Our main support lies in the machine guns and light minenwerfers that have been brought quickly into position. If possible the first minenwerfer men must arrive with the charging infantry. These men select and mark the positions, while the regiments send forward ammunition. Orders for this must have been issued even before the decision for the assault is arrived at. The artillery will endeavor to regulate its stationary barrage for defeat of counter-attacks in case our infantry does not go beyond the position, and if possible, verify its correctness by airplane observation; however if the attack is to be carried further a change of position of our artillery will generally be necessary for proper fire support.

If the attack miscarries, it is the duty of all commanders to bring the men, retreating under the hostile fire, to a halt. As a general rule the halt is made at our artillery. But a halt probably cannot be thought of if the hostile fire is very effective. Only at the nearest cover, or where there is no cover, only at long range, when fatigue brings the retreat to an end or when the hostile fire is no longer effective, can a halt be made. This distance is the greater, the longer the enemy, not being interfered with by our fire, can make full use of the ballistic qualities of his arms, unless the attacker's artillery prevents him from doing so. The general rule must be to give up as little as possible of the terrain that has been once captured. Wherever the troops come to a halt they again form, and intrench if the hostile lire effect permits. They must then try their very best to attain, under protection of darkness, what could not be attained during daylight. An attack in the late evening, after the decisive fight has not been quite completed, has always had success.

Influence of Fog

Examination of a large number of operations shows that bad weather, fog, snow storms, heavy rains accompanied by thunder, beating into the enemy's face has never under various excuses been fully utilized by troops in war, to carry out an attack. An exception is the dust storm on March 9, 1905, at Mukden which facilitated the attacks of the Japanese wherever they were attempted. Fog is never cited as a motive for attack, but almost without exception as an excuse for inactivity or failure.

The difficulties connected with executing attacks in fog and carrying them to completion are well known; the direction is easily lost, and frequently detachments will fire on each other. The fear of running into an ambush creates a feeling of insecurity. On September 9, 1917, we started a well prepared attack against Hill 344 at Samogneux (Verdun). The attack went to pieces in the fog, though the troops were excellently trained in executing night attacks. The assaulting troops lost the direction and the connection with a successful column could not be kept up as no signals or signs could pierce the fog. We must calculate in an advance in fog or on the fog rising or dispersing suddenly. While close order formations are preferred in an advance under fog and all distances are to be shortened and special measures taken for keeping up connection, all subordinate commanders must, upon the dispersion of the fog, independently take all measures that are necessary, as in an advance without cover, viz., formations with more intervals and distance. Fog is a valuable ally for well trained troops.

Fighting in Woods

Woods have different influence on the attack as well as on the defense depending upon their extent, density, conformation of the ground, and season. In all cases they permit placing troops in readiness and shifting them, unobserved by the enemy's terrestrial and aerial observation. Possibilities for surprise always exist, as reconnaissance is difficult. During protracted bombardment the trees gradually disappear and the view is facilitated. In case of large woods the artillery has at the start little possibility of producing much effect, but this effect will be materially increased by application of all technical means — especially if the battle is protracted.

If woods prevent the enemy's gaining a view, they will prove very valuable in the matter of supporting points and flanking works, and in many cases will become the critical points of the battle. If, on the other hand, they can be seen from afar, they easily attract hostile artillery fire and soon become useless as cover against observation. Woods facilitate the defense by an inferior numerical force, favor the delaying battle by permitting troops to be disengaged, and deceit as to strength. They generally compel the attacker to employ relatively large forces, and therefore he will generally seek to avoid them.

Experiences in war have taught us that only minor importance is to be attached to infantry fire in woods, that the flight of the bullet is easily deflected by striking twigs, etc., and that not the bullet but cold steel is the decisive weapon in forest fighting. Anyone engaging in protracted fire fighting in woods will only lose time. The defender seeks to gain time, while the attacker must seek to bring the forest fight to an end as soon as possible. Hand grenades in forests are generally more dangerous to the thrower than to the enemy.

From the above we find:

> 1. Close order is discontinued only if the condition of the woods demand it; the denser the woods, the closer the troops; only thus can the officer retain control over his men.
> 2. Dense woods must not be circumvented; the troops must work their way through them, unless they want to run the risk of losing march-direction.
> 3. The less noise troops make passing through woods, the better; all shouting, and signaling must cease. Only in clearings and at spots where the woods are very clear and devoid of brush can firearms be resorted to, otherwise the decision is sought by sharp attack with the bayonet.
> 4. Experiences have taught that a decision may be gained in forest battles by exhaustion of the enemy, but that the decision can be more quickly reached by making attacks with fresh detachments

against the hostile flanks.

5. There is special danger in the infantry attack of units becoming dispersed and the consequent loss of control by officers, thus frittering away the attacking power.

The French, having wired the edges of the woods, preferred the system of posting small posts and machine guns there, and arranging a disconnected defensive position, with low blockhouses connected with wire, in the interior. Obstacles were placed from the edge into the interior so as to lead the attacker into blind alleys dominated by machine guns. Sharpshooters and machine guns lodged in trees kept paths and roads under fire. Much use was made of sound detectors which gave notice of the approach of the enemy. In the Vosges the Alpine Chasseurs, lodged in trees, gave the alarm by imitating the cries of birds. The defense was made offensively (ambush), the principal intention being to fall on the flank of the careless pursuer. The artillery fire at the start was barrage fire, with ravines, crossroads, paths, and roads through the woods systematically kept under fire.

If woods are of small extent we will push through them rapidly, but such procedure has its danger if the woods are large. In the latter case it was found better to push into the woods some 50 meters, then halt and establish order. Pursuing patrols advance along all roads, combat patrols are stationed at the edge and outside the woods with orders to keep up connection with the troops on the roads leading into the forest. After fixing the march direction and properly securing the service of information, the advance is made slowly under protection of patrols. Clearings and roads, where hostile fire may be met, are avoided, shock troops with flame throwers are held back by battalion and company commanders, machine guns are posted at roads and clearings to be ready to fire along them. Hand grenades and light minenwerfers are but seldom suitable in forest fighting.

It depends on the kind of forest in what formation the troops must traverse it. Forests with no underbrush permit advance in skirmish formation, but in dense woods, skirmish lines are not easy to control and have little power of resistance, so that a detachment advancing, in close order, can overrun them.

In forests, detachments will encounter each other at ranges hardly more than 100 meters, so that rapid fire, and energetic attack with cold steel will secure to the troops all the advantages resulting from surprise, and consequently success. The reason for this may be found in the fact that the opponent, unable to see, allows himself to be frightened by the attack, overestimates the hostile strength, and, hearing loud shouts from all sides and confused by the reverberating sound of rifle fire, turns to hasty flight, believing his line of retreat cut off. He has not been given a chance to think of offering any serious resistance.

Attack with cold steel must become second nature to the troops; it requires a formation that allows rapid fire and a rush in close formation; such a formation might be the company in line, but as line formations on the move are difficult in woods, and as men in skirmish line can easily evade the supervision of their officers, and furthermore, as the skirmish line has no power of resistance against troops in close order neither line nor skirmish formations seems suitable for the purpose.

For traversing dense woods platoons of the company in line abreast of each other, or echeloned, each platoon formed in double column of squads is recommended. It is not so good to advance in double column by platoon or half-platoons abreast of each other, as the columns are too long, deployment too difficult, and intervals hard to maintain. Squad columns on the other hand will be near enough to keep in sight of each other, and they can more easily work through the forest than can detachments in close order. Deployment for purpose of delivering fire and for the assault can be easily accomplished. A disadvantage is their lack of resistance against a flank attack or against an attack coming obliquely; in that event we need support of flank echelons. Columns of greater depth which require a longer time for deployment, have the disadvantage that intervals may be lost in the endeavor to keep proper direction. Front and flanks will have to be protected by patrols and by detachments in echelon, so that any hostile flank attack is itself flanked by detachments moving to the front. In rear of this first line follows a second line in close order, where practicable along roads. The patrols must not be so far away that they cannot see the troops they are protecting. A stop is made at all crossroads, when direction and order is reestablished. Of course, this formation, halting and reestablishing order, takes time, which however is offset by the increase in order and security. To prevent connection with the retreating enemy from being lost at the edge of the woods, strong pursuit patrols must be started along roads after the enemy.

It is advantageous to signal the progress of the infantry to the artillery and to the commander by flares, which, by the way, easily remain hanging on the tops of trees.

In an attack upon a forest we do without the stationary barrage. At the start we throw shells on the edge of the forest for a depth of some 200 meters, then, at the moment of the charge, the fire is lifted to 400 meters and the infantry advanced to the edge of that fire, then the fire again lifted some 400 meters, and so on. All available means of communication must be utilized for connection with the artillery. For communication within the battalion, we will have to be satisfied with runners.

It has always been of advantage to mark the lines along which battalion and regimental headquarters moved forward, when entering woods, by posting runners.

Woods are of advantage to the defense in that they conceal to a large extent the works, prevent aerial observation and increase the difficulty of the enemy's artillery locating them. Surprise works, such as blockhouses, offer in woods good opportunities for the counter-attack against an enemy that has entered the position, as the defender knows the ground well. Obstacles from branches of trees are poor, they soon dry out and can be easily set on fire by hostile patrols or artillery fire. They suffer much in a bombardment. Men familiar with woodcraft, such as foresters and wood cutters, should be employed on listening posts. By observing many indications, such for instance, as the conduct of birds they can ascertain the location of observation posts in trees or the approach of hostile patrols. In the retreat woods facilitate disengaging troops from the enemy. Even sharply pursuing detachments can be held up by weak but skillfully handled rear guards until the main body is marching in the desired direction undisturbed, or has made its preparations for a counter-attack. Rear guards generally have no trouble in drawing the enemy into a direction favorable for the counter-attack.

The Infantry Attack in Open Warfare

Village Fighting

Localities such as villages at all times during the war exerted a fatal magnetic power on all troops. In vain were all precepts and regulations of all armies to occupy villages, for the defense, only with weak forces and to defend villages only when their occupation offered tactical advantages; to avoid in any attack village fighting, but to seek the decision beyond their limits, in the open terrain. Aspern, Ligny, Bazeilles, and Le Bourget are merely examples of how little the teachings helped. Beaune la Rolande with 1510 meters extension was held by 2300 men with a loss of only 5.6%. Frequently the defender gave way to the conflagration rather than the attacker. The hope entertained prior to the World War that the increased artillery effect would make village fighting superfluous, was incorrect.

The World War can cite many instances of tenacious village fights carried on around complete ruins that once were villages, but which still were capable of being defended. I shall mention only Combles and Sailly in the Somme battle, and Mondidier in the Summer of 1918. On the Eastern theaters of war a number of tenacious village fights could be cited. In the Masurian battle a bitter house to house fight took place in Johannisburg held by two Russian regiments; the place fell into the hands of troops of the 2d Infantry Division brought up from three sides.

Par. 435, 1. D. R. pointed out that tenaciously defended, massive villages might become the key point of the battle, and occupation and arrangement of the edge of the village occasionally facilitated the rapid creation of a defensive position and an increase in the enemy's difficulties in perceiving the strength of the garrison. The disadvantage of the ease with which the hostile artillery could find the range should be well considered also, so that it would often be better to place the defensive line outside the village. Fortification of the flanks of villages is not to be neglected and the rear edge should be opened so far that the counter-attack by reserves would not be made more difficult.

Riflemen's positions when the village is within the range of effective hostile artillery fire, should be in massive buildings or in houses that are covered by a rise in front, or by other portions of the village. For this reason the French recommended that the defensive line be withdrawn into the interior of the village, using the portions lying between the village and the enemy's position as a protective cover against the hostile artillery fire. As early as the Campaign of 1870 it appears that, the defense of Bazeilles was planned with this intention. "Defensive arrangements in the interior of the village must be made so that each sector, and each enclosure can be defended. Broad streets, open places, or brooks, running through the village parallel to the defensive line favor defense by sectors." (Pioneer D.R., par. 344.)

In the World War the difficulties of village defense were increased by aerial reconnaissance, by the increased size of projectiles of the attacking artillery, and by the employment of flame throwers. On the other hand the defense of a village was increased by the introduction of machine guns which permitted the replacing of numerous men by machines. Utilization of minenwerfers favors the attacker as well as defender. In the fights for the fortress-like Armentiers on April 9, 1918, the German infantry declined to make a charge against the strongly occupied village, which had been covered by a hail of shells and gas bombs. The village finally fell (the British falsely state that they voluntarily evacuated it) when taken in flank and rear. The spoils were 50 officers and 3000 men as well as 45 guns, and a clothing and ammunition depot. The place had cover, toward the side of the enemy, so that the artillery, which was given the mission of throwing flanking fire came from neighboring sectors. In many cases the British understood how to post machine guns in buildings in the vicinity of and visible to our artillery positions. These were so hidden they could be located by our airplanes only with difficulty, and by frequent change of position they were able to even escape our flash and sound ranging squads.

A peculiar village fight happened on April 24, 1918, around Villers-Bretonneux, east of Amiens, which was held by the British. After an artillery preparation lasting two hours and a half the German infantry supported by tanks attacked the village. The first attacking wave of infantry stopped in front of the village, which was still under fire, while infantry, and tanks, gained ground in the open terrain to one side of the village. Tanks cleared a supporting point at the southeast corner of the village for the assault and then opened fire on the village street, later they turned off to the north edge of the village and from that point produced good effect against its interior. Still later the tanks advanced towards the railroad station and church of Villers-Bretonneux, where the British in vain endeavored to hold out.

These examples sketched in mere outline, show that a tenacious defender cannot be driven out by artillery fire from a well prepared village, if it has been supplied with deep shelters and that an artillery bombardment does not assure the possibility of avoiding a bitter fight in the interior. Fights in streets and houses consume forces and time. We will cite the capture of Messines on October 31st, of Wytschaete the same day and on November 1st and 2d, 1914. A later study will have to show, if with all the heroic valor of the troops it would not have been possible to shorten these fights. If that is impossible, nothing remains except to give troops flame throwers and accompanying artillery.

The surest means for the attacker to take a village, is in locking the place in by fire and troops. Villages completely surrounded by troops are almost always taken quickly, with rich spoils in prisoners and with little loss on the part of the attacker. Rapid penetration of the village, immediately in rear of a rolling barrage frequently breaks resistance without losses. If a house to house fight results, the attacker must gain a foothold just as the defender, in houses and ruins. He must avoid the streets, work his way through gardens and yards, and thus slowly but surely break the enemy's resistance.

Defensive arrangements of a village take much time and troops. Works that can be fired on by artillery will be destroyed in a short time and do not pay for the trouble of constructing them. But the ruins still offer, to the stubborn defender, a possibility of continuing the battle. Battle positions, in front of the village, are hard to hide from the view and camera of the airplane, they require special works for bomb-proof shelter, while connecting roads with the village take much labor, and invariably will betray the position. Thus it is an open question if the defense of the edge of the village would not be better. Cellars are numerous, and even if they require reinforcement, the labor connected therewith is slight in comparison with constructing bombproofs and connecting trenches. Only works that are hidden from view of artillery and airplanes are a reinforcement to the defense. Thus it may well be accounted for how the tenacious resistance happened on November 11, 1914, by the left wing of the Guard Division in the Chateau Veldhoek in the forest of Herenthage. Positions, hidden from hostile fire and aerial reconnaissance, from which a fight can be advantageously conducted, require especially strong garrisons and materiel. They turn into critical points of the battle, on which the entire defensive system may be constructed. Obstacles and bombproofs have precedence over earthworks, which in a bombardment, are generally annihilated beyond recognition in a very short time. Supporting points are for the purpose of holding out, even if the surrounding country has already fallen into the enemy's hands, but whether or not completely surrounding them with obstacles is correct, requires special consideration in each instance. Probably it will always be well to do it!

Chapter X – Cavalry

Cavalry Prior to the World War

After all wars of modern times — from Blücher's sharp condemnation of the activity of the Prussian cavalry during the Wars of Liberation down to the reproach for the breaking down of the Russian cavalry in Eastern Asia — the same complaints were heard concerning the small achievements of the cavalry in the face of the enemy. Besides the increase in fire power, we must seek for the cause in the continually increasing discrepancy in the strength of cavalry and infantry. The only exception of this is shown in the American War of Secession; unfortunately we delayed making use of the experiences of Stuart, Sheridan, and Forrest; in any case we could have arranged for similar achievements as early as the Franco-Prussian War by timely change in armament and training. We were quite justified in concluding from the Russo-Japanese War that only first-class cavalry pays, that cavalry has to be trained for mounted and dismounted fighting, that it must by no means be allowed to sink to the level of mounted infantry, which means poorly riding riflemen like the British in South Africa. Cavalry has to be able to fire especially well. The Russian cavalry in Eastern Asia, except a very small fraction thereof, did not come up to the standard in training, equipment and armament of modern cavalry; it did not seek dismounted fighting; it fell into inactivity. Cavalry that can be employed in war cannot be improvised, it must be systematically trained during long peace years. Then, however, the army leadership must set cavalry clearly defined tasks and pitilessly demand definite results. Field Marshal Oyama stated after the Battle of Mukden: "If I had had but two or three cavalry divisions, the Russians would never have gotten northward after the defeat of Mukden, or at least their right wing would have fallen victim to the pursuit of the army cavalry." In Germany and France we considered the dismounted action only a makeshift and sought employment on the battlefield by the charge against all arms. Little attention was paid that the Turkish cavalry, trained according to German principles, had sought in the Balkan War of 1912-13 the attack, but had to be satisfied with very successful participation with fire arms in the actions of the other arms.

Our conception was confirmed by the fact that the British cavalry, after some hesitation, then the Russian cavalry after the Russo-Japanese War, adopted the belief that the days of the cavalry charge were by no means past; that cavalry rather, was clearly destined for mounted fighting; that the attached arms in many instances relieved the cavalry from the necessity of fighting on foot. The German cavalry drill regulations with the same maxims were adopted by Japan in 1895.

If the cavalry has not sufficiently achieved success in the face of the enemy there are two good reasons. First, a lack of individual commanders capable of requiring the higher efforts of cavalry under favorable conditions without regard to probable losses, and second, the supply of horses on the battlefield, by no means fulfilled the requirements clearly foreseen in time of peace.

The extension of the battlefield increased the difficulties of reaching the flanks and rear of the enemy. But if cavalry desires, through its charges, to accomplish a decisive influence on the course of the battle, nothing remains, in consideration of the growth of modern armies, but to attack in mass. However, the increased fire power of rifle and gun increased the difficulties of placing cavalry in readiness and bringing up larger units. It is very probable that charges in regimental and brigade formation in favorable terrain are still possible, but attacks in division formation are out of the question. In the machine gun the infantry has received an arm which is absolutely annihilating against tall and broad targets. In addition, increasing cultivation, and covering the terrain with industrial works, fencing the fields with barbed wire, are increasing the obstacles to the mounted use of cavalry.

Views on Cavalry Attacks

Regulations of all armies lay stress on the necessity in time of peace of cavalry employing the *arme blanche* in action to drive off the hostile cavalry and to open a road for our participation. Thus, in the World War we ought to have seen numerous cavalry charges, but the very opposite happened. The Russian cavalry — without success — several times attacked the German infantry; but in the West the cavalry declined to attack. Equipment with the lance, and our well trained horses, undoubtedly gave our cavalry a superiority and our opponents well knew the capability of our well trained cavalry in movements and maneuvering in larger units. Minor contacts showed the difficulties, due to the increased fire power, of keeping the cavalry close enough to the firing line, to be able to fully and quickly utilize rapidly passing opportunities for participation. The rapid wearing out of the trained horses, hard to replace, worked against a probable costly employment on the battlefield. Replacement of trained horses will probably be difficult in the future, but by no means impossible. As long as wars are conducted with impressionable humans, so long will a suddenly appearing cavalry mass have its effect on infantry that has suffered physically and in morale, and where training has not given it the proper stability. On the other hand, the organization of infantry favors success of a charge. Arms become effective only in the hands of men; but these men appear more than ever susceptible to moral influences on account of the increase of urban population. Because favorable opportunities were not grasped, or because cavalry was not just at the right place, or because the commander had been deceived by the "parade" aspect of the enemy, or because the commander was unable to see that the infantry opposed to him was ripe for a charge, we have no justification for concluding that the attack was impossible. Uncertainty, which leads to inactivity, taken in conjunction with the difficulties in reaching the decisive place at the correct time, has frequently saved broken and demoralized infantry from the charge.

Charges against marching batteries, surprise attacks against flank and rear of artillery in action, or even against the front of artillery firing from under cover, against artillery that is not fighting in connection with infantry, can frequently have great success. Frequently it is advantageous to silence batteries if only for a short time. Successes against ammunition columns are also to be valued. Present day cavalry must therefore be able to fight mounted as well as dismounted; it is entirely too costly to sink to the level of rapidly moving infantry.

The moral impression produced by charging cavalry remains undisputed (Custozza, Mars la Tour), and even its mere presence has a weakening effect on the enemy.

The leader will have to consider that the losses in a charge of cavalry against cavalry will probably be very small, and against other arms extraordinarily high, while the losses inflicted on the enemy are generally relatively small. The leader must consider this in arriving at a decision whether to resort to the charge or to dismounted fighting, especially when, by fighting on foot there is a possibility of causing the enemy great loss. But in no case must the fact that a dismounted action can quickly and easily be broken off, be permitted to affect the decision to make a mounted charge, when it would cause a quick and decisive result. Prerequisite for a favorable attack lies in sudden appearance. In any case we will probably have to prepare the success of a mounted attack by the firefight of carbines and machine guns. Tanks also can perform valuable service here. Frequently battle airplane echelons and escadrilles will have the same effect as a mounted attack. The mounted attack, which utilizes celerity and shock power to ride down the enemy, has lost in importance in modem war, though plenty of opportunities will offer for successful charges. The larger the cavalry unit, the greater the difficulties of coordinated action and the more will cavalry have to seek opportunity to participate by fighting dismounted in the battle, to which the cavalry must be trained, and without paying any attention to the neighboring troops to solve independently its task in any terrain and at any hour of the day. Due to increased attachment of fire arms of all kinds, in conjunction with its mobility cavalry will more than ever be assigned to operate against the enemy's flank and rear, in which hostile cavalry must be quickly swept aside, if possible by mounted attack, and not by the slower method of fighting on foot.

As the hostile cavalry will have the same tasks, both parties will naturally endeavor to bring about a rapid decision, to uninterruptedly continue their tasks. Thus cavalry engagements will result; and only the inferior cavalry will resort to dismounted fire fight to accomplish its task. This resistance has to be overcome by dismounted offensive attack. The cavalry has to be ready day and night for the "offensive fire fight," to be able, after the victory over the hostile cavalry, to move against the flank of the enemy, against the line of communication, or against cavalry.

The cavalry must never wait for opportunities to attack, it must not delay its activity until it is let loose for the pursuit, but must participate with all means at hand in gaining the victory and carry its strong fire power rapidly to the weak points of the enemy's line. This advantage of being able to rapidly cover short distances to occupy important points, was not properly valued prior to the war. Efficient cavalry can always mislead the enemy and can also thereby make him afraid. The long continued battles and the dependence of the armies on uninterrupted supplies of ammunition and provisions, mostly brought up by rail, make operations against communications to the rear of decisive importance. Without rail connection modern armies rapidly lose their fighting power and freedom of movements. The raids, condemned before the war by C. D. R. 527, gain thereby special value.

It is probably to the point to here point out the raid, undertaken with strong cavalry in September, 1919, by General Mamontoff. The end of August he pierced the Bolshevist line south of Moscow, was enabled to live, without supplies from home, in rear of the 8th Bolshevist Army, off the country, and supported the advance from

Moscow against Orel.

Employment of Cavalry in War

Let us try and sketch the tasks of cavalry in war. The *army cavalry* performs all the duties that an army demands; the generally weaker *divisional cavalry*, frequently reinforced or totally replaced by cyclists, performs the duties required by smaller troop units. In conjunction with the aerial observation forces the cavalry carries on reconnaissance, screens movements of the army, and secures the connection between separated portions of the army. After the contact of the armies the cavalry seeks employment in flank or rear of the enemy, against important railroad junctions, prevents the enemy from bringing up supplies and attempts to keep approaching reinforcements from the battlefield. The development of wireless and of the airships make it possible to supply distant cavalry with orders and facilitates co-operation with the armies in retreat and in pursuit. The cavalry participates with all arms in battle and finds special employment in retreat and in pursuit.

Reconnaissance

Aerial reconnaissance, in so far as it is not influenced by weather, supplements the cavalry reconnaissance and indicates the directions to the cavalry in which it is to reconnoiter. Cavalry reconnaissance always has the advantage of gaining by personal contact (prisoners) important points for the leader's decisions. The cavalry reconnoiters with weaker detachments (officers' patrols) which are followed in support by reconnoitering squadrons; reconnaissance with stronger forces ("patrol rides by cavalry divisions") leads to frittering away the forces.

The general rules laid down in peace time for the service of reconnaissance, for far, near, and battle reconnaissance, have stood the test. We reckoned only too little with the fact that the Russians as a general rule appeared with stronger cavalry patrols and made more use of deceptions than we foresaw. The strength of a patrol is governed by its task and the probable number of messages to be sent back. The weaker the patrol, the easier can its road be blocked and the quicker will it use up its forces. It was proven wise to attack hostile patrols and reconnoitering detachments whenever the situation permitted. Armament with the lance gave the troops superiority and all reports prove that the intrepid attack of our reconnoitering detachments always had good success. Of course, heavy losses resulted sometimes by overhasty action. The leader will solve his task mounted if practicable, otherwise dismounted. This requires a certain strength of the patrol. It is advisable in close reconnaissance — to save the horses — to move the patrols forward in waves from sector to sector. The relieved patrols assemble first as message centers along the route of march and finally join the advance guard cavalry. In this manner the sending back of messages is best assured. Good reconnaissance is the first requirement of security.

For the purpose of furnishing rallying points and supports for distant patrols, reconnoitering squadrons were of advantage in 10 to 20 kilometers broad reconnaissance strips. Light radio stations performed the service of communication; we cannot caution too strongly against sending messages uncoded. We found in Maubeuge and Namur copies of our own wireless messages which the enemy had picked up with his wireless. In order to overcome hostile resistance the reconnoitering squadron requires a certain fighting power, and that is increased by the assignment of cyclists, machine guns, and even single field pieces.

Screening the Movements of the Army

At the opening of the World War screening the movements of the army was so successfully performed by both cavalry corps that the advance of the 1st and 2d Armies had a completely surprising effect on the allied leadership, in spite of the fact that participation in war in Belgium by the population increased the tasks of the cavalry.

Similarly in October, 1914, the Cavalry Corps Frommel (5th, 8th and Austrian 4th Cavalry Divisions) succeeded in screening the march to the left of the Army under Hindenburg to the vicinity of Thorn.

Employment Against Flank and Rear

In July, 1915, the 5th Army Cavalry Corps accompanied, with its 2d, 6th and 8th Cavalry Divisions, the attack of the North Corps of the Niemen Army against the right flank of the Russian Army in position on the Dubissa and upper Windau as far as the vicinity of Popeljany. The advance of the German cavalry against the Russian flank was decisive. In no case could infantry have operated at such a distance from its main force. The greater the distance, the greater the effect.

In September, 1914, during the "race to the coast" there were concentrated on the German north wing — on a narrow space: the 2d Cavalry Corps, v.d. Marwitz, consisting of the 7th and 9th Cavalry Divisions; the 1st Cavalry Corps, V. Richthofen, consisting of the Guard and 4th Cavalry Division, and the 4th Cavalry Corps, v. Hollen, consisting of the 3d, 6th and Bavarian Cavalry Division.

At the present writing it cannot be stated whether the cavalry could have caused more delay to the march of the British or could have pushed into the hostile communications zone. Lack of infantry compelled the army leadership to employ this brilliant cavalry in position warfare.

What will ever remain as a brilliant cavalry achievement, was the employment of the Cavalry Corps Garnier (the 1st, 3d, 4th, 6th and 9th Cavalry Divisions took part) after the fall of Kovno against the rear of the Russian army at Wilna in September, 1915, Smorgon September 15th, Solg 16th, and Wilecki 16th), all of which were taken in dismounted fighting in the face of continually reinforced Russian infantry, which was being brought up by rail. In the face of this infantry the cavalry could not take Molodeczno, so that finally the Russians were able to also break the resistance of the rapidly brought up 75th and 115th Reserve Divisions. In a captured Russian order appeared the following praise: "The cavalry must take example by the energetic, brave and rapid action of the German cavalry; I consider it sufficient to call back to mind to the cavalry, especially to the Cossacks and their commanders, the former valor of their predecessors — definite, bold reconnaissance under the nose of the enemy, especially in his rear, full freedom to raise havoc among his batteries and columns, to fall on his tired infantry — which is history with which each commander must be familiar in order to cite examples of the Russian cavalry, which the German cavalry now so eagerly emulates."

If cavalry has once reached the rear of the hostile army, then only relentless action without any regard to losses can attain large success.

Connection Between Separated Parts of the Army in Retreat

After the first battle of the Marne the gap between the 1st and the 2d Army was closed by German cavalry.

Mounted Participation in Battle and as Mobile Foot Troops

Cavalry, by surprise, can bring its strong fire power into effect.

Cavalry Divisions

The cavalry division is the fighting unit of the army cavalry; its organization and composition must be in accordance with the new tasks. It is true that the formation of 3 brigades of 2 regiments, taken over from the Franco-Prussian War — principally designed for mounted action and for reconnaissance — has proven itself excellent, but the regiment nevertheless requires another machine gun troop of 6 guns besides the 8 to 12 automatic rifles assigned each troop. If cavalry desires to solve its problem, it requires an absolutely strong equipment with automatic arms, as the horses rapidly decrease — as we have learned. In present day employment of cavalry after deducting reconnoitering troops and far patrols, 1 regiment will not be able to insert more than 200 carbines, 1 cavalry division no more than 6 troops. Each trooper must be an excellent marksman; the small number of carbines must be increased by automatic arms. For this employment we have too many headquarters (staffs) and it should be considered if the demands of dismounted action cannot be better met by organizing brigades of 3 regiments and to increase the number of troops in the regiment to 6. Attaching good marching infantry to the division and not to the cavalry corps, say about 1 battalion to the brigade with necessary autos to carry the knapsacks, is recommended; in addition too, infantry cyclists are indispensable even on an Eastern theater of war.

All men that cannot be mounted temporarily because of loss of horses, are to be formed within each brigade into bicycle detachments. As has been learned, bicycles are always available. In Italy every cavalry regiment had 1 cycle platoon. The cyclist companies can occasionally also be organized into battalions.

In the attachment of artillery, the lack of light field howitzers was sorely felt, and also the lack of long range guns. Attachment of heavy field howitzers and 10-cm. cannons, frequently demanded, may occasionally be of advantage, but would seriously affect the mobility of the troops. It is also wrong to carry along more than two calibers. Attachment of anti-aircraft guns was demanded with justification.

In the matter of mounted pioneers (supplied with explosives carried on pack animals), 1 company with cavalry bridge equipment was found sufficient for the division. It was found best to mount the pioneers, in place of equipping them with bicycles, on account of the explosives they had to carry along. Information detachments should be equipped with light radio stations for the reconnoitering troops, heavy radio stations for the brigade and division; this is absolutely necessary. The service of information in a regiment had best be performed by one platoon. Subsistence and ammunition columns should be changed from horse-drawn to motor-drawn.

Cyclists

In organizing cyclist companies (collapsible wheels) with the Jäger battalions on October 1, 1913, the dislike to the employment of cyclists in Germany had been overcome. At the opening of the World War Great Britain had cyclist battalions (coast guard), Austria (with single Jäger battalions), Switzerland (to reinforce the weak cavalry). Italy and France also had cyclist detachments. Preparations had been made in Russia to supply the cavalry divisions with cyclist detachments. At the close of the World War each Italian cavalry division had 1 cyclist battalion of 3 companies and in addition each cavalry regiment had a cyclist platoon of 30 men. Each British army corps had 1 cyclist battalion (230 men) of 3 companies with 6 automatic rifles carried on cycles. In mobile warfare each division was to receive 1 bicycle company, as there was no longer any divisional cavalry toward the close of the campaign — only corps cavalry still existed (3 troops). The French cavalry division had a *groupe cycliste* of 3 *peletons* of 3 officers, 15 non-commissioned officers, and 90 men each.

In Germany the cyclist companies were doubled shortly after the commencement of the war, and then ersatz companies were organized in addition, which were brought into the field as mobile troops. Cyclist companies were enabled to utilize their rapidity to good advantage during the quick advance through Belgium and Northern France, and because the road net was excellent, they could perform tasks independently, and did excellent service in the holding of important sectors, especially in the retreat from the Marne, and offered a rallying point to the cavalry far in front. The fear that through the permanent assignment to cavalry corps and cavalry divisions their movements would be retarded, did not prove correct as long as the roads were good and the road net favorable. In the East cyclist detachments also performed excellent service. During the course of the campaign additional cyclist companies were organized based on the good results so far shown. The cyclist companies not attached to the cavalry corps and cavalry divisions were employed for duty at army headquarters, army corps and single divisions, and in part also formed into cyclist battalions of from 5 to 7 companies and 1 machine gun company of 6 guns, model '08, on auto trucks. 6 of such battalions (4 Prussian, 1 Bavarian, 1 Saxon) later on formed the 2d Infantry (cyclist) Brigade, which performed most excellent services at different times, the last time in the Autumn of 1918, on the retreat in the West.

While in time of peace a cyclist company consisted of only 3 officers and about 110 noncommissioned officers and men, its strength in war — corresponding to the demand — was increased to 3 officers and 150 noncommissioned officers and men and each company was assigned 1 passenger and 2 supply autos as well as 3 wagons. Such a strength was necessary as the company in mobile war in encountering the enemy was left to itself and because we had to count on detachments for patrols and messengers and personnel for the trains, as well as on losses in battle.

In cyclist troops the desire was expressed to have machine guns to increase their fighting power, and in the summer of 1918 a portion of the cyclist companies were supplied with 3 automatic rifles, which with spare parts and ammunition were carried along on cycles.

The strength of a cycle detachment is dependent on the march depth and on the fact that in mobile warfare half of the men are designated to bring along the wheels of the skirmishers. The folding wheel did not show up well with us. If we calculate, in addition, on detachments for supply trains, subsistence and headquarters service, wheels getting out of order, etc., it will be seen that it is not correct to attach to a cavalry unit less than 1 company of cyclists of 2 platoons, of a strength of at least 2 officers, 22 noncommissioned officers and 160 men. The baggage necessary for daily use is carried on the wheel, the remainder on wagons. If the cavalry division wants to make effective use of its cyclists, at least 1 battalion of from 3 to 4 cyclist companies and 1 machine gun company should be attached. Units of this strength proved themselves to be effective. Marching in the West usually was in column of threes, in the East generally in column of files. Method of movement and rate of speed require that the cyclists be taken out of the march column and moved from sector to sector. In the battle cyclists are to reinforce the fire power of the cavalry and to relieve the cavalry as much as possible from the fire fight.

French Views Concerning Employment of Cavalry

At the opening of the World War French cavalry divisions were not equal to the German cavalry divisions because of the latter's superiority in machine guns and attached Jäger battalions. Men's equipment, horse equipment, and means of communication, were in favor of the German troopers. In the Autumn of 1914 the French cavalry officers' corps was rejuvenated, infantry was attached to the divisions, and in November portable intrenching equipment and bayonets were supplied. In the Spring of 1916-17 Cuirassier regiments were changed into "Cuirassiers dismounted" organization and strength of foot troops, and in addition dismounted *groupes legeres* were formed from other regiments. Grenade rifles (*Vivien Bessieres*) were introduced, the number of cartridges carried by individuals was increased, and the number of automatic rifles increased first to 3 and later to 6 per troop. Automatic rifles were given to combat patrols as a general rule. Their employment in attack and in reconnaissance was specially emphasized. To each regiment was attached one 37-mm. cannon with tripod mount (range 1500 to 2000 meters). Attached were also motor guns and motor machine guns; and in the Spring of 1918, also light tanks. The auto guns were not to be considered as fire reserve, but were to be energetically inserted with utilization of their mobility and their protection against infantry and shrapnel fire, to precede the detachments, to cut off the enemy's retreat, and to be employed in attack and in defense for sudden fire from flank positions. In effective fire zones they were to keep up connection between commander and advanced detachments. At night, motor guns and machine guns were not to be used. Employment of long range heavy cannon had also been considered. The object was to create quickly moving fire groups which were to make use of the success attained by the other arms in trenchless terrain. While for mounted employment the requirements of C.D.R. of 1912 were fully to be adhered to, three regulations were published consecutively in 1916, which looked on the dismounted fight as the normal employment of cavalry. The final precept was the regulations dated May 26, 1918: "Celerity, mobility and ability to maneuver are the inherent qualities of cavalry, as long as it is a question of marching and maneuvering. But to reach objectives, which are assigned the cavalry, to solve its tasks, the cavalry will have to fight. In most instances these fights will have to be carried on dismounted, for there is no longer any German cavalry on the Western theater of war Cavalry tactics will have to correspond to the fire power of modern battle, and its organization and armament give it the possibility to fully use the fire power. Therefore cavalry, supported by artillery, must be able to fight on foot. But nevertheless the mounted fight also has to be considered and prepared for. For that opportunity is offered against cavalry which seeks to attack or accept attack, against infantry surprised or disheartened in terrain devoid of trenches or ditches, against artillery on the move, or when it can be attacked in position from the flank or rear. The cavalry is a fragile arm, its reconstruction is slow and far from easy. It therefore must not be sacrificed to the impatience of a leader under conditions in which its inherent qualities cannot be utilized."

After December, 1916, the cavalry troop consisted of 3 platoons of 3 squads each; the dismounted platoon, like infantry platoons, suitable for a protracted fire fight according to armament and organization. In the Regulations of 1918 it is stated: "Under present day requirements for battle the dismounted fight is the normal procedure for cavalry. It is important that, if the cavalry dismounts to fight on foot, it forms each time when possible units corresponding to infantry formations, as those possess all means for the fire fight, for movements and for connection in consonance with well known experiences." Thus, the cavalry platoon dismounted was to correspond to the infantry section, the dismounted troop to the infantry platoon or half-company, the dismounted regiment to 2 infantry companies. The men trained for special purposes (rifle grenade throwers, automatic riflemen) were distributed equally to the platoons. 1 platoon inserted 14 skirmishers, the remainder serving as horseholders and for reconnaissance. 1 brigade formed a foot battalion with 1 machine gun company. The led horses of a troop were under charge of 1 officer; he has 2 noncommissioned officers and 32 troopers, including 6 litter bearers. The led horses of a half-regiment with the combat train of the machine gun platoon were conducted by the captain second in rank, and the led horses of the troop were generally posted separately. The following points were laid down for the tactical insertion: "In the dismounted fight the celerity and mobility of the cavalry must come to the top, to fully utilize the surprise and the possibility of turning against flank and rear of the enemy. Where the enemy makes a stand, he will be held in front by fire, and mounted portions of the command press forward in the direction our task lies. The troops are formed into dismounted detachments, led horses with combat train, mounted reserve (up to one-fourth of the total). The mounted reserve secures the flanks and maintains connection with neighboring detachments, gathers the fruits of success by rapidly throwing forward detachments for the fire fight against flank and rear of the enemy or pursues, mounted, the enemy, covers the now mounting detachment that has fought on foot, and informs it of everything important for the continuation of its task."

The corps cavalry and the divisional cavalry secure in the offensive battle the attainment of success, and the army cavalry secures the fruits of success. In the defensive battle cavalry is enabled to materially lessen the effect of a penetration. Corps and divisional cavalry participate in gaining success in battle; if that is attained, they keep touch with the enemy, reconnoiter and cover the exit of the troops units into the terrain that is free from trenches. The following tasks are set the cavalry: To attack retreating infantry and artillery; to increase the point of entry by rapidly bringing up fire echelons with automatic arms against the flanks of detachments that still make a stand. "It will be the general rule to bring the frontal fight of dismounted detachments into consonance with the appearance of detachments, that are especially strong in machine arms, against the flank and rear. In the defense these cavalry detachments will secure the approach of reserves and occupy important points in advance. The army cavalry will overtake the gathering of the fruits of victory, will increase the effect of a tactical and operative surprise, and will secure the movement of armies. Celerity, mobility and its fire power give the army cavalry an opportunity to solve tasks which infantry divisions cannot solve with the same rapidity, and which corps and divisional cavalry cannot solve with the same power. Such tasks are after a penetration: Threatening the rear of the hostile troops, rear attacks, against parts that still make a stand, reconnaissance and attack on approaching reinforcements and rear guard positions, to prevent the enemy to again make front in a position in rear, to hold positions until the arrival of the infantry, to execute important demolitions, to take possession of provision and ammunition depots. Assignment of airplanes, means of communication, light tanks, artillery, infantry units and labor troops will frequently be necessary. Again and again emphasis is laid on the necessity to not allow itself to become entangled into serious frontal fights, but to turn with fire arms against flank and rear of the enemy, but still adhering to the general march direction and then to inform the commander of the situation by using all observation and communication means. The cavalry division will divide itself into reconnaissance detachments, into a *detachment d'exploitation* for pursuit, into the portions designated to utilize its mobility, and into infantry support. In the defense the larger units are mainly designated in accordance with a kind of mobile reserve, to close up a gap should the enemy have succeeded in entering the position. The cavalry divisions have the advantage of being composed only of rapidly moving portions, so that on their arrival on the battle field they can participate in full numerical strength with their guns, their automatic arms, and their ammunition. In that lies the value and the justification of existence of cavalry divisions." In this rapid insertion as a unit lies the advantage of cavalry divisions as contrary to infantry divisions, the hasty insertion of which is possibly only gradually, foot troops and vehicles separated.

The French cavalry, without entirely doing away with the mounted attack, turned into mounted infantry, which sought to solve its main task on the battlefield in participation in the battle. The corps cavalry and the divisional cavalry was to fight also as a general rule. Generally frontal fire fight was to be connected with an advance against the enemy's flank and rear, so that artillery and automatic arms could be inserted against the most sensitive points of the enemy.

Chapter XI – The Artillery

Organization and Combat Principles

Infantry and artillery tactics, in so far as concerns the employment of light and heavy artillery cannot be separated; but as has been already pointed out, we can here only treat of them together along general lines and we cannot discuss special questions.

Before the World War, when only open warfare had to be considered, the quantity of artillery for one army corps operating as a part of a larger unit, was determined by the number of guns that could be placed into position in the corps zone of action, which amounted to 24 batteries to each 5000 meters front. The deployment of the artillery, except the light howitzer batteries, was to be in a single line. As a result of experience it was believed in marches that, in relation with the infantry, the proportion of artillery could not be too great. The march length of the artillery columns, with the light munition trains included, was at the beginning of the World War, 5600 meters for a division, as against a march depth of the infantry at normal strength, of 4800 meters. Before the campaigns started there were for each 12 battalions of infantry 12 batteries, that is for full war strength there was for each 1000 men one 6-gun battery, as against 2 guns to 1000 men, the amount provided in 1870. As campaigns proceeded this proportion had changed; for example, the 10th Army Corps had at Vionville 4.16 guns per 1000 men; at the time of the capture of Metz this proportion was 5.8; at Beaune-la-Roland 6.4; on December 3d (1870), 8.8 and on the 9th of December, 11.4.

The Second Army at the beginning of the World War in 1914 had 3 active corps; 3 reserve corps; an army cavalry corps of 2 divisions; 2 Landwehr brigades for lines of communication duty; 4 battalions of mortars; 1 battalion 4.2 guns; 2 heavy coast mortar battalions, and 2 pioneer regiments. Each active army corps, 24 battalions strong, had at the beginning of the World War in each division 12 infantry battalions, 12 light batteries, of which 3 were howitzers, besides 4 heavy howitzer battalions belonging to the corps artillery. The assigning of only 4 heavy batteries to the army corps was entirely too small in view of the superiority of the French light artillery gun; each division should really have had heavy artillery, in order to itself solve its own battle missions, especially when the question to be solved was to deploy the guns under the protection of the heavy artillery. The necessity for employing heavy artillery in the attack soon became apparent, although the regulations had assigned them only a mission in the defense. In former wars, the fact that inferior infantry required stronger artillery was not given consideration. We can never foresee that during the development of war the inferior troops, such as the Landwehr and Landstrum organizations may not obtain the more difficult missions. At the beginning of the war the reserve corps, for example had no heavy howitzers and only 12 gun batteries. This was an entirely too weak artillery strength for any task. For lines of communication purposes the Landwehr brigades had a strength of 6 to 8 battalions with 1 or 2 batteries mostly of an old type, but they were often called upon to fight alongside active corps equipped with entirely different material. In any case, reserve and provisional organizations should have rather a stronger than a weaker proportion of artillery. The reserve corps in October brought into the field, divisions with 9 batteries, of which 3 were light howitzers.

In the rapid and noteworthy increase of the army it soon became necessary to adopt the 4 gun battery, without any disadvantages appearing, such as had been feared in time of peace, and then also to adopt the 3 unit organizations for the division infantry and to assign to each infantry 6 light gun, and 3 light howitzer batteries. Finally, when position warfare commenced, it became necessary to assign high angle fire artillery to the divisions, and each division therefore received 1 heavy battalion of 2 heavy howitzer batteries, and 1 10-cm. battery.

These formed the basic strength of the division and allowed exhausted divisions to be replaced by fresh troops. But it was desirable that the heavy batteries while under division control be assigned to the sector and left there until relieved by the army artillery. In the development of our tactics the experiences on the west battlefields had a major influence. In mobile warfare the battle was fought from concealed positions, exposed positions being exceptional. An artillery fighting principally from defiladed positions could not be neutralized, and only partially damaged. At the beginning shrapnel was the principal projectile. Its effect against vertical targets was annihilating, especially when these were in unsuitable formations, while the effect against skirmish lines taking skillful advantage of cover was remarkably low. The French artillery distinguished itself by close co-operation between the artillery and the infantry and by employing their guns up to the limits of their range. The German principles concerning combat proved to be correct; but we soon felt the superiority of the hostile artillery, which could not be offset by the use of our high angle guns.

Soon the strength of the hostile artillery forced us to organize an advanced guard artillery with the usual disadvantage of meeting the enemy suddenly and having to take unfavorable positions. For security on the march and during an advance against an enemy in position, single guns with the advance guard were sufficient, but not when a meeting engagement took place. It was necessary to coordinate the action of the infantry and the artillery. In reconnaissance it was first necessary to select observation posts, the gun positions being regulated on these. Often the caution had to be given that reconnaissance must not be so made as to draw fire upon our troops. In general the artillery had to fire over the heads of the infantry. It could not always be avoided that, at increased ranges, our troops were fired on by our own artillery, because of inattention or inability to determine the location of the dispersed formations. This bad feature could never be overcome in spite of all efforts. Our enemy also complained of the same trouble.

In the attack the principal factor was to neutralize the enemy's artillery, and to place our fire with full strength on the hostile infantry, in order to permit our individual skirmishers to arrive within short range of the enemy's position without firing. Artillery fire to accompany the infantry attack was indispensable; caution had to be given as to carelessly taking exposed positions, as this, in the West often caused us heavy losses. In the defense it was advisable to decrease the effectiveness of the hostile fire and the possibility of being seen from the air by closely hugging the ground. The deployment of the artillery in a single line, to which we had become accustomed during peace time, quickly disappeared. The employment of single entrenched platoons or sections in flanking positions, was soon adopted.

The further development of the German artillery took place under the requirements of position warfare, shrapnel was replaced by shell and also the range of the guns was increased with employment of high-angle fire artillery; also the effect of the shells was increased by the use of gas projectiles. Germany paid especial attention to the development of high-angle fire artillery, whereas the Allies laid preponderance upon heavy, flat-trajectory guns. In addition both sides took up the employment of railroad artillery on special railroad mounts, either for standard gauge or narrow gauge railroads, to be fired from specially constructed sidings, for very long ranges.

The effects of artillery fire was constantly increased by co-operation with the air service on observation of fire, reconnaissance and report of shots and by reducing and finally suppressing the employment of trial shots, which were replaced by theoretical calculations based upon daily atmospheric conditions. This method was fully employed only in the last year of the war, and our enemy had a start over us in this respect. A prime requirement was an accurate map of the targets and the batteries.

The Artillery

By the introduction of artillery position finding troops (flash and sound registry), who plotted observations of hostile batteries on a plane table (captive balloons could also be used to give data) results of observations free from all daily factors could be rapidly obtained.

The trigonometrical determination of positions of batteries and infantry positions was the foundation for this work. Sound registering troops, who were independent of the terrain, could distinguish between actual and false positions, although both sides sought to mislead such observations. Also in open warfare, the observation of reports of single shots by sound registering and flash observation troops of the light position finding troops, could be counted upon within three to six hours. It was necessary for these troops to have a reliable information service and the trigonometrical position of hostile batteries and observation posts, promptly transmitted to the proper headquarters.

In the defense timely steps could be taken to trigonometrically determine suitable points along lines in the battle zone leading towards the rear, from which points measurements could later be made.

Co-Operation of Infantry and Artillery

It was found that co-operation between infantry and artillery was very important. During the Franco-Prussian War, it was a matter of honor for our artillery to have a proper understanding with the infantry based on visual observations. Such support was possible as the battles took place at short ranges and as both sides could readily be distinguished by their uniforms, which, in spite of the clouds of smoke that lay over the firing lines, were clearly visible to the batteries fighting in the open. All our pre-war regulations required co-operation between the arms but it did not explain the means or methods by which this was to be accomplished; the infantry relied on the artillery, and the latter believed that it was the duty of the infantry to call upon its sister arm at the proper time for assistance against a designated objective. This question had received special consideration by our enemies and a correct system had been arranged to secure co-operation between the two arms in which nothing was to be left to chance. In supporting the infantry the artillery must keep down the fire of all hostile troops, both infantry and artillery, directed on its own infantry. To be practicable such support had to be given at particular moments, which only the attacker could determine, and also on particular points, which could be partly designated by the attacker but which, on the other hand, were partly dependent upon the movements of the enemy. On the defensive, the infantry must designate exactly the targets on which its artillery is to fire. A good system of liaison is therefore required. The foundation for such a system is obtained through orders and battle plans which designates the task and place for co-operation between designated infantry and its supporting artillery. In general the method of issuing orders remains unchanged, but exceptionally designated artillery units may be placed, in close terrain, under the infantry, and always so for accompanying artillery on special tasks such as village fights and suppression of machine gun nests. In the absence of a battle plan, co-operation between infantry and artillery is seldom possible even if both parties do their best to obtain it. In such cases, in vigorous rivalry, each arm looks after itself, leading to a lack of co-operation.

 The basis for combined tactics is the battle plan; cooperation between the two arms proceeds by mutual agreement between subordinate commanders through which the nature and location of targets is designated, and by direct requests from the battle line to obtain artillery fire at a designated point at a definite moment. If artillery fire control is not to be completely dropped, then only previously designated batteries should receive such requests, not from each infantry platoon commander but from the higher infantry commanders. These agreements must be made between the two headquarters. In no case must the infantry allow itself to be misled, by not taking advantage of favorable situations when there is no artillery support available. But the artillery must depend on its own observations, even when the infantry does not request special support. Thus battle plans and observations supplement and support one another. The battle plans operate only for prearranged tasks. Even with the assistance of the best means of communication, co-operation between the two arms can be attained only when the commanders have thoroughly studied the method thereof, and have determined the best method through combined exercises. Without special preparations, co-operation of the arms depends entirely on the good will of participants, and this always leads to disillusionments and losses of time.

The infantry can only be properly supported when it can make its actual battle lines known to the artillery beyond any doubt. As to location of the front line by the Air Service, a burning of colored lights and the exhibiting of infantry panels upon demand of the infantry airplane, as well as at pre-determined hours, has proven valuable; photographs can be utilized only after a longer time. Good results in marking front lines has been given by flags about 60 cm. square, white, black, red, red-yellow or yellow-red, but the side of the flag facing the enemy must be of some neutral protective color. The English prescribed that these flags were to be paid attention to only when they were moved back and forth, or when shown at pre-determined times; it was feared, not without good reason, that flags left standing by the enemy might lead to errors. As a matter of course, the front battle line only was to be so marked. It was found advisable upon occasions to burn bengal flares when the line designated in orders had been reached.

In the autumn offensive in Champagne in 1915, the French infantry wore linen cloths on their backs, to prevent their own artillery from firing on them. This method was not successful, as in spite of it, the infantry were heavily fired on by their own artillery during the advance. Mistakes can never altogether be avoided; we can only attempt to reduce them to a minimum and for this, information as to the plan of attack and good observation of the battlefield is necessary. Often enough, in close terrain, single detachments coming to the rear will be taken for enemy detachments advancing. Besides signals for "fire in front of us," which should be different for different units of the army, there should be the signal "We are fired on by our own artillery!" Often will the infantry mistake hostile shell fragments flying to their rear, or shells coming from a flank, for bad marksmanship of their own artillery. To avoid such errors during position warfare, artillery trench patrols were sent forward, and even better was the sending of battery commanders or battery officers to the infantry trenches. They here had opportunity to verify their own observations, to discuss matters personally with the infantry; to hear their requests and complaints, and to exchange information with them. Thus it was easy to secure co-operation of the arms, the infantry learned to meet the artillery half way in providing liaison, to take care to have good observation positions, and to assist observers materially by giving them their own observations. In any case an artillery observer, posted with general and superficial instructions, and to whom no one thereafter pays much attention cannot accomplish much in supporting the infantry. When a critical situation arises, where the infantry does not find the expected support, the infantry should not blame the artillery, but should seek the reason for the failure in their own conduct. In this manner artillery liaison officers sent to the front can perform good reconnaissance service.

Co-operation between the artillery and the infantry rests on artillery liaison officers who should be liberally supplied with maps and means of communication. The preliminary instructions given them should refer mainly to the battle missions of all batteries which are the barrage batteries for the sector, what batteries are available for fire within the sector, and finally how these batteries can be reached. Knowledge of the capability of the various guns is naturally necessary. As these officers have knowledge of the orders and information received by the infantry, they are in a position to recommend proper artillery support, inform their own commands as to the general situation, so that they may quickly prepare for coming missions. Their duty is especially to orient both arms in mutually informing them as to the whole situation. Frequently, it is desirable to communicate directly with the forward artillery observers, especially when targets are to be fired upon on request of the infantry.

The duties of observation and liaison officers are sharply separated, even when observation officers are in a position to transmit requests from infantry for artillery support. It is well to attach to each infantry battalion headquarters an artillery liaison officer, and supply him with necessary information. Never can the artillery count on using the infantry lines of communication which are always overworked. In position warfare the liaison officer is

The Artillery

detailed permanently to a battalion, and lives permanently with the battalion staff; in quiet sectors he will often be charged with the service of observation also within the battalion sector. The heavy artillery will have one artillery liaison officer detailed to each regiment; it is very desirable that artillery groups should conform to infantry subsectors, the co-operation of arms is much enhanced thereby. If the respective artillery commanders are in the vicinity of the headquarters to which they are attached, this will facilitate personal consultation of staffs and co-operation between the arms. Even when it is expected to have to meet an attack, timely consultation between the respective infantry regiments and the corresponding artillery units is thereby facilitated.

Co-Operation Between Artillery and Air Service

Close co-operation between the air service and artillery in order to locate targets, and in order to observe fire, is always a prime requirement for success. It is always very desirable to attach air service officers to the staffs of artillery commanders. Artillery airplanes supplement the service of the flash observation and sound registering troops; air photographs make it possible to definitely determine the effect of fire, by proving in a short flight the accuracy of the artillery adjustments and the results of the fire. Of the greatest importance is information of those hostile batteries which have been firing most or have been silenced, as well as good or poor fire by our artillery. Only those airplanes which are equipped with radio sets can remain in uninterrupted communication with the artillery without stopping their flight. Firing for effect with aerial observation requires a previous understanding and good communication between the observer and the battery commander. Previous discussions cannot cover long engagements and in such cases each observation airplane must, through its radio, call on batteries for fire. Artillery equipped with radio for receiving information, and the air service must have a firm determination to co-operate; in such cases all difficulties will be overcome. On the defensive it is necessary to designate certain batteries to receive information from the observation airplanes, which batteries should have particularly good communication. The positions of these batteries must be such that it will be possible for them to cover as much as possible of the battlefield, their range should be such that they will be independent of the movement of the infantry in order to avoid frequent changes of position and arrangements must be made with the air service at each station under all kinds of weather, so that quick decoding of radio messages may be made and transmitted to the proper headquarters or directly to designated batteries. Should no intelligence messages be received for his own command the radio officer must listen in on messages from airplanes to neighboring units for his own orientation.

The Decisive Battle in Position Warfare

In the first months of the war, an insufficient supply of ammunition made difficult the systematic employment of the artillery in the attack. The artillery on the defensive was divided into two classes; guns in concealed battle positions and forward guns; the latter were often in the first line in masked or covered positions and were to fire only when the hostile assault took place. These guns were generally destroyed early and a belief arose in an automatic defensive barrage, which was to be brought down by means of bengal light signals. The front of a defensive barrage for 1 battery was not to exceed 200 meters; but such a width was generally exceptional. This proceeding misled the infantry into relying too greatly on the artillery support, and to call too frequently for this support. Through the loss of guns during the enemy's artillery preparation, the defensive barrage was never as strong as intended, often came too late, and without endangering the defender could not be brought close to the front line trenches. Even when defensive barrages lasted only 2 to 3 minutes, it increased the expenditure of ammunition. In the same way reprisal fire did not serve any good purpose. "It was designed to square the account with the hostile artillery by annihilating fire on the respective sectors of the opposing hostile lines and so to prevent him from deploying and advancing to his attack position." This was the method we still adhered to in the battle of the Somme. This procedure was of no value. We found out that air superiority and the efficiency of the position finding troops was essential in the artillery duel. New regulations prevented reprisal fire, substituted annihilating fire for defensive barrages, and prescribed for each kilometer front an artillery strength of 5 to 7 barrage batteries, 4 to 6 high angle batteries, and 1 to 3 heavy gun batteries.

The strength of the artillery defense does not lie in making the barrage and annihilating fire denser, but in attempting to foresee the enemy's movements. In a new edition of the Regulations dated September 1, 1917, this idea was further discussed, and no mention was made of a systematic calculation of the artillery strength. It was required that timely preparations be made, when the artillery deployment is undertaken, as to the artillery battle, without regard to the damaging of guns during the artillery battle, because such a battle would at least delay and weaken, possibly decisively, the enemy. The difficulties lay in the nature of the targets; well concealed batteries can withstand a heavy bombardment; in the greater number of and mobility of targets, the enemy made more frequent changes of his battery position and of his artillery reserves than we did; finally there was the difficulty of observation. As terrestrial observation is in most cases impracticable, artillery superiority is closely connected with air superiority. Very naturally two groups arose, one for long range fire into the enemy's back areas and the other a close defense group, just close enough to take under fire the enemy's battle trenches. These designations were not well named, the close defense group was as a matter of fact the furthest to the rear. Grouping of the artillery in several lines was recommended, the reinforcing batteries, which arrived generally only during the progress of the battle, being placed in the second line. Orders must, from time to time, be given as to how long the artillery battle is to continue against a threatened attack, and where and when the annihilating fire is to be laid down. In any case the general principle is that the artillery fire should be laid down as late as possible. It was much to be desired that our artillery should be strong enough to lay down annihilating fire against the hostile infantry and at the same time, with a part of it continue the artillery duel. For such a purpose there was needed heavy gun batteries, from 18-cm. caliber upwards, which deployed in depth, could with assistance of special balloons and airplanes, undertake to neutralize distant hostile batteries. By separating the artillery into a distant and close defense group there was a natural depth formation. Against a penetration this greatly decreased the effect of surprise, as well as furnishing flank support for adjacent sectors. The great difficulty in the transmission of orders and information soon became very clear.

Fire against the hostile infantry is the second mission of the artillery in the defensive battle. In this we must be free from the thought that it is possible, or necessary, to destroy all of the hostile infantry positions. The question is, during the development of the hostile attack, to select the tactically most important targets such as infantry, mortars, command and observation posts, support trenches, bomb-proof dugouts; to fire either in order to destroy them or else prevent their occupation. Daily bombardment of unoccupied trenches is useless.

The artillery defense against assault is by pre-arranged mass fire, in more or less rigid form, annihilating fire, or barrage fire. Annihilating fire is directed against the rear echelons of the attack, if possible against supports of the assault troops; the barrage is laid down on the enemy's approach lines to strike down the advancing infantry. Withdrawing barrage fire to our own front line should be avoided due to the fact that our infantry, at the moment of the hostile assault, must be saved from the demoralizing effect of short shots coming from their own artillery. Where the hostile trenches are only a short distance away and when artillery cannot cover dead angles in front of our trenches, the artillery fire is replaced by trench mortars and rifle or hand grenades. In these cases, the artillery directs the mass of its fire in rear of the foremost hostile lines. Trench mortars are under the command of the artillery to insure proper regulation of the barrage. When the opposing trenches are far apart, the higher commanders prescribe the line in No Man's Land on which the barrage fire is laid; it is best to have this line where natural obstacles will delay the enemy. It must be possible to lay down the barrage on all parts of our front and in front of adjacent sectors. Should the enemy penetrate into our position, supporting the infantry fight, is difficult. It will often only be possible to limit the amount of penetration and by firing gas shells at the hostile artillery prevent them from assisting the attack. A mobile artillery reserve is of great advantage; it is brought up and employed as prescribed for open warfare.

For calculating the strength of the artillery we have but few rules to go by. The number of guns required is naturally dependent on the enemy's artillery strength, but this can only be determined by its effects. It is then usually too late to provide reinforcements. In such cases, we would have to renounce the superiority in the artillery fight. The strength of the field fortifications also has a material effect as to the strength of the artillery. The weaker our position may be the greater should be the proportion of guns. The commander must start from a definite basis; it is never possible to be too strong in artillery. As a guide it was prescribed that for each 400 meters of hostile trench, 1 high angle fire battery for annihilating fire was to be provided, and that the barrage fire was to be laid down by machine guns, light trench mortars and the infantry. For destroying 1 battery, according to Par. 254 Battle Regulations for Artillery, 300 rounds from heavy howitzers or 200 rounds from mortars were required; and by Par. 268, same Regulations, for each division sector at the commencement of the attack, 1 to 2 mortar batteries; 2 to 3 heavy howitzer batteries and 1 to 2 heavy gun batteries were required for the artillery battle. Light artillery was used against casual targets. The difficult situation of our troops compelled us to operate generally with materially smaller forces than our enemy. Usually in quiet sectors for each kilometer of front, each division besides its 9 light batteries had 2 to 4 heavy howitzer batteries, 1 mortar battery and 2 heavy gun batteries. This was not enough. It did not suffice at all and besides, the division sectors were generally noticeably wider than given above.

No steps had been taken in Germany to prescribe a rule for the occupation of a battle front by the artillery. This was determined by the strength of the hostile artillery and the method of conducting the battle. In active sectors, when an attack was foreseen, there was provided for about each 4 kilometers front (when a counter-attack division was provided for each 2 division sectors whose artillery was available) the following artillery was provided for each kilometer of front:

3.5 to 5 light gun and 1 light howitzer batteries,
1.5 to 2.5 heavy howitzer batteries,
1 to 1.5 10-cm. gun batteries.

This made a total for a 4 kilometer sector of 14 to 20 light batteries, 6 to 10 heavy howitzer batteries, and 4 to 6 heavy gun batteries. In addition, it is desirable to have an artillery reserve, and a mobile artillery repair shop in rear of the front.

The Offensive

The first attacks were, to be true, erroneously based on destroying the hostile artillery in preparation lasting many hours, surprise being unobtainable. Until we came to the point of neutralizing the hostile artillery at the moment of the assault, when we decided to do without bomb-proof cover for the battery positions, and when we were able to avoid range finding and trial shots by substituting therefor theoretical calculations based on daily weather conditions and accurate measurement of distances between battery and target, then only could the high command count on the possibility of obtaining surprise for the decisive action. This was made the easier by the number of battery positions that had been constructed along the entire front during the years of war, and subsequently by the introduction of tanks.

Batteries designated for counter battery work can be kept back; the artillery employed to support the infantry assault has, however, to be held close in hand, and these should, as long as possible, utilize the full possibilities of range and not make a change of position, especially when a counter-attack may require artillery support for the infantry. Only effective support will keep the assault going; as a matter of experience the infantry only gets as far as its artillery fire reaches. As a general rule it must be held that the artillery preparation should be as short as possible; with one blow the resistance of the enemy must be overcome. Almost always will there be the accessory mission of destroying the hostile

The Artillery

liaison and intelligence communications.

Gas shells, which at the close of the war were loaded with stronger bursting charges, were the more effective as they were the less perceived by the senses (being odorless and colorless). After a "green cross" bombardment the terrain can again be entered within two hours. The effect of "yellow cross" gas shell is noted gradually for hours and days, the effectiveness continues a long time in good weather, especially in villages and woods.

In a large attack for penetration, the following missions fall to the artillery:

    1. Destruction and neutralization of hostile artillery and trench mortars.

    2. Neutralization of the hostile trench and supporting positions.

    3. Firing on reserves and rear communications, on observation and command posts, parks, balloons, transportation and munition centers in rear beyond the objective of the attack.

    4. Supporting the assault by a rolling barrage.

    5. Accompanying the infantry assault with infantry guns and light artillery to break up local centers of resistance by direct and close shell fire.

    6. Protecting the infantry after reaching the objectives by a standing barrage.

    7. Repulsing hostile counter-attacks, and distant approach of reserves.

For counter battery work at the beginning of the attacks there should be provided for each division sector for observed destructive fire, 1 to 2 mortar batteries, 2 to 3 heavy howitzer batteries, and 1 to 2 heavy gun batteries; this number must be reinforced for neutralization of the hostile artillery in order to obtain a quicker success. Only seldom will the general situation justify a delay. It is better to employ over the entire terrain gas shell and high explosive shells to neutralize the enemy's activities. In gassing areas the quick fire guns of the light artillery are more suitable than the heavier projectile from the bigger guns. In order to neutralize 1 hectare, by gas, the following ammunition is required:

100 rounds light artillery, or 60 rounds light howitzer, or 10-cm. guns,
25 rounds heavy howitzers,
10 rounds mortars.

In order to neutralize by gas 1 square kilometer from 1 to 2 hours, there is required 10 light batteries, 17 10-cm. batteries, 12 heavy howitzer batteries and 10 mortar batteries. If the enemy's artillery is contained in a zone 2000 meters wide and 800 meters deep, or in area of 1.6 square kilometers there would be required for neutralizing by use of gas:

12 light batteries (of which 6 batteries have not previously fired),
3 light howitzer batteries,
2 10-cm. guns batteries (neither having previously fired),
5 heavy howitzer batteries (1 to open fire for surprise effect later).

At the moment of the assault these batteries neutralize hostile artillery with gas and high explosive shells. In this mission attack airplanes can greatly assist by attacking hostile batteries with machine gun fire, and by bombing. Single batteries remain available for the second period as surprise batteries, waiting for the attack to develop in order not to be previously known to hostile barrage batteries. The English Regulations for the defensive against a strong attack provided for special "silent" batteries; the French similarly provided "dumb" batteries.

To prepare a position for assault for each 100 meters of front penetration, 1 high-angle fire battery is needed. Places which are not to be assaulted are neutralized by the smaller caliber gun. A part of the preparation is taken over by the trench mortars with 1 heavy or 1 medium trench mortar for each 40 meters front. For 3 division trench mortar companies, containing all kinds and including 12 heavy and 24 medium trench mortars, with 10% of spare mortars, a front for penetration of 1600 meters can be assigned, and in 1 hour they can fire 280 heavy and 900 medium trench mortar bombs. As for the artillery, where the second line must cover neighboring sectors, they must cover with their fire 1200 to 1500 meters of the front to be penetrated. Details cannot

The Artillery

be given here without considering a definite case of attack. Par. 267, Battle Regulations for Artillery, prescribes the following ammunition as required for the artillery preparation preparatory to an assault:

"In about 3 hours a position can be prepared:

	One battery	One line of trenches width in meters	Number of rounds
Light Howitzer		100	800
Heavy Howitzer, Model 13		150	600
Heavy Howitzer, Model 02		100	400
Heavy Howitzer, Model 96		75	300
Mortar (3 guns battery)		100	225

"The above ammunition includes that required for the destruction of bomb-proofs; also for the destruction of obstacles which are not more than 30 meters from the line of trenches fired at. Against more distant obstacles, special ammunition and time must be allowed. In a contrary case their destruction will be accomplished through the dispersion of shells directed at the trenches. By use of flank fire, which also always gives a moral effect, the amount of ammunition prescribed above may be reduced one-third. Whether all the lines of defense of a position are neutralized simultaneously or successively will depend upon the number of available batteries."

There will be required for example:

3 light batteries each covering 100 meters front firing 800 rounds each, giving a total of 300 meters front with 2400 rounds.

7 heavy howitzer batteries each covering 100 meters front firing 700 rounds each, giving a total of 700 meters front and 4000 rounds.

4 mortar batteries each covering 100 meters front firing 400 rounds each, giving a total of 400 meters front and 900 rounds.

However, this number of batteries alone is not sufficient to prepare one position for assault. Adjacent sectors must also as far as possible be neutralized by use of gas or smoke in order to prevent them from using enfilade fire or making counter-attacks. A secondary mission is the firing on the positions in readiness of the reserves, lines of approach, command and observation posts, munition dumps, balloon ground stations.

As the main point of defense rests not in the less easily found intermediate lines but in the less conspicuous built machine gun nests between lines. General Nivelle in 1916 introduced the rolling barrage. This after the first jump was to permanently precede the infantry at the rate of 100 meters in about 4 minutes and was to halt for a time beyond designated attack objectives as a standing barrage. In this manner, all defensive positions in the entire terrain, such as machine gun nests are effectively neutralized until the infantry with their own weapons can attack them themselves. Frontal counter-attacks should be broken up by the barrage fire. But it is necessary that the infantry should closely follow the rolling barrage, that the infantry should not stop its advance, which would result in the rear lines over-running the front lines, nor that the advance should proceed too rapidly. The latter case is the most unfavorable, as then the positions being attacked would be free from fire too soon, and machine guns and reserves could then undertake a counter-attack. The limit for the rolling barrage is the effective fire of the guns which is about 4000 meters. This requires the artillery to be posted immediately in rear of the line of departure, and then that the batteries advance rapidly to the position penetrated. If the rolling barrage is to provide effective protection for advancing infantry, the latter must adhere exactly to the prescribed program and closely follow the points of burst of the shells. Consequently, it follows that in the first line, gun batteries are most suitable, that howitzer shells may be employed as a pace marker but cannot be used in the barrage on account of the backward flight of the splinters of their shells. Infantry can be taught to overcome the fear of closely following the barrage by thorough training, in which at the start they follow the barrage to one side. The closer the infantry follows the better. The best formation to follow is small narrow columns, so as to reduce losses from back flying shell splinters. Attempt to regulate the advance of

The Artillery

the rolling barrage by the advance of the infantry has not been successful.

It was found that often in variable terrain the rolling barrage had been set at too fast a speed, so that it got away from the infantry and could not be stopped. It therefore was determined that the barrage would advance slowly from one line to another. In general 1 light battery is needed for 100 meters front.

The infantry must never rely on rolling barrage alone, but must advance through the strength of their own weapons. Especially must they depend on the infantry accompanying guns. Each regiment of infantry has at least 1 accompanying battery assigned to it, which is entirely detached from the artillery command, and which is distributed among battalions by sections or platoons, each gun having 2 caissons filled with shells. It is to be noted that the guns of reserve battalions are given 2 extra caissons per gun for replenishing ammunition. These form an ammunition section. Considering the great demands, selected teams must be provided, and for each gun and each caisson at least 6 extra horses are necessary.

The possibility of watering the horses during the advance must not be lost sight of. The quickest method for crossing trenches is to fill them in. The battery commander remains with the infantry regimental staff, but may temporarily join his guns. Sending junior officers to infantry regimental staffs is never advisable, as they may not receive the same respect, and may have less tactical training and experience. The battery commander will recommend to the regiment to have necessary roads marked by streamers, by signs or by paper markers. The attacking infantry cannot, by any means, be called on to furnish labor detachments, but the division should attach at least 1 pioneer squad to each gun and to each caisson. For each man 1 long handled shovel or 1 pick axe is required. The intrenching tools on wagons serve as a reserve. In addition materiel is carried along for camouflage against airplanes (wire netting is too heavy and too rigid to shape). By using natural cover (as for example shell-holes for the teams), and guns protected by camouflage nets against airplanes, they are ready to have teams quickly hitched and accompany the attacking infantry. Occupying a position in readiness can ordinarily be done at night only after the roads have been carefully reconnoitered, so as to avoid unnecessary fatigue for the teams. About 15 minutes before the concentration or assault the teams are hitched up, otherwise the guns will only be left behind. Crossings over our own trenches (in this case it is best to utilize bridges provided in advance) are to be made during the artillery preparation. Crossing places must be watched by details and kept in proper repair. The difficult movement across shell torn terrain while at the same time keeping up with the infantry behind the barrage, is hard for the artillery.

The gun commander (to be generally an officer when single guns are detached to battalions) remains with his vehicles, and sends a noncommissioned officer forward to the battalion to prepare timely information through patrols of machine gun nests to be fired at, as these are the principal targets. Whether it is practicable to fire over the heads of the infantry in front depends on the situation; often the infantry on pre-arranged signals will have to clear the field of fire of the guns. Fire is opened only when the infantry can no longer advance or when hostile counter-attack is noted, or when tanks start to attack. Generally the fire will be at short ranges and from open or partly covered positions. Positions from an elevation above that of the infantry which allow of direct fire without danger to the infantry are especially valuable. A caisson is unlimbered near each gun, but the ammunition is not removed therefrom so that no loss of time occurs when the advance is resumed. The following dispositions of the battery are generally suitable:

    1. The battery commander with his special detail remains with the infantry regimental commander.

    2. 1 officer and 1 noncommissioned officer is with each gun, and 2 caissons and 18 extra horses with each battalion acting as accompanying artillery in the front line. Battle missions are: to support the infantry in the first line against machine guns and tanks.

    3. With the reserve infantry battalion: 2 guns and 6 caissons. Battle missions: advance from one covered position to another prepared to defend against counter-attacks.

The light ammunition column must plainly mark its position; agents sent to the rear by batteries to obtain ammunition are to be

The Artillery 257

directed to guide caissons to their batteries.

The losses in personnel of accompanying batteries have been relatively small, while the loss in animals has been often very great, without, however (thanks to providing sufficient reserve horses), interfering with the mobility of the artillery vehicles.

The inconvenience during the advance of the infantry in the rolling barrage becoming gradually thinner, can only be overcome by the timely advance of the artillery. This then gives a second artillery approach march having the following features: early special reconnaissance and air observation, bringing forward and installing the artillery position finding troops and providing artillery orientation, observation service, firing positions and the quick construction of lines of communication, the re-establishment of the battery stations, orienting battery positions and aiming points, selecting targets, and determining ranges and organizing the meteorological service for the artillery. So far as concerns a new prepared attack: drawing up the orders for the development and advance of the batteries, the ammunition supply and location, the battle missions for single guns, barrage tables, etc.

All the foregoing tasks are supervised by the division in accordance with instructions from higher authority and the preparations are to be completed before the first penetration. The carrying out of the order must proceed as soon as the first line stops, without waiting for information and decisions as to further intentions. If reconnaissance, range finding, etc., proves to be premature, or unnecessary on account of the attack continuing forward or because the attack has been discontinued, the fact that the artillery formation has been changed, etc., is of no importance; it is better to start these preparations early rather than too late. The systematic carrying out of missions must not be interfered with by unnecessary rapidity of movements.

Altogether the artillery for an attack on a division sector whose zone of action was 2 kilometers wide is as follows:

	Light Gun	Light Howitzer	10 cm	13 cm	HV How.	M
Neutralizing hostile artillery with gas	6	3			8	0
Surprise batteries (may also be used for firing gas)	6	0	2	0	1	0
Standing barrage fire	0	0	4	2	0	0
Artillery for preparatory fire	0	5	0	0	7	4
Accompanying artillery	3	1	0	0	0	0
Total	15	9	6	2	16	4

We thus have for each division sector 24 light batteries, 8 heavy howitzers, and 2 mortar battalions with 26 batteries. Altogether 52 batteries. Before the World War no one of us thought of the amount of ammunition. Orders for the deployment of artillery, for its occupation of positions, and for furnishing ammunition could be developed only gradually. In 1917 the English for 1 division sector, with a zone of action, 2 kilometers wide, had artillery of 3 divisions, 24 light batteries and 33 heavy batteries. Ludendorff provided for each kilometer front of attack 20 to 30 batteries, that is for a division zone of action 40 to 60 batteries. Generally in most battles 3 divisions were posted, one in rear of the other, each provided with 13 to 20 batteries. The question as to the proportion of the artillery is no longer: "How many guns for each thousand men should be provided?" but far rather: "How much infantry will be required to utilize the success of the fire of the artillery?" But is not the infantry still the principal arm as heretofore? It is no use to argue this matter. General Ludendorff writes in his memoirs: "The artillery suffered as much as the infantry. The longer the war lasted, the greater were its losses in the defense as well as in the attack; it became more and more the bearer of the burdens of the battlefield and the hold-fast of the front.....It is right not to dispute the question that the infantry is the main arm. There are no longer principal arms. Each arm has its use, all are necessary."

Chapter XII – The Year 1918

Transition from Position to Mobile Warfare

The year 1917 finally brought the campaign in Russia to an end. The troops relieved there furnished the means for an offensive in the West, in which the experiences gathered concerning the penetration battles in Eastern Galicia, on the Düna, in Roumania and in Upper Italy found excellent use. The general situation demanded the offensive, which the troops also greatly desired. "In the same measure in which the defense depressed the troops, the offensive raised their morale. In defense the army had finally to succumb to the hostile superiority in men and munitions of war, while the offensive had always been the strongest role of the army." The attack is the most powerful form of war, and brings the decision; and a modern defensive battle is far more costly than the attack. With a superiority of from 25 to 30 divisions over the enemy, the offensive could be started.

When thus the situation of the German armies demanded the offensive, the principal question could, however, be only that of a penetration, considering the extensive of the hostile front, from which action there could follow later on, in case of a favorable decision, an enveloping attack of the separated hostile wing.

The penetrating attack had been about rejected in Germany prior to the war as, of course, it was harder to start and harder to execute, and certainly furnished smaller results than an enveloping battle as Count Schlieffen had described it in his "Cannae" procedure. From the ill-fated penetration at Liaoyan it was concluded: "The ill-success only furnishes proof that with modem fire effect and modern field fortifications tactical penetration has little hope of success."

The question as to whether in the selection of the point of attack strategic demands should be placed above tactical requirements, — the affirmative being demanded by the "Criticism of the World War" but denied by Ludendorff — cannot be discussed here. I agree with Ludendorff in his statement: "Tactics should have been placed above mere strategy. Without tactical success strategy could not be accomplished. Strategy which does not think of tactical success, is condemned in the very start to failure. Numerous examples for this were furnished by the attacks of the Entente in the first three years of the war."

In the penetration we could attempt to break in at a favorable point for maneuver, to annihilate the reserves streaming together here, and to bring to an end through this victory the operation in the quickest possible way; or, we could, through operations intended to deceive, draw the reserves away from the decisive point, and utilize our superiority in numbers to enlarge the tactical entry and to conduct the final battle against the gradually appearing reserves. Brussilow adopted this procedure in Eastern Asia, his false operations extending to the lower Düna, his penetration starting on the right wing of the attack zone and then continuing south. A German counter-attack broke the Russian offensive.

The German leadership selected the first, and shorter road, as it hoped; it had learned by experience how very difficult it is, in view of the great development of aerial fighting forces to deceive the hostile leadership by trying to execute double attacks separated in time and space. Preparations for further attacks took place along the entire front, as well as feints on a smaller scale. The German leadership had made its decision; all it had to do now was to see that the attacks would not come to a standstill at strong hostile positions. Did the forces suffice to have a second attack immediately follow the first? "It will be a giant struggle," writes Ludendorff, "commencing at one point, continuing at another and which will take a long time."

However, the infantry had a far different value than had the infantry with which we executed the offensive at the opening of the World War. Battalions and companies were commanded by young, for the greater part by very young, officers who probably had had by then experiences in the field, but who still lacked those qualities which had formed the strength of our officers in peace. Thoroughly trained to meet all situations, indefatigable in their care for the subordinates, an example in danger as well as in enduring fatigue and hardships, our old officers' corps was the best proof of the correctness of our peace training. The difficulties of filling up the gaps in our officers forced us to husband our trained officers and to cut out a "leader reserve" prior to each battle. But, nevertheless, there still was excellent spirit in the ranks, and the men followed their leaders in full confidence. Of course, the training was no longer the same, as we could not accomplish in six months what had taken two years in time of peace, which was especially true of the use of the rifle as a firearm and as a shock arm. The troops were younger, and added to the lack of training was the fact that the youthful recruits were neither fully developed physically nor trained. The youthful recruits, who had grown up without the parental influence because their fathers were in the field, were spoiled by high wages and manner of living, and were lacking in morale as well.

Methods of Hostile Defense and German Offensive

On the Allied side an attack on a grand scale was expected — but by no means before April. Just as was the case with us, the decrease in moral value of the troops was felt by the Allies. In Regulations for the Defense the Entente sought development of the then accepted German views in adopting the mobile defense. The leader was to designate:

1. Whether the attack was to be accepted in the first or the second position, or,

2. Whether the attack was to be avoided, in order to launch a well-prepared powerful counter-attack during the enemy's advance, and, at the time that he would not have the support of his artillery, or,

3. Whether voluntary retreat should take place to a position in rear, to profit, at some other point, by the delay the enemy's attack would encounter in such a movement.

The condition of all works, badly shot to pieces, was accepted as a fact that could not be helped, and thus we declined to keep up a defense of "trunk" lines, which the troops up to this time regarded as a prerequisite for a successful defense. After a protracted drum fire the only question could be of tenaciously holding a few critical points; these the commanders attempted to establish inconspicuously under mutual fire support; the trenches situated between them, with strong obstacles, were to divert the attention of the enemy from the combat groups, which, grouped behind or beside each other, were consolidated into strong points in company sectors, and these latter again into battalion centers of resistance. The trenches were only for the purpose of facilitating communication in quieter times. A battle group, usually of the strength of half a platoon, consisted of 1 machine gun with some artillery observers, riflemen, and hand and rifle grenade throwers. In this manner formation in depth and an intermediate terrain defense had been prepared, the importance of which we, as attackers, found out to our cost. Special weight was laid on the counter-attack and flanking fire was specially recommended for the reason that it would in this manner be possible to save rifles. Only one general difference from the German Regulations was adopted, in this case the medium and heavy flat-trajectory guns with the corps artillery and a few high-angle fire batteries remained under the orders of corps headquarters, which latter thus retained control of fighting the hostile artillery. The divisions kept only their field artillery, the stationary tank defense guns and a few high-angle fire batteries. We will point out here, that, on the part of the enemy, the flat-trajectory artillery — different with us since we had a preference for batteries — was preferred for tactical and technical reasons (minor weight of gun, less powder charge).

The divisions occupied sectors of from 2 to 4 kilometers breadth; first and second positions were separated by a distance of from 6 to 8 kilometers, so that in any case the attacker would be compelled to again deploy his artillery. The main fighting trench is the most important work of any defensive position; security detachments are placed in front of it, and in rear lies the *parallele de soutien** at a distance of about 200 meters as an exit for counter-attacks. Within the trench were bombproof shelters capable of defense, while in the main fighting trench there were small shelters. The construction of deeper and stronger bombproofs in the main fighting trench was prohibited. Besides the connecting trenches, inter-locking trenches and intermediate lines were constructed, as well as numerous rallying points independent of the trenches. In front of the batteries was an artillery protective position consisting of strong points connected by trenches. False positions and protection against aerial reconnaissance were specially valued.

The fire activity had almost completely discarded the retaliation fire; the stationary barrage fire was left mainly to the infantry auxiliary arms; greater importance was assigned to the daily destruction and annihilation fire (counter preparation) in which the minenwerfers participated. High angle fire was directed against fortifications, fighting positions, observation positions, bombproofs and crossings of trenches; batteries were attacked by flat- trajectory guns; routes of approach stopped by machine guns. The defensive method demanded tenacious resistance on the part of all detachments and also of the ones that had been dispersed, so that points of resistance sprang up which could cause the attack confusion and thereby prepare the success of counterattacks. Reserves that were not designed for counter-attacks, according to the defensive plan, prepared themselves for defense just where they happened to be. "It is important that the reserves remain in readiness for employment at the places originally designated."

The German commanders distinguished between attacks with a limited objective (for purpose of bettering the position, relieving

---

* "Parallel support."

the main attack through deceiving the enemy), and the penetrating battle which could develop after entry into the hostile position into the battle of maneuver. In spite of extensive preparations the penetrating attempts on the part of the enemy had come to a standstill after the relatively easy beginnings; the German penetration was based on the maxim that the hostile artillery had to be taken the first day. This required an entry of at least 10 kilometers. Emphasis was laid on the great value of surprise. The extensive preparations for attack could, however, hardly be hidden from the hostile aerial observers and this information was augmented by statements of deserters and prisoners (and for that reason, we, as well as our enemies, stopped all minor attack operations prior to the battle). Though we received in this manner timely knowledge of each hostile attack, we had to assume that the enemy received the same in regard to our intentions. To keep the operation secret as well as strict control of the troops in shelter, on the march, in deploying and in the service of communication, remained one of the most important tasks of leadership.

The Battle of the Somme had furnished an illustration of the slow "eating through" process of a stabilized situation; the longer this took the more time the defender gained for his counter-measures. That had to be avoided at all cost. After the first entry, quick attack was essential so as not to allow the enemy to come to his senses. The hostile attacks never were able to progress beyond the fire zone of their own artillery fire; thus the attack fell through. A deeper entry could have been accomplished only by rapidly advancing the artillery, inserting reserves, relieving the shock troops from the care for the flanks and rear, and then the utilization of tanks.

While the regulations of the Allies laid emphasis on the necessity of depth formation and narrow fronts in attack, we sought to find the proper mean between the demand for the pressure of fresh forces from the rear (narrow front) and the possibility of advantageously posting the artillery, as well as the necessity for assigning to each division in the first line a good road for bringing up supplies (broad battle fronts). From this it resulted that it was not considered correct in a deep attack to obtain less than 2 kilometers' breadth of a battle front for the division, while in an attack with a limited objective the breadth could be 3 kilometers. Even with a decrease of numerical force a battle breadth of 2 kilometers was found not to be to large, as the power of fire arms had been materially increased and as the gun carriers in the first line were designated to utilize fire effect. But if, on the other hand, the number of rifles decreased too much we had to limit ourselves to holding the enemy and first gaining terrain supported by the progress of a stronger neighbor. The necessity was perceived furthermore of disregarding some single well fortified supporting points, around which, we had learned, protracted fighting would ensue and holding them down for the present and taking them later on by an attack from flank or rear. As was the practice in Eastern Galicia and on the Isonzo, it was believed to be advantageous to conduct the attack so that preparations were made on a large scale in the earliest assignment of the troops for an enveloping attack against single supporting points. In the further development of this thought, not all parts of the hostile position were to be attacked equally, but the center of gravity was to be laid on such points the possession of which had to be decisive in the further conduct of the battle.

Two to three division sectors were placed under one corps headquarters; in the second and third line followed divisions for relief, to be inserted after the leading troops had expended their force. The thought of placing them under the orders of the leading division was rejected, as that method would merely have hastened their premature use. They were to remain as a reserve in the hands of the highest commander. Their insertion in any case was proper only where the attack made good progress. As we had learned, taking full advantage of a success best helped the troops that had remained behind or even had suffered reverses. In any case they had to be kept close at hand, but did not need to reach the assault terrain until the very day of the assault.

Based on our experiences it was deemed correct to have a strong artillery preparation lasting for about two hours, with a full utilization of gas. A shock-like fire preparation might well be suited for minor or medium operations, but attack without fire preparation could be successful only under specially favorable conditions. Carefully thought out distribution of tasks for the artillery and minenwerfers as well as separation of targets was required. Minenwerfers were placed under the orders of the artillery and, on account of their limited range, directed their fire only on the nearest trenches, especially on obstacles.

The longer the artillery fight lasts, the harder will it be to accomplish surprise; the more difficult will it be to protect the assaulting troops in their places of readiness. The artillery fight commences at dark, so that the infantry can start the assault in the early morning hours after a powerful bombardment of the hostile position. We must prove in every case how few guns we require for the artillery action and how many can be employed to prepare the hostile positions for the assault. We must avoid creating spaces near the trenches which suffer nothing from the bombardment and into which the enemy may withdraw. The major battles have shown that the defensive power is by no means broken by changing the trenches into a field of shell-holes; but the hostile morale is most surely destroyed by creating fire pauses, then advancing the fire and finally bringing a burst of fire back upon the point to be entered. It is entirely wrong (as the French and British did) to create the conviction in the infantry that through this fire it would be saved from close range fighting; this kind of fighting can only be shortened and made easier.

After the position has been entered, the infantry demands:

1. Artillery support in the position when overcoming the hostile resistance (machine gun nests and rallying points) by attaching about 1 accompanying battery per regiment.

2. Fire protection during the advance, — "Creeping barrage." A further success lies only in the rapid advance — commencing with the entry — of an artillery wave, with teams hitched, that has been kept back for that purpose, and the entire force of teamed minenwerfers. The difficulties of the ground have to be overcome and proper steps taken to prevent the roads from getting blocked up. It is also necessary to bring forward, besides the artillery, mortars and long range 10-cm. guns.

3. If the infantry has reached the objective of the attack, the creeping barrage changes into a stationary barrage (which gradually decreases and is again called for at places of counter-attack).

4. Until the forward movement is resumed, the fire activity of the

artillery is to be regulated according to the points of view of defense; advancing reserves are to be kept off and counterattacks, as soon as perceived, are to be annihilated by timely action.

The artillery receives a very material support by the attack squadrons and the observation airplanes of the aerial fighting forces.

The deeper the entry is to be made, the earlier must the time for the assault be fixed. It depends on the time required for artillery preparation whether the infantry leaves the assault position prior to the artillery fire during the night or, in case a longer artillery preparation is planned, during the artillery fire. Losses by hostile artillery fire have to be reckoned with in the latter case. It is unfavorable if the preparations extend over several days; for, in spite of all destructive artillery fire, the enemy can recuperate during the night and shift his forces. The longer the artillery preparation, the more favorable for the attack. "Placing the assault infantry in readiness is the first crisis of the attack." Danger lies in a too extensive crowding together of men, which increases the difficulties of hiding all noises in movements and which increases the losses in sudden fire. Complete clearness must obtain concerning the procedure in case the enemy has perceived the position in readiness and attempts to destroy it. The commander must regulate exactly what equipment the troops are to carry. The troops are placed in readiness in very compact formation to rapidly run under the barrage fire, and assumes depth formation only during the advance. If infantry is placed in readiness in great depth formation the first lines must be made especially strong, as we have to reckon with the rear waves being cut off by sudden barrage fire, and the leading waves in that case must be strong enough to force the decision. Whether the infantry attack is to be executed in thin lines or in lines of squads must be carefully considered in each instance. If the enemy's resistance is strong, each line of trenches will as a rule consume the attack power of one wave, so that the number of attack waves should be fixed by the number of lines of trenches to be taken; but, in no case, must the leading wave halt at the first trench; what can proceed forward, must keep on till the attack objective is reached. As the opponent will no longer occupy his trenches in a dense battle line, we might eliminate the entry in a dense skirmish line. In this manner the entry in close swarms, in "shock-squads" was developed. But we cannot do at all without a skirmish line as a battle formation; formation into shock squads is merely a makeshift. In the skirmish line, supervision is easier; the skirmish line facilitates the greatest deployment of fire power. The skirmish line must be formed prior to the time that the entrenched terrain is reached. More important than the formation of a definite attack procedure is the celerity of the advance. Infantry must become accustomed to having machine guns fire over its heads and also through gaps between detachments. But by this manner of advance, the question has also been answered whether troops are to advance in long or short rushes. As long as possible the walk is continued, and only when the enemy's fire becomes effective, are short, irregular rushes taken by squads and individuals. The farther off the attack objective, the less attention will be paid to the trench garrison; they are captured by the "mopping-up" detachments. It would be an error for the leading line to move toward a flank to assist a neighboring detachment; that would merely promote the loss of the march direction. Only succeeding troops engage in action towards the flank, and minor detachments may be successful by a mere attempt to do so. The farther the attacking troops have gotten beyond the attack objective, the more effective has been their shock, and the less chance of meeting a new front. The number of machine guns must be brought into consonance with the number of rifles; to 1 platoon of 40 men 2 automatic rifles would generally be attached, and a materiel reserve should be held out, in addition. "The automatic rifle was and had to be (considering its fire power as against that of a rifle), the main and increasing reliance of the infantry fire fight, especially as it was improved in design. This is not to say that the riflemen must not fire, — to the contrary, the greatest value was laid on such action." (Ludendorff.) Machine guns are to provide permanent fire protection for the infantry. A few machine gun companies are placed in ambush prior to the infantry start, while the others advance with the infantry to quickly reach important firing positions, which, in position warfare, can easily be reconnoitered in advance. Single machine guns serve for airplane defense. Light minenwerfers which are made mobile for the attack and also for direct fire during the advance are attached to the battalions for attacking strong objectives.

Simultaneous breaking forth of the assaulting infantry, entry immediately behind the last projectiles fired into the position — generally with time fuse — then in one rush piercing to the attack objective, was always found effective. After reaching the attack objective measures must be immediately taken for warding off a counter-attack, and the infantry given stability by mobile minenwerfers and artillery. Rapid attack can frequently cause positions farther off to fall.

Regimental headquarters must make arrangements for bringing along the accompanying guns, must arrange for locating the bearer squads, regulate the police service, supply of ammunition for machine guns (in belts), for rifles, grenade rifles, light minenwerfers and hand grenades. It is the duty of division headquarters to regulate the movements of the combat trains. Telephone communication to brigade and artillery headquarters remains of special importance, as well as wireless. Connection between regimental headquarters and the battalions is generally had by runners and dogs, but an attempt to establish communication by light signals must not be abandoned.

The Spring Offensive

All conditions for the success of the planned offensive battle had been met. Information of the insertion of the 18th Army (v. Hutier) between the 2d (v. d. Marwitz) and the 7th Army (v. Böhn), the creation of numerous flying fields and troop camps in the vicinity of Laon had of course not escaped, since March 4, 1918, the observance of the hostile aerial reconnaissance, but had not been sufficiently evaluated by the hostile command. In reserve, the defender had 16 British and 35 French divisions. General Foch as president of the Supreme War Council made preparations for the organization of a reserve army of 30 to 60 divisions, but declined to get ahead of the German attack by an offensive on his part. There were probably 6 divisions of Americans present, but still under training. During the night of March 18-19th two Lorraine deserters went over to the French and, as was ascertained later, betrayed the German intentions. The evening of March 20th the concentration was completed. Though the fine spring weather in the second and third week of March had favored reconnaissance, the screening had not yet been successful. Great thanks is due the aerial fighting forces; they increased the difficulties of the hostile aerial reconnaissance while they themselves took many photographs of positions in rear; and, continually watching over the traffic in the terrain in rear, could report their impression that the enemy did not expect an attack. The infantry could be instructed by means of the aerial photos of all details of the position to be assaulted, of each machine gun and of each minenwerfer location. In the second half of the month rainy weather softened the fields and the roads, and with sorrow did the assaulting troops watch the fog roll down during the night of March 21st. But the high command insisted on the execution of the attack.

The attack along the 70-kilometer front by the 17th Army (Otto v. Below), the 2d Army (v. d. Marwitz) and the 18th Army (v. Hutier), started principally north of the junction between the French and the British, was, at that time and at that place a complete surprise, as an attack was not thought of before April in the terrain of the Somme battle which offered such unfavorable conditions after the retreat into the Siegfried position. The British commander-in-chief was home in England. It was the task of the shock troops to pierce through the three main lines of the British position system to a depth of from 12 to 15 kilometers. As the 17th and 2d Armies advanced from the bend of the Cambrai arc in southwesterly direction, and the 18th Army, on the other hand, advanced westward, a concentric attack resulted, which was brought into a straight line during the course of the first movements by the 18th Army pushing sharply ahead and by the stubborn resistance offered by the British Army in the north.

At 4:40 A.M. March 21st, — that is when it was still completely dark — the artillery battle opened along the entire front between Croisilles and La Fere with gas and high explosive shells. At and after 6:40 A.M., the concentrated fire of the short range battle groups swept the 3 British positions. The failure to find a gradual weakening of the positions through days of effective fire had to be offset by a doubled energy of the fire wave lasting for 3 hours. The incomparable shock-power of the infantry (which broke forth at 9 A.M.) was so instrumental in securing success that, in spite of fog and mud, the second hostile position was reached the evening of the first day of battle and partly captured and partly over-run. The foremost trenches were taken comparatively easily by the deep-formed phalanx under cover of the fog; at the most difficult points, such as the south exits of the city of St. Quentin, flocks of tanks reinforced the momentum of the shock. Thereafter, however, a net work of numerous supporting points had to be overcome with the help of machine guns, minenwerfers and batteries. The fog, though it had materially favored surprise, now increased the difficulties of orientation, and slackened the rate of the attack. At many points in the afternoon, when the weather had cleared, and when our pursuit and battle squadrons threw themselves on the enemy, we had to wait for the arrival of the field artillery working its way under unbelievable difficulties through the bottomless mud of the terrain (which was merely a mass of shell-craters), in order to overcome stronger bulwarks.

Most of the airplane detachments moved their flying fields to correspond with the progress of the action forward, some of them even to places heretofore used by the enemy's airplanes. The captive balloons, without being drawn down, followed the infantry at 4 to 5 kilometers distance and constantly reported to higher headquarters the course of the action. Anti-aircraft guns were brought close in rear of the foremost infantry line to fire on low flying battle airplanes, and there found opportunity to accomplish good results against the fleeing infantry and other ground targets at short range. In the first days the hostile battle airplanes found little opportunity for counter-attack.

The shock between the Scarpe and the Oise struck the British 9th Division on the front line with the 8th Infantry Division and the 3d Cavalry Division behind it. At the time the British 3d Army in the north (Byng) made a stand in the face of the attack by the 17th Army, the resistance of the 5th Army (Gough) broke quickly and entirely unexpectedly. An unsuccessful counter-attack was started on the 22d by foot troops without artillery support, who were brought up by autos from the vicinity of Senlis and Compiegne and who belonged to the French 9th and 10th Infantry Divisions and 1st dismounted Cuirassier Division, supported by the 25th Infantry Division from the vicinity of Chauny. During the evening of the 22d, the Army of Hutier had broken through the third hostile position, while the 17th Army (Otto v. Below) rested in front of the British 3d position. The evening report of the 23d read: "We are fighting in a line about north of Bapaume, Pèronne and Ham." The penetration had been successful as well as the pursuit connected with it; and thus the dead point of all previous penetrating battles had been overcome. During the night of the 24th Bapaume fell; the day after, Noyon; in vain did the 55th Infantry Division, hurriedly brought from Paris, attempt to ward off fate there. Farther north, around Cambrai, the British troops also gave way. The French forced to insert their divisions as they came up, were thrown into the general retreat. "The support of our battle airplanes was specially effective during the infantry attacks on Bapaume and in the charge against Ferme la Maisonnette at Pèronne which had been attacked before. At Albert they attacked fleeing columns with bombs and fired more than 80,000 rounds from machine guns. Our bombing squadrons continued night after night the fight against the lines of communications, the troop shelters, and the flying fields of the enemy. In the attack against railroad stations behind the front they frequently flew at altitudes of less than 100 meters. Hits in the midst of railroad works and on trains and heavy explosions and conflagrations were the result of their audacity. In the three nights after March 25th a total of 100,000 kg. of explosives was thrown down."

The most important event of the day was the final appointment of Foch as commander-in-chief of the Allies. Countershocks by British divisions brought from Flanders made themselves felt. A counter-attack on a large scale started by Foch encountered a rapidly formed new German front Mondidier — Lassigny — Noyon. The French reserves had been held back to the fullest extent, since the German progress was naturally not so clearly defined as in the first days. The German front had approached within 15 kilometers of Amiens. The gap between Ancre and Oise was closed by British reserves and by the army under Fayolles brought from Flanders. A continuation of the attack which had been expected by the Allies did not take place, so that the Allies on April 4th advanced from Amiens to an attack, which, however, had no success.

In the very first days of the attack the Army Group commanded by the Crown Prince of Prussia which had been designated to carry forward the attack of the 2d and 17th Armies in the direction of Albert and Abbeville had 15 divisions, which were quite fresh yet, but of the second and third line. But the High Command held the view that to succeed quickest was to attack where the enemy had given way easiest. It was indisputably confirmed that the hostile resistance was stronger than our power. A battle of attrition ought not to have been fought. This was precluded by our strategical as well as tactical situation. The High Command had to come to the exceedingly grave decision — in conjunction with all headquarters concerned — to definitely stop the attack on Amiens. At the same time, while the attention of the Entente was completely engaged at Amiens, on the opposite wing, on April 6th, the 7th Army started the offensive and was enabled to bring its right wing to the Ailette and to the Aisne — Oise canal by the battles at Aurigny and Coucy-le-Chateau.

The indicated shifting of the British Flanders reserves and the expectation of finding along the Flanders front less efficient units (Portuguese) or even tired out divisions, was (in addition, the possibility of exerting a pressure on the British communications leading from the canal ports), the inducement for a new attack in Flanders. Unfortunately, we lacked fresh forces to execute the shock with full vigor. April 9th the 6th Army (v. Quast) attacked on the line Festubert — Armentieres, not bothering with the latter place in the start, which later on, on the 12th, fell into our hands. This time there was a short preparatory fire from 4:15 to 8:45 A.M., then excellent artillery support for the infantry, so that most of the enemy's machine guns were unable to get into action. As early as 10:00 A.M., the third position of the enemy was taken. The difficulties encountered in the completely sodden, shell-cratered terrain, appeared almost insurmountable, but we succeeded on the first day in bringing up several heavy guns, though after

The Year 1918

unbelievable labor. Early on the 10th, the 4th Army (Sixt v. Armin) commenced the attack under the same difficulties farther north between Armentieres and Hollebeke, while in the next few days the 6th Army gained more ground in the direction of Hazebrouck and Hollebeke, so that between the 16th and 18th our successes in the Ypres arc made themselves felt also on the right bank of the Yser. On April 21st the number of prisoners taken was 117,000, 1550 guns had been captured and more than 200 tanks. The amount of ammunition, subsistence, supplies, and equipment captured could not even be calculated. In the course of 4 weeks the British not only lost what they had gained in the half-year battles on the Somme and the rest of their success at Cambrai, but also about two-thirds of the terrain they had bought so dearly in 16 battles in Flanders. On April 25th the battles ceased by the well planned and brilliantly executed capture of Kemmel. Had headquarters arrived in time on the hill, continuation of the attack would have been possible before the hostile reserves could come up. German patrols had reached without danger the Scherpenberg, while the troops occupied a very unfavorable line which they had been ordered to hold. Thus we contented ourself with the mere capture of a corner pillar of the important Flanders position. "The attack fulfills its purpose as long as it causes the enemy more damage and loss than it does ourselves. That is always the case in the first stages of a successful surprise attack. Here the main point is to engage the enemy without fear of losses, but not neglecting fire support and fire preparation. The commander must determine whether the effect of the hostile reserves is becoming stronger. If that is the case, the attacks must gradually become more systematic; strong artillery preparation with plenty of ammunition develops more and more until the transition to defense on the part of the victor becomes realized. By his insufficiently prepared 'counter-shocks' and counter-attacks the opponent will suffer material losses in the face of a skillful defense, while we save our forces. With us the question hardly ever is to gain terrain at any price. We must strike down the enemy; we must save ourselves. Our military feeling must in this regard become even firmer; we are inclined to attack in the later days of an attack with entirely too insufficient means and are inclined to fight for the purpose of gaining ground, which is entirely immaterial to the whole situation." (Reference — High Command on June 9, 1918.) In these expressions lies the entire system of our battles in 1918.

Our new method of attack had been still farther developed. It consisted in surprise, by short, powerful artillery preparation directed on single points and in rapid advance of the infantry with co-operations of its auxiliary arms.

On March 21st the principal question was of an attack that had been planned by Great General Headquarters in quietness and with the utmost care; in its fortunate execution the German troops struck newly organized fronts, or fronts that were still under construction. Every delay in time might bring the success of the undertaking into question; the subordinate commanders had to act quickly and independently, and General Headquarters had to bring the different operations into consonance with the whole. 3 to 5 divisions had been placed under the orders of Corps Headquarters; 2 to 3 of these divisions were to execute the attack in the first line, under proper artillery support, as long as possible. The attack frontage of 2 kilometers proved too narrow in most cases for properly leading the division and therefore an extension to 3 kilometers was recommended. Strong resistance was to be overcome by inserting more artillery but not by increasing the density of the infantry, which would only increase the losses. 20 to 30 batteries were inserted per kilometer. Their effect was supplemented by medium and heavy minenwerfers. The artillery attached to the divisions by the war organization tables was reinforced in most cases by a second field artillery regiment, one or more heavy field howitzer battalions and 1 mortar battery. If the reinforcing artillery was taken away from some one division, then arrangements had to be made to have that artillery return at the proper time to its own division. The Group (army corps) had the disposition of a number of field batteries of the army artillery, heavy field howitzer battalions, mortars, and heavy flat-trajectory batteries, which were attached to the division in the front line according to requirements. Assigning such artillery was to be kept within limits, so as not to create specially difficult conditions by the insertion of an unweildy mass. The number of guns had to be brought into proper consonance with the increase of the ammunition supply. "Too many guns in relation to the amount of ammunition is very bad. The fighting power of troops is lessened, not increased, since the difficulties of leadership are increased by the voluminous carriages and vehicles of the numerous guns, which cannot be properly used. And probably what the troops need more is denied for that very reason."

Success of the attack does not lie in the number of infantry units inserted, but in the manner of artillery preparation and the immediate utilization of the moral impression created by our fire effect and in the use of the auxiliary arms (machine guns, light minenwerfers, flame throwers and accompanying guns) that accompany the infantry. We had but very few tanks, and could do without their assistance. The German industries could have constructed a sufficient number of tanks by neglecting other means of fighting. We adopted a tank gun (13-mm.) which unfortunately was very heavy and required two men to handle. Important services were performed by battle airplanes. Technique now also had the same importance as tactics and psychology.

The machine gun had become the main arm of infantry and formed the skeleton of each battle formation. A fifth machine gun was now furnished the companies. The skirmish line takes a back seat now in the fire fight; we had absolutely broken with the meaning of a "powerful skirmish line" with which we entered war under other conditions. In the start great objection was put forth against this innovation; for in the first battles the skirmish lines were still too dense. "Overcoming machine gun nests had caused difficulties beyond expectation at many points and delayed our attack. The independence of our infantry squad had been found wanting frequently, as well as its co-operation with the auxiliary arms. It had become especially difficult for the troops to form again for defense after the completion of an attack and especially to perceive that a continuation of the attack could have no further success." But, in the end, the number of men carrying rifles will determine the result. It is questionable if that number might not decrease too much; "the danger is the greater because a weaker unit requires the same administrative staff, same number of information troops, and same train as that of a stronger unit, but has only a smaller number of rifles. It was necessary to consider whether it would not be best to overcome this difficulty by consolidating two divisions." Another difficulty was the new attack method. Heretofore the entire attacking space was filled with dense skirmish lines. Battle leadership, which had to pay attention only to the hostile skirmishers, or at most to a few machine guns, was relatively simple. Everybody went straight for the objective. At the present day, however, there can be no thought of an equal distribution of the infantry in the terrain. The troops divide according to the breadth and depth into sub-detachments and lose themselves in the terrain — but all must work toward one objective. The auxiliary arms also demand depth formation; if they are once let out of hand, the infantry will soon be unable to get forward. The new method of attack puts especially high demands on the subordinate leaders. If these give out, the attack stops; heretofore we could carry it forward again by inserting strong skirmish lines led as units. But this — and therein lies the danger — no longer is possible in the new method, which expresses itself in a slow forward movement in overcoming hostile centers of resistance. It will be the main task of battle training from now on to assure rapid, decisive co-operation between the separated portions within the whole of the battle action.

Infantry advances in files, in swarms, as "shock squads" or in skirmish line; its fire power lies in the machine guns and light minenwerfers, the protection of which it assumes. Overcoming hostile machine gun nests takes much time. Frontal attack leads to nothing. In view of the checkerboard like distribution of the nests and in consideration of the strength of the supporting points, attacks from flank and rear were but seldom possible; the use of gas proved useful; the troops also soon learned to estimate the value of the rifle grenades adopted from the French system. Difficult situations arose when machine gun nests were discovered too late, so that their attack could not be prepared under cover, and when the accompanying guns had heavy losses before they could fire even a single shot. The accompanying guns were able — even if only slowly — to follow up the infantry by the help of pioneers and laborers, being partially protected by gas masks. Proper attention also has to be paid to watering the animals during the advance.

Finally the infantry storms the terrain still held by the enemy, but adheres to its depth formation until entry of the enemy's position and then seeks to re-establish that depth formation immediately after reaching the attack objective — generally toward the front. It has not always been easy for infantry to regain this depth formation. Detachments in rear take over the fire protection against counter-attacks and secure the flanks or turn to the side to help the neighbor.

The commander endeavors to achieve surprise with all means at hand. Though success is accomplished in hiding the attack preparations from the enemy by well thought out orders, strict discipline and development of oral examinations and instructions of all concerned, it is by no means assured that the enemy will not receive a warning of the storm about to break through statements of deserters. But the statements of single prisoners can hardly ever give a complete picture; they are usually received so late, that the leader can utilize them but seldom, even disregarding the fact that false statements are mixed up with true statements, and that probably no credence will be given to the true ones. It was impossible to stop communication between the army and home, "the mania for talking and boasting, so inherent to the Germans, brought the most important and most secret things to the knowledge of the press and consequently also to the knowledge of the enemy."

If we must count absolutely on the defense of a "foreground," it may be of advantage to take possession of that foreground even before the assault and to gas more effectively those hostile batteries that fire standing barrages during the advance.

The infantry attacks under protection of the creeping barrage which advances in lifts of about 200 meters each, at the rate of 40 to 50 minutes per kilometer. In spite of the slow progress of the creeping barrage it has in many cases outstripped the infantry; it also proved to be too rigid, to correspond to the progress of the infantry. The danger was very great that in disruption of the barrage, some batteries would fire on our own infantry. It was of course entirely out of the question to bring a creeping barrage back, as the location of the infantry could not be definitely shown to the artillery. If the infantry was able to follow close at the heels of the barrage, it could in most cases over-run the hostile machine gun nests and supporting points before the latter could become effective. But if the barrage continued its way and outstripped the infantry, then the latter was obliged to break the stubborn resistance of the enemy with its own means — accompanying guns and teamed minenwerfers. The infantry must never come to believe that its very existence lies within the creeping barrage. The existence of infantry much rather rests in the fighting value of the troops and the skillful utilization of its auxiliary arms. The desire for more accompanying artillery was heard everywhere; in many cases a 96-mm. gun battery (the 16-cm. was too heavy) and 1 platoon of light field howitzers were attached to the regiments, and single guns with several caissons to the battalions. Often heavy field howitzers were desired. It was quite natural that the regiments finally received in addition to their accompanying batteries an artillery group consisting of 2 96-mm. gun batteries and 1 light and 1 heavy field howitzer battery, while the rest of the artillery remained at the disposal of the divisions. This was correct as the regiments because of their gradually decreasing effective strength (companies frequently had but three men carrying rifles) were required to cover materially greater spaces with the number of rifles available. Due to these broad attack sectors, the battle generally resolved itself into partial fights which were conducted by "mixed" regiments in the front line. The division commander was able to bring his influence to bear on the battle only through his reserve regiment and his artillery. This dissolution of the attack into partial fights was an unavoidable and bad feature which had to be abandoned when the situation permitted systematic attack or defense. The first step in that direction was to deprive the regiments of their artillery.

After the position is entered, the divisional artillery is brought up; and, to avoid congesting the roads all vehicles that can be spared, even the field kitchens, must be kept back.

Resuming the Offensive

The German offensive in Flanders had succeeded in at least one object; it had contained strong hostile forces, it had filled the enemy with fear for his canal ports and had aroused the last remnants of the Belgian state. It is probable that it did have a farther reaching objective. Based on the recommendations of the Army Group commanded by the Crown Prince of Prussia, Great General Headquarters first sought a success in the attack in front of the 1st and 7th Armies, and then to again transfer the decisive attack there as soon as the first attack had had its effect on the situation in Flanders. Though prisoners taken on May 25th and 26th had divulged everything they knew concerning the time and place of the attack, the attack of the 7th Army on June 27th at the Chemin des Dames and farther east to Brimont was very successful; in conjunction with the 1st Army (Fritz v. Below) it was able to accomplish the capture of the heights of Reimes and Epernay. The French high command had ordered early readiness for gassing and had placed its reserves (13th Infantry Division) on the heights between the Aisne and Vesle.

At 4:40 A.M., on the 27th, after a short artillery preparation, the German troops broke forth to the attack from their positions between Landricourt and Brimont. The attack struck battle-worn British divisions, which lost about 15,000 prisoners, and then encountered several fresh French divisions. As early as the first day of the attack a depth of 18 kilometers was reached inside of the hostile position by the irresistible center of the attack. In the next few days the wings of the attack could not keep up with the advancing center. On the 3d day of battle, Soissons was taken, the number of prisoners increased to 35,000; on May 30th the Marne was reached south of La Fere en Tardenois, the number of prisoners being 45,000; and, on the 31st heavy battles took place near Soissons.

The French leadership saw the cause of its defeat in the error of having deployed all its batteries in a single line, so that the artillery was annihilated in a short time; in addition, the French did not utilize the advantage to get ahead of the recognized German artillery preparation by a timely counter-preparation. It was quite different in the succeeding battles! The leaders abandoned the rigid holding of terrain, and evacuated portions of the position when it was impossible to lay a barrage to 100 to 150 meters in front of its own line. Such positions show themselves to be untenable. Untenable positions are defended only when it is absolutely unavoidable. It is an advantage only if the new position is not exposed to the destructive fire of the light artillery and minenwerfers, so that a new deployment of the artillery becomes necessary. The troops should fight in a position of their own selection, not in one selected by the enemy.

From June 6th the two new front line positions of the Germans, Chateau Thierry — Villers Cotterets — Noyon and Chateau Thierry — Dormans — Reims were under the desperate counter-attacks of the enemy but the situation did not change. The Army Group commanded by the German Crown Prince had taken up to June 6th; 55,000 prisoners (of these, 1500 officers) 650 guns and more than 2000 machine guns.

A fourth German offensive shock by the 18th Army with four corps (9th, v. Ottinger, 62d, v. Webem; 8th, v. Scholer; 28th Reserve Corps, Hoffman), led to the *Battle of the Matz* between Mondidier and Noyon, with the determined intention to take the forest terrain of Compiegne which possessed permanent danger for the Germans. It was a rare coincidence that the commander-in-chief of the French 3d Army, General Humbert, claims to have had information as early as June 4th (the orders of the attacker were dictated only that day). It is, of course, true that the army had expected an attack here since the end of May and had sought by all means to prevent a surprise. A deep foreground had been ordered, defended by many machine guns, from which the guns were at the proper time withdrawn. The first position, the foreground, was said to be strongly defended by 8 divisions disregarding the existence of a second position. This first position was to be the exit point for counter-attacks of the corps reserves. The 10th Division of the army reserve was to be brought with its leading elements as far as the second position.

The German attack was to be started by gas shell fire, but in 1 division of 1000 throwers only 150 could be placed into position because of strong destruction fire, and, of these, 70 were destroyed.

The attack preparations commenced at 12:50 A.M. with a surprise fire of gas and bursting projectiles lasting 10 minutes against the main hostile batteries, observation and command positions (which however had been withdrawn during the night) and against the shelters and routes of approach. Between 1 and 2:30 A.M. a stronger artillery preparation; between 2:30 and 4:10 A.M. destructive fire against the hostile positions in such manner that each time two lines were taken under fire, while the hostile artillery remained under fire of the long range batteries. At 4:20 A.M. a powerful fire shock was to give the signal for the assault, which was to be preceded by a creeping barrage (1st lift 300 meters, than 10 minutes for each 200 meters) up to the line Ecouvillers-Atteche Ferme. The infantry worked its way up to within 300 meters of the leading hostile trenches, ran under the barrage squads, formed within the hostile trenches for further advance and also advanced the artillery at once. The execution of the attack had been well planned; in spite of superior forces the German divisions gained ground, and could gain ground everywhere. In this battle, the infantry naturally did not have the full support of its guns, while being exposed to the concentrated fire of the hostile artillery. Rapid deployment of the artillery against this new line of resistance was the principal requirement for success, while the infantry had to be halted as soon as it reached the artillery protective position. The French counter-attack executed on June 10th, 11th, and 12th, and supported by tanks and airplane squadrons, had no success worthy of the name.

The German leadership would have been able to break the resistance prepared here only with heavy losses, and it therefore decided not to continue the attack at this point. It was correct in any case for both opponents to seek the further decision in the Champagne between Rheims and Chalons. The German attack, with 15 divisions in the first, and 10 in the second line, started on July 15th against a fully prepared enemy. The 4th Army, Gouraud, claims to have made preparations as early as July 12th in the Champagne, and to have occupied its leading positions only with detachments, in rear of which were single strongly wired supporting points to catch the shock in the line Pournoy — Prosnes — Perthes, while the decision was to be sought by a counter-attack on a large scale against the front Chateau Thierry — Soissons. The day, place and frontage of the attack had been known to the Entente since the 13th. Prisoners taken on July 14th divulged all further details of the attack. At 12:10 A.M. July 15th the artillery fire was to start and the infantry was expected to start for the assault at 4:15 A.M. The French counter preparation started at 11:00 P.M. on the 14th.

According to British statements, the outpost garrison had materially delayed the German attack, and the French artillery, in rear positions, brought heavy losses to the assaulting troops and the batteries that had gone forward too soon. The 5th Army (Berthelot), connecting on the left, held the advanced line between Rheims and the Mame in the Montagnes de Reims, but could not prevent the German 1st Army (Fritz v. Below) from taking the heights north of Venteuil and the Ardre valley to include Poury. On the German right wing the 7th Army had experienced greater successes and had been able to gain ground. On July 16th the German headquarters directed the cessation of the attack, at 5:30 A.M. On the 18th, between the Aisne and the Mame a completely unexpected French counterattack came from Belleau (near Chateau Thierry) — Fontenay (west of Soissons) . This counter-attack was made in superior force, with great depth, and directed against the right flank of the Chateau Thierry — Reims front, and was executed by the Army Group of Fayolle (6th and 10th Army) . It was preceded by a short fire preparation which immediately continued in the shape of a creeping barrage accompanied by numerous fast tanks. The tanks, favored by the tall standing crops in which our machine guns could produce no effect, plowed through our lines, unloaded their passengers with machine guns in our rear to form machine gun nests, and then the tanks returned to bring up reinforcements. Loss of ground was unavoidable as our troops were battle worn, but, nevertheless, the scheduled flank attack was frustrated. Reserves rapidly brought up with auto trucks re-established the situation by a strong attack (20th Infantry Division). We will here again point out the difficulties encountered when the foot troops are separated from their guns and vehicles while using auto trucks. The French did not utilize their initial success and thus saved us from a heavy defeat. The German offensive had passed its zenith; the enormous losses in leaders and trained men were not to be replaced as quickly as the situation demanded, and the value of recruits fell greatly. Even the best army cannot be victorious if it is not supported from home.

The German conduct of the offensive up to then was based on the assumption of surprising the enemy and that the enemy would remain in the terrain dominated by the German artillery. Any attack method that is correctly formed breaks the enemy's resistance. Surprise makes this easier. The attack must disintegrate if the enemy defends an outpost zone of some kilometers with weak forces, and takes a position in readiness with strong forces outside the effective fire zone of our artillery, like Humbert did for the first time on the Matz and the Army under Gouraud in the Champagne. Now, could not the preparation for a change of the battle plans have been ascertained by aerial reconnaissance? Against such a battle formation a long artillery preparation merely meant squandering ammunition and allowed the infantry without sufficient artillery preparation to enter into the unbroken artillery fire of the defender. From these reflections result the fact that the hostile outpost zone should have been taken after a short artillery preparation (possibly only by medium and heavy minenwerfers) in the afternoon before the attack on a broad front (for instance 3 to 4 army fronts) and that only at the assault points should the assaulting troops be placed immediately in front of the main line of resistance during darkness. Prior to the infantry attack the second artillery deployment into the hostile outpost zone should commence. This will not be possible without resorting to the mechanical truck trains (caterpillar trucks). Only a portion of the artillery with the required amount of ammunition should be placed in readiness in our outpost zone. Simultaneously with the infantry attack the gassing of the hostile artillery commences; almost the entire artillery participates in this; the infantry has to break the hostile resistance with its own accompanying arms; this becomes more necessary since it will hardly be possible to start an effective creeping barrage. Obstacles in the positions in rear have to be flattened and torn down by tanks. The attack has become more difficult through this battle method. The defender can materially delay the second deployment of our artillery through harassing fire and gas attacks; he can bring to naught the preparations for the attack by nightly sorties on a large scale, and can himself take the offensive at other points.

We are obliged to admit that the French Army has shown a greatly increased offensive power in these battles through mass insertion of airplanes, ammunition and tanks. As large forces of American troops had already arrived, the supreme command decided to evacuate the Marne to hold for the present the Aisne — Vesle line.

The Last Defensive Battle

After the defeat of the German July offensive, Marshal Foch had given the task to the British Army which on July 28th the 1st French army (Debeney) was subordinated; i.e., to press in the projecting arc east of Amiens. For this attack Marshal Haig designated the 4th Army (Rawlinson) which, with 7 divisions in the first line and 4 divisions in the second line (starting on a 17-kilometer front from the line Hangard — Morlancourt), waa to reach Le Quesnil (9 km.) — Mericourt sur Somme (6 km.) as its first objective. 1 cavalry corps (3d Cavalry Division) brought up by night marches, reinforced by 1 cyclist battalion and 2 motor machine gun battalions, was to push forward along the Amiens — Roye road. The French 1st Army, connecting on the south, was to attack about one hour after the effect of the British attack made itself felt. Marshal Foch retained at his disposition the French 3d Army farther to the south. By means of well planned false movements and wireless messages sent out to mislead the enemy, it was the plan to create the belief that the attack would take place in Flanders. It appeared that an operation of the German 27th Infantry Division on August 6th south of Morlancourt did not clear up the situation for us. Favored by a heavy fog that had, in addition, been artificially thickened, the artillery fire suddenly opened on August 8th; this fire soon changed into a creeping barrage, immediately followed by tanks and infantry. Surprise against the leading division of the 2d Army had succeeded. The entry nearly reached the objective, that is, between Albert and Pierre-pont on the Avre, a depth of penetration of 14 kilometers had been reached, though, with the exception of organizing the position, everything that could be done for defense was done, including narrow division sectors with excellent depth formation and plenty of ammunition. The hostile tanks annihilated our machine gun nests, and, followed by cavalry, entered deep into our position system spreading disorder and confusion — even headquarters were surprised in their quarters. Valuable documents were lost. 7 German divisions, considered absolutely fit for fighting, were annihilated; the enemy had but little loss; but the increasing bad morale of our poorly trained recruits became a decisive fact. Under such conditions, there could be no longer any mention of tactics. "The 8th of August is the black day of the German Army in the History of this War." It was very fortunate that the attack of the Allies was not continued on the 9th in the same strength.

Further attacks between Ancre and Avre pushed back our lines without disrupting them. Gassing in conjunction with fog, mass insertion of tanks, and insertion of strong airplane battle squadrons were the causes of British success. Based on the estimate of the situation General Ludendorff perceived that in the face of the relative strength of both sides no victory could possibly be gained by the Central Powers. The Government of the Empire was obliged to start negotiations for peace, the army high command was forced to try and prevent a penetration of the German lines, in order to gain time, and to avoid unnecessary losses, and to save the living power of the army for subsequent tasks, which could be solved farther in rear on a shorter line. Thus the troops were forced to hold the enemy, to cover the bringing away of the materiel, and to gain the time required for preparing a new position. Tenacious defense of the extensive foreground delayed the enemy's advance. These foreground battles gave the defender time for his preparations and furnished important viewpoints for estimating the offensive intentions of the enemy. In many cases it could not be prevented, having the fights extremely stubborn in the foreground zone. Foreground and mobile defense with countershock proved excellent in the defense. A British attack undertaken on August 21st at 6:00 A.M., with a 16 kilometer front between Croisilles and the Ancre, against the 17th Army, according to the arrangements of August 8th, was driven off. 104 tanks alone had been inserted on the Bucquoy — Achiet le Petit road. On the 22d an attack on a larger scale succeeded, and then the British continued their attacks the next few days. "The characteristics of the attacks were narrow, but deep, entries by tanks after a short but exceedingly heavy artillery preparation, in conjunction with artificial fog. Mass insertion of tanks and artificial fog remained our most dangerous enemies in the future. They became more and more dangerous the more morale became lowered and the more tired and weaker our divisions became. The depth of the entry, but not its entire extent, were soon seen. Correctly inserted counterattacks by the reserves generally offset these entries. But there was danger that the local command employed its troops in an overhasty manner and not in close order."

The decisive battle was from now on carried on in the mobile attack method only where success was assured. If deep indentures occurred in a position, then the entire portion of the front was taken back rather than exposing the troops to heavy loss by flanking or envelopment.

Frequently, the enemy was deceived concerning the evacuation of a position, which fact led him to attack the void left by the abandoned position. The differences between empty positions and positions only temporarily defended by rear guards offering serious resistance, frequently misled the attacker into rash attacks, so that he subsequently suddenly attacked fully occupied fire fronts. In Army Reports of July 21, 1918, it is stated: "On the south bank of the Marne the enemy conducted attacks against the positions evacuated by us during the preceding night (19th20th); these attacks were made yesterday (20th) in the forenoon after an artillery preparation lasting four hours, and were executed under heavy fire protection and accompanied by numerous tanks; the latter attacked but smoke in the empty positions. Our fire from the north bank, in part flanking, caused the enemy heavy losses." "Our task" said General Ludendorff after the army high command had ordered the retreat to the Siegfried position in July, 1918, "is not for the purpose of gaining terrain nor to hold it at any cost, but to reduce the fighting power of the enemy." Possession of the terrain is in itself a visible sign of success, of course, but was greatly overestimated at home. But possession of the ten-ain can never justify remaining in a tactically unfavorable situation; however,

The Year 1918

timely evacuation of unfavorable portions of terrain may well offset the gain of time if it compels the enemy to undertake a new deployment or to an advance across difficult terrain under our uninterrupted fire. However, we must not fail to recognize the moral gain to the enemy when he attributes the voluntary retreat to the effect of his own measures. But, if we could hold or abandon terrain without material disadvantage, conditions were different for the enemy. The recaptured terrain was to him native soil, the reoccupied localities gave some measure of the extension of his power. The German defensive method was something of an innovation which was demanded by considerations of expediency. The "mobile defense" makes enormous demands on the troops. A retreat never raises the self-confidence of troops, for whatever remains behind in men, materiel and arms, falls into the enemy's hands.

On September 18th attacks by large units on the part of the British were begun; the weak German troops still proved their tenacity and desire to attack; heavy fighting took place around the debris and ruins of Gauzeaucourt and Epehy. In spite of the use of all available means, no deep entry was made on September 21st. But the German losses had been very heavy. The troops had executed a task that was superhuman. The hostile attacks were based upon the employment of tanks, followed by infantry with great depth, in many cases with hesitation. The artillery preparation consisted principally of a short powerful fire shock, which changed at the appearance of the infantry into a creeping barrage. The appearance of tanks in large masses demanded a formation for tank defense arms in great depth, as we could not expect that all tanks could be defeated by a single line, especially when their advance was also screened by fog. Thus, a certain "tank defense zone" was created between the main line of resistance and the artillery protective position in such manner that, in front, machine guns and "tank guns" were formed in groups, farther in rear light minenwerfers and field guns which possibly gave opportunity for effect towards both flanks.

Directions from Great General Headquarters of August 8th pointed out the probability of surprise attacks. Protection against those was not to be sought by making the defense more dense but by holding forces, in rear, in readiness. "Their location must be determined with a view to meeting hostile surprise attacks. The activity of the units placed in the front line together with their decisive conduct in the battle zone, must facilitate timely readiness for action on the part of the forces held in rear; these latter forces must attack the enemy with a countershock during his sudden entry and in conjunction with the divisions in the front line, drive him back beyond the battle zone." The question of the foreground also was made clearer: "In open terrain, when the view is good, the position can be relatively open. In close terrain and when there is a bad view (night fog) the garrison must move closer together within the foreground; whether the movement is forward, toward the center, or toward the main line of resistance depending on the terrain. In all other portions of the foreground, patrols must suffice in such situations. The strength runs all the way from a simple chain of sentries to the deep, organized outpost position, with artillery and minenwerfers. In battle the foreground garrison conducts itself like outposts. It will drive off hostile patrols or capture them. The foreground garrison does not conduct this fighting rigidly, but with mobility and by using every opportunity for favorable movements. In hostile attacks (to this also belong patrol operations on a larger scale prepared by artillery fire) the foreground garrison, as a general rule, falls back fighting — and in pursuance with a prearranged plan and according to instructions from the commander — on the main line of resistance — also laterally, towards the wings. If the hostile attack is driven off, the foreground will again be occupied as before unless the commander directs otherwise. The recapture of the foreground is conducted independently by the fighting troops, in so far as possible; but that demands (if the enemy has gained a strong foothold there), a systematic counter-attack which must be ordered by the higher commander and which requires stronger forces than the foreground garrison."

It was quite correct to point out that, as soon as the morale of the troops will be endangered thereby, defense of the foreground should be abandoned as a general rule.

The artillery was to conduct its fight in a formation with depth and as a mobile force; it was cautioned against "gun fanaticism;"

was informed that ammunition was of more importance than number of guns, and that concentrated fire against the important targets was of great importance. Systematic defense by stationary barrage was discountenanced absolutely. "Barrage fire is without any effect, seldom is correct in its adjustment, is too thin, starts usually too late, requires a great deal of ammunition and materially endangers the infantry in a mobile battle. Stationary barrages should in all cases be strictly forbidden in ordinary position warfare. Their place should be taken by a concentrated fire of annihilation."

Again Great General Headquarters pointed out that losses could be materially lessened without endangering the battle objective by the creation of an extensive foreground, 1 to 3 kilometers deep, and by systematic, well planned depth formation. The designations "foreground zone" and "main battle zone" are primarily designations of command. It can only confuse troops if they have to differentiate between these designations. In speaking to troops the expression "foreground zone" and "main battle zone" should not be mentioned, but the troops should receive directions in each case as to what zone they must hold. That is their "battle zone." Positions in rear thereof, are, for the troops, merely "positions in rear." In the sense of an "elastic defense" the troops must free themselves from an overestimation of the possession of terrain. In any case it must be made clear to the troops in orders, whether they must give up ground and how much, and what terrain must be in their hands absolutely at the conclusion of a battle. Keeping up the fighting power and the offensive spirit are more important than possession of a few villages all shot to ruins, and of a few trenches; for that reason, the higher and the subordinate commanders must very quickly decide clearly whether a counter fire shock or a counterattack is required, and if the losses suffered in any attack are commensurate with what we hope to attain by gaining ground. We never succeeded at all points in organizing positions in rear in sufficient extension. The fighting troops required rest, and in addition they were required to fight, march and then intrench. It was quite comprehensible that the troops were only too willing to do without trenches, especially as the hostile aerial reconnaissance could not then ascertain without considerable trouble where the main resistance was to be made. Obstacles and bomb-proofs were of greater value than trenches. It was the old fight between shell crater positions and rifle trenches. The advantages of a well constructed trench system however show themselves immediately as soon as the troops are forced to remain for a considerable time at one place. Again and again the high command was obliged to point out the importance of thoroughly constructed positions. Time for recuperation could not be granted to the tired troops during this fatal period; the strength of the companies in many instances sank to about 40 men, and supplies failed to suffice for the demands either in numbers or value.

I quote the following excerpts from a letter written in the field:

> The man is supposed to work and fight. That, which he has created today, is lost the very next day. Supply from the rear is going to pieces, there is a shortage of rations. Actual rest the troops enjoy but seldom. For three weeks training has been very fatiguing for the officers. The men on furlough do not return at the proper time; they loaf around railroad stations and around the cities and appear probably seven days after the expiration of their furlough. If they are punished therefor, we lose their work; if we let them off without punishment, discipline suffers. And then the traffic and theft! The young officer is undoubtedly brave, but training is lacking in the officers' corps. He cannot treat his older men properly. The older gentlemen (officers) are for the greater part no longer equal to their tasks; they break down, and the battalions and regiments pass from one hand to the other.

And again from another letter prior to the revolution:

> The army has been fighting for six weeks continually on the retreat, partly in dissolution, thrown out of one position into the other, the troops without relief, played out, airplane attacks by day and by night, firing on the quarters, lack of ammunition in consequence of the railroads going to pieces, — that was the picture offering itself to the eyes of the man behind the scenes. The men lived only in the thought: why should I let myself be shot to death, peace will soon come, and so they gave themselves up as prisoners. Our enemies of course soon perceived this state of affairs. Therefore their continual desire is to gain time, so as to completely annihilate us. Would we

The Year 1918

have acted differently? But the answer of the enemy to our offer for an armistice has had a very different effect on the entire front than the enemies thought. The men perceived the hostile desire to annihilate us and had come to their senses. For the past eight days I believe that an entirely different sentiment has taken possession of the men. We have learned to organize the retreat, there are again troops present, and ammunition, and everything runs smoothly along tranquil roads. The front holds out. Our positions are adapted to the attack methods of the enemy. The enemy will find that out. Our men again have confidence, and then we will be superior to every opponent.

The much abused "militarism" misunderstood by its opponents at home but well known and feared by the enemy, has stood the test splendidly in these dark days and proved its justification.

Conclusion

The World War found a premature end through political events in Germany, without additional battles having been able to prove the correctness of our new defensive method. Great General Headquarters had the fullest confidence in these general rules, though it did not underestimate the value of the hostile procedure of the offensive, the influence of superiority of numbers, and the importance of the hostile fighting means. The high command reckoned on success, or at least on gaining time, in the defense of the expected Antwerp — Meuse position and also in further battles. But things happened differently! The army at home knifed the undefeated field army in the back, like Hagen of old did to the unconquerable valiant hero, Siegfried. The lessons of history were not written for us, our peoples trusted to the "goodheartedness" of unforgiving enemies, who concealed their hatred under the banner of the League of Nations. Our peoples were to find out for themselves "*Vae victis!*"[*]

Supported by weak allies, the German army had opposed for

---

[*] "Woe to the vanquished!"

Conclusion

almost four and one-half years a world of enemies, who had at their disposition all means of industry and technique, of foodstuffs and raw materials. If we seek for the criminal responsible for our fall, he should be sought, not in the army, but he should be sought in the ranks of the leaders of our political parties, in the ranks of the men who placed pursuit of their own ends above the weal and woe of Germany. In the territory of the enemy, the army has secured its greatest achievements, and was very near in reaching an advantageous peace. In the foregoing pages no one should seek for errors; they are only for the purpose of information of what we have done, so that the reader may proudly look back on the achievements of our people under arms. The ignominious peace of Versailles is for the sole purpose of making us helpless and consequently no longer dangerous. Can the annihilation of our peoples be God's will? We do not believe so. Our peoples have given too many proofs of their efficiency to permit a stroke of the pen of the Entente to annihilate them. In spite of all difficulties piling up in front of us, I firmly believe in the future of our peoples. German power may be lamed for years, but the German spirit cannot be killed. The German Spirit will continue to live!

When later on a new aurora of history embellishes our days, then may our peoples remember also our heroes of the World War. Work, suffer, and fight like they did, and thus Germany's future will be secure. And then, also, the blood of our heroes who fell in the belief of Germany's victory will not have been spilled in vain!

About the Author

Konrad Friedrich August Henry William Balck (1858-1924) was a Prussian General and internationally renowned expert on tactics. His six-volume textbook, *Taktik*, saw multiple editions and was translated into English, in which it was acclaimed by numerous officers in the American Army, including its Chief of Staff.

In the First World War he commanded the 13th Landwehr Division from 1915-1916 and the 51st Reserve Division from 1916-1918, during which time he was wounded in action and earned Prussia's highest military honour, the *Pour le Mérite*.

www.ingramcontent.com/pod-product-compliance
Lightning Source LLC
Chambersburg PA
CBHW050103170426
43198CB00014B/2445